RECONSTRUCTING THE MIDDLE EAST: POLITICAL AND ECONOMIC POLICY

Editor

Gyles Fletcher

Socialy Press
AN IMPRINT OF SCITUS ACADEMICS

Reconstructing the Middle East: Political and Economic Policy

Edited by **Gyles Fletcher**

This Book is Printed on Acid-Free Paper.

ISBN: 978-1-68117-781-6

Library of Congress Control Number: 2017938809

Socialy Press

(An Imprint of Scitus Academics),

616, Corporate Way, Suite 2, 4766,

Valley Cottage, NY 10989

www.scitusacademics.com

Notice

Printed in United States of America.

Preface

Political economy studies the relationships between individuals and society and between markets and the state, using a diverse set of tools and methods drawn largely from economics, political science, and sociology. Political economy emerged as a distinct field of study in the mid-18th century. From the mid-1990s, the field has expanded, in part aided by new cross-national data sets that allow tests of hypotheses on comparative economic systems and institutions. In the large and growing literature on economic reform in the Middle East and North Africa, social policy has often taken a back seat. It is treated as a residual, or an afterthought to economic reform, in the shape of safety nets or safeguards to reintegrate marginalized groups dislocated by the reform process. Given the vast energy resources that form the backbone of western economies, influence and involvement in the Middle East has been of paramount importance for the former and current imperial and super powers, including France, Britain, USA and the former Soviet Union.

Reconstructing the Middle East: Political and Economic Policy provides political and economic perspectives on social policy and its evolution in the Middle East and North Africa. The compilation offers unique historical and comparative data, as well as a gender analysis of social policy, that will be of relevance to specialists in social policy, development and the Middle East. The framework also provides immediate insights into emerging problems and offers policy guidance that, if heeded, could avoid countless failures and the loss of goodwill throughout the region.

The aim of this compendium is to analyse and explain the dynamics of political economy in the contemporary Middle East. There is a focus on how political actors and social forces influence, and in turn are influenced, by political economy structures and development strategies. Specifically, the effects of state institutions, international actors, social classes, and new groups such as private sector businesspeople are assessed, and their roles considered in the context of political economy theoretical approaches. Case studies focus on recent trends in the region; the processes and outcomes of economic reform; the impacts of globalisation and foreign penetration of the region; and the ways in which new industries and technologies are shaping the political economies of the region.

Table of Contents

1
CHAPTER

The Arab Uprising and the Future of the Region

Marwan Naser

Department of International Development, The London School of Economics and Political Science LSE, Houghton Street, London, UK

ABSTRACT

This paper examines the political and economic vulnerabilities behind the Arab Uprising. Social justice and the provision of basic needs were at the top of the demands of the revolutions in Arab Word. Arab who took to the streets sought to topple a regime, which failed to deliver on political and economic reforms, and applied policies that increased poverty and inequality. Three years after the revolutions, the record of the Arab governments in meeting the socio-economic demands of the revolutions is mixed, at best. Not a few numbers of scholars have noted that the socio-economic policies of the current government do not differ from those of previous regimes with their bias towards the interests of the business class, failure to address social injustices, and dependency on western capital and International Financial Institutions' prescriptions. The question is: why hasn't the revolution achieved its goals? And why do the new governments continue to face crisis after crisis?

Keywords: Economic development; Political economy; Conflict and political transition

CONTEXT

The Arab state has attempted to institute reforms in various guises, but these have mostly ended up centralizing power, rather than dispersing it. Whether it is the Tanzimat reforms under Ottoman rule, nationalization of the 1960s or neo-liberal **ECONOMIC REFORMS** of the 1980s, they have all served as vehicles for refurbishing the state's power. It is useful to note that the revolution [1] did not end the reign of corruption and tyranny only, but it has also ended the era of Pharaoh and launched the freedom of societies; in addition to an end to the minority rule and the return of the masses in order to determine who is better to come to the helm of power, but why hasn't the revolution achieved its goals? And what next?

The Arab world [2] lies at the cusp of a new era. It is witnessing an unprecedented demographic transition resulting in one of the "largest youth cohorts" in its history [3]. The future of the Arab World crucially depends on whether it can convert this youthful transition into a productive transition. This requires Arab rulers to concede not just political space, but also greater economic access. Unless accompanied with a distribution of economic power, **POLITICAL REFORM** alone will not be sufficient. Borrowing the conceptual formulation of Douglass North, what the Arab world needs today is an "open access order. The Arab state has typically created rents by restricting access to economic opportunities to a dominant coalition, and used these rents to sustain order.

The region's centralized and segmented administrative structures have restricted economic access and prevented the diffusion of economic rents through **ENTREPRENEURSHIP** and trade. Importantly, a segmented state apparatus has prevented the emergence of a business class that has direct stakes in more open regional markets. This has given rise to massive coordination failures, with the result that Arab governments and firms today are particularly deficient in capturing positive externalities and productive spillovers. This centralized bureaucratic rule has a long historical lineage, dating back to the Ottoman rule. The Ottoman Empire and its successor Arab states have been particularly efficient at promoting and guarding their autonomy from society. But, in this quest for absolutist control, **BUREAUCRACY** has been turned into an irritant for the growth of bourgeoisie and regional economic integration [4,5].

Through centralized economic control and restrictive economic barriers, Arab governments have erected a system of economic apartheid that systematically excludes people and firms at the margins. Although, the Middle East has modest levels of measured inequality by global comparisons, its central challenge is the inequality of access. Everywhere in the region there are strong advantages of incumbency. To create an open access order, a new governance paradigm needs to be imagined that brings people from the margins to the mainstream, offering them ladders for economic **MOBILITY-LADDERS** that are defined by merit and competition, rather than (wasita) or connections. This requires that economic rewards are distributed through achievement rather than ascription, and that elite privileges are transformed into universal rights.

Arab economies [6] have long been greased through revenues from oil, aid and remittances. There is now a need to generate alternative revenue streams through trade and private sector development [7,8] that can replace patronage with production. But it is inauspicious to talk about the necessity of economic reform at a time when the region's political climate is decidedly anti-business. The private sector is at once the most despised as well as the most desirable aspect of reform. Business in the Arab world is often comfortably embedded within the state, with the result that it invokes images of crony capitalism. At the same time, an estimated 100 million jobs need to be created in the MENA [9-11] region over the next decade or so. This employment challenge cannot be addressed without a strong private sector. And, without a strong private sector the human capital gains that the Arab world has achieved over time cannot be translated into solid productivity gains.

An independent business sector will also serve a vital political function: it can generate a middle class that can serve as a powerful constituency for political reform. A **ROBUST** private sector is thus both an economic and political imperative. But this requires a radically different business life. It requires a private sector that is open, competitive and can operate outside the royal circle. This can be achieved through a genuine infitah (economic opening) that dismantles entry barriers, replaces privilege with competition and ensures a decentralized and rules-based framework for decision-making. Viewed in this light, the struggle for a new Arab World will be won or lost in the private sector.

There is an overlap in the assessment of the revolution and the governance, whether it is influenced by media campaigns that have alienated people from the revolution and focused them on its downfalls instead, or the continuing crisis facing the new regimes in power that led people [12] to forget the achievements of the revolution.

It seems that decades of tyranny did not only destroy the present of these countries' politics and economy [13-15], but also spontaneously destroyed its future too. This was reflected in the majority being excluded from political life and its monopoly through one group or faction that was chosen by the President. As a result of this monopoly, other political groups did not have a chance to qualify for the state administration, nor take part in the advancement of the nation through its various institutions.

Given this background, it is obvious that the crisis of governance refers to several factors; the expected unrest that follows any revolution that has brought down a previous regime and establishes an alternative one, the heavy legacy left behind by the previous regimes due to the destruction of political, economic, social and state institutions, the unsuccessful leadership of the new regimes in power, the immature and poor performances by the opposition, the division of the components of the society as well as the rest of the political groups, the role of followers of the former regimes who are still in positions of power within the new regimes, and the impact of lawlessness on economic activities, and the external pressures mainly through negative **MEDIA CAMPAIGNS** and economic blockade.

Most of these factors were expected, but what was disappointing is that the Islamic movements that came to power as a result of the revolutions did not live up to the expectations of its people. It has not exercised the required and expected **TRANSPARENCY**and has been slow and unsure in making key decisions. Recidivism promises has also exasperated the crisis of confidence. This has created a gap between the authority and the society, and had an impact on the revolution and its goals.

The arrival of Islamic movements to power is not surprising considering the years of oppression, marginalization, exclusions from political life and the fear to return to prison and exile. Being in power presented a safety net to the movements but at a hefty price. It would have been more worthy for these movements to focus on the principals and the success of the revolution, the democratic transition and the implementation of the demands of its people instead.

The rush to be in power has led the Islamic movements to make unrealistic electoral promises and expectations in all areas, including economic, political and social. This has forced these governments to look for foreign aid and loans as well as political support rather than focusing on putting their countries on the path of reform which is a strong blow to the principal of revolution that is against any regime where dependency represents one of its fundamental pillars. These movements have suffered a blow to their reputation, credibility and popularity.

To ensure a successful transition, all parties including the opposition and the governments in power must work together and participate in the crucial stage of building the state institutions based on strong fundamentals. This has not been the case in the Arab countries after the revolution where race for power rather than reform was the focus.

It has become apparent that if the Muslim Brotherhood were successful in running their parties, they have not had the same luck with running their countries. This is the essence of the current crisis that brought their countries to almost a political stand still. The current regimes seems to be stuck and don't know exactly where they are going amid adversity that is hitting them from every direction. To resolve this crisis will require a high degree of wisdom, courage and foresight. The revolution remains greater and deeper and far-reaching that the governance. The spirit of rebellion has reached countries where there hasn't been a change in power where voices are heard loud protesting oppression, corruption and social injustice.

There should be a distinction between two kinds of uprisings [16]; the **BUSTLING SPRING** and the **SILENT UPRISING**. The first is publicly announced and can lead to the change of political systems. Whilst the Silent uprising expresses itself through the means of social communication, that are traded in quietly, and aims at reforming the regimes and the regulations and not necessarily to change them. This model is considered as reformist and not revolutionary.

In this context, many Gulf countries including Saudi Arabia have called for political reform through the release of detainees, and change to the way and methods the police use when dealing with frustrated citizens who are fed up and suffer from poverty, unemployment, financial and administrative corruption, declining interest in health and education. Such message is the most important and prominent in recent times in the region. The so called Arab spring [17] is an indication of the start of a historic change in the region, and special attention should be paid to its nation who is asking for social justice [18,19], right of participation and inclusion in political life as well as defending its dignity.

From this angle, the Arab nation is facing a real dilemma that must be recognized and dealt with. At a time that the region is going through a radical change, instability and insecurity hangs on the Arab arena. When considering the scene there are only three projects, Economic development in Turkey, Political development in Iran and the settlement expansion in Israel. It does not stop at this point, because there are significant shifts occurring on the ground that suggest that the region is re-mapping, and could be on the way to what is new Sykes / Picot. The situation on the ground manifests the following observations;

Iraq is being divided after the demolition practiced by the American occupation. The Kurdish region has separated from Iraq and will soon achieve full independence; There is currently a strong call for the division of Iraq into three regions, one for the Kurds, the second for the Shiites, and the third for the Sunnites.

Evidences show that Syria is about to enter into the same stage, especially in light of the severe vibrations that hit the pillars of the regime, and the anticipation of the establishment of the State of Allauiites on the coast in the case of the fall of the president Assad. According to available information assets have been transferred to the Central Bank of Latakia, the airport and seaport being equipped for this purpose. However, President Assad has denied this during many interviews.

The fall of the Syrian regime will have a direct impact on the balance of power in Lebanon, notably a negative impact on Hezbollah, with this in mind the new situation in Syria will be antagonistic to Iran in particular. This may encourage the Suniites in Iraq to rise up against the regime. With this in mind Turkey has preceded it and reached a reconciliation agreement with the detainee Kurdish leader Abdullah Ojalan, to avoid the opportunity to use the Kurdish case fomenting unrest in Turkish territories.

Israel has apologized to Turkey and reinstated relations after ties were cut for three years; this seems to be in anticipation of the situation after the fall of the Syrian regime. There are many interrogation points about the status of Iran at some point after the fall of President Assad. And the potential of a military strike by Israel has not been ruled out yet.

South Sudan separated from the north, and calls for separation are strong in southern Yemen too. The Amazigh community in Morocco is showing some developments, which indicates that, the achievements in the cultural field, is in the process of transition to the process of political demands.

At the present there are confrontations between the Salafists and the Renaissance movement in Tunisia, tension in Egypt between the Salafists and the Muslim Brotherhood, and high tension between the last and the army, confrontation between the Salafists and the state in Algeria. These confrontations create tension between Liberalism and Islamic groups, which is sharp in Egypt, Tunisia, and to some extent in Morocco. In the absence of a prospect of any solution to the

Palestinian cause in the foreseeable future, the prospect of a third intifada in the occupied territories is stronger than ever despite the geographical separation between the West Bank and Gaza.

Turkey has reached to understanding with Israel, and Tehran reached to understanding with Washington and questions arise about the prospects of final agreement between Tehran and Washington, especially as the current U.S. Secretary of State is in support of the idea. This agreement became more achievable after the departure of Mr. Ahmadi Nejad in the last presidential elections. So in the case of such agreement being achieved, the Arabs would be in a weaker position, if such agreement isn't reached at the detriment of their interests in any case.

There are many possible scenario cases, but the danger is that they take place without taking into consideration the interests of the Arab nation that could have catastrophic consequences in the region and its people. These indicators are sufficient to demonstrate that the map of the Arab world is being redrafted.

REFERENCES

1. Bishara M (2012) The Invisible Arab: The Promise and Peril of the Arab Revolution.
2. Browers ML (2009) Political Ideology in the Arab World. Accommodation and Transformation, Cambridge University Press, New York.
3. Tripp C (2007) A History of Iraq. Cambridge University Press, New York.
4. International Monetary Fund (2014) Regional Economic Outlook Update. Middle East and Central Asia, Washington, D.C.
5. Al-Atrash H, Yousef T (2000) Intra-Arab trade: Is it too little?. IMF Working Paper 10, International Monetary Fund, Washington, D.C.

6. Noland M, Pack H (2007) The Arab Economies in a Changing World.

7. Tarek M, Yousef (2004) Development, growth and policy reform in the Middle East and North Africa since 1950. J Econ Perspect 18: 91-115.

8. Industrial Development Report (2009) United Nations Industrial Development Organization. Oxford University Press, Oxford.

9. The World Bank (2008) MENA Economic Developments and Prospects: Regional Integration for Global Competitiveness. Washington, D.C.

10. Nugent JB, Yousef TM (2005) Does MENA defy gravity: How MENA has performed in its intraregional, EU and other trade. EUI Working Paper 2005/26, European University Institute, Florence.

11. International Crisis Group (2011) Popular Protest in North Africa and the Middle East (VI): The Syrian People's Slow-Motion Revolution. MENA Report 108, Brussels.

12. Tripp C (2013) The Power and the People: Paths of the Resistance in the Middle East. Cambridge University Press, New York.

13. Carapico S (1998) Civil Society in Yemen: The Political Economy of Activism in Modern Arabia. Cambridge University Press, New York.

14. Henry CM, Springborg R (2010) Globalization and the Politics of Development in the Middle East. Cambridge University Press, Cambridge.

15. Hudson MC, (1998) Middle East Dilemma: The Politics and Economics of Integration. I. B. Tauris, London.

16. Pace M, Cavatorta F (2012) The Arab Uprisings in Theoretical Perspective - An Introduction. Mediterranean Politics 17: 125-138.

17. Bradley JR (2012) After the Arab Spring: How Islamists Hijacked the Middle East Revolts. Palgrave Macmillan, Newyork.

18. Halpern M (1963) The Politics of Social Change in the Middle East and North Africa. Princeton University Press, Princeton, NJ.

19. Heydemanm S (2000) War, Institutions, and Social Change in the Middle East. University of California Press, Berkeley.

2
CHAPTER

Analyzing Direct and Indirect Effects of Economic Sanctions on I. R. Iran Economic Growth: Focusing on the External Sector of the Economy

Morteza Ezzati

Tarbiat Modares University, Tehran, Iran

ABSTRACT

In this paper, we analyze direct and indirect effects of economic sanctions on I. R. Iran's economic growth from 1979 to 2012 focusing on the external sector of the economy. Our data for variables except for sanction are derived from 1966 to 2012 and a dummy variable is used for each sanction's beginning years. The designed model is based on the endogenous growth models in which we analyze the effects by 2SLS econometric method. Our findings indicate that economic sanctions have not directly affected Iran's economic growth so much. These effects have been indirect through restricting total imports, capital goods imports, imports of intermediate goods and primary products and also the export leading to decreased economic growth of the country.

Keywords: Sanction, Economic Growth, I. R. Iran, External Sector

1. INTRODUCTION

One of the economic and political means of imposing the demands of a country or in other words, meeting its interests by another country is the use of sanctions. In this case, a great and politically and economically influential country may be able to impose economic and political costs on a smaller state through implementing restrictions on that smaller and less influential country and this can be intensified if other great actors of the world of politics and economy cooperate with that sanctioning country, a situation that may be expected for the sanctions imposed on Iran's economy. Considering the importance of this issue, in this paper, we will look into the effects of economic sanctions on Iran's economic growth.

In this article, at first we have a look at economic sanctions against Iran and review research literature. Then, we analyze growth models and so the model for this study is developed based on the theoretical assumptions and frameworks concerning economic growth models. Then in the methodology section, the self-explanatory models with broad intervals and also unit root time series are explained. According to the selected method for estimating the research model, the model is explained as a dynamic, long- term and short-term model. The variables used in the research model are then checked in terms of the existence of unit root using generalized Dickey-Fuller test; the two models are estimated within the system of equations concurrent with dummy variables representing sanctions.

2. HISTORY OF SANCTIONS AGAINST IRAN

2.1. History of United Nations Sanctions

Economic sanctions are mostly known as alternative to war and coercive force. Different countries use limited economic sanctions against target countries to achieve their own political purposes, but this kind of sanctions has been generally ineffective. Diplomatic and economic sanctions have been rarely done on the part of international organizations. The community of nations which during the years between the two world wars had the ruling role in coordination of the world affairs, attempted to impose sanctions only four times that was successful only two times. Also, before sanctions against Iraq in 1990, United Nations has made a comprehensive set of sanctions only for three times. After Iraq sanctions, UN Security Council has imposed other sanctions against countries, people and groups; among those sanctions, the most important are the following ones:

Liberia (2003), Democratic Republic of the Congo (2004), terrorist groups and non- state actors (2004), Ivory Coast (2004), Sudan (2004), The suspects in the murder of Hariri (2005), Democratic People's Republic of Korea (2006), and then Iran sanctions since 2007 [1] .

In addition to UN sanctions, countries themselves also impose sanctions against other countries unilaterally or multilaterally. US has applied these sanctions more than any other country. Just Clinton's association made unilateral sanctions against 35 countries. These countries constituted 42 percent of the world's population and 19 percent of the world's exports consumers. United States itself has suffered much damage by these sanctions. According to Heritage institute estimations, economic sanctions against 42 countries have decreased United States annual exports about 19 billion dollars and have abrogated 200,000 jobs. Also, the export sector workers have lost a billion dollar of their wages.

2.2. Classifying Sanctions

Sanctions can be classified by different approaches. Here, we just mention a number of classifications.

Regarding the context of economic sanctions, sanctions are classified into two categories:

1) Trade sanctions where exports to and imports from the target country is restricted or cut off.

2) Limit or cut off financial ties.

From the perspective of sanction targets, sanctions are divided into two categories:

1) Economic sanctions with strategic purposes and,

2) Sanctions for other economic or non-strategic purposes.

Sanction for strategic purposes is often an alternative for the war option since it costs less than war and so justified for them.

In other way, sanctions are classified to economic and non-economic ones. Non- economic sanctions start before the economic ones, aimed at encouraging policy change in the target country. Non-economic sanctions are different depending on the country and the situations.

On the other hand, sanctions can also be classified according to their adopting and performing agents. Thus, sanctions can be grouped in three distinct branches:

1) Unilateral sanctions like US sanction against Iran.

2) Sanctions by some countries or unions such as the European Union sanctions against Iran.

3) Sanctions by UN Security Council like Security Council sanctions against Iran.

This latter classification can be of higher importance in terms of universality and efficiency and is more compatible with our study.

2.3. Sanctions against Iran

The greatest sanction against Iran is the nuclear ones which are provided by UN security council and binding to all countries. Besides, American and European Union's sanctions are applied separately. In the following Tables 1-3, these three groups of sanctions are listed along with their beginning years.

3. RESEARCH LITERATURE

Iran's nuclear sanctions have little background. However, good academic studies have been done on the effect of sanctions on the Iranian economy in recent years; we will refer to these studies.

The effect of sanctions on Iranian economy can be of different natures. A number of experimental academic researches dealing with sanctions against Iran have tried to explore and analyze some of these effects. Now we mention these studies.

Yavari and Mohseni [2] evaluated the effects of US financial and commercial sanctions on Iranian economy in a historical study. They have tried through a statistical analysis to survey the effects of US trade and financial sanctions against Iran in 2000 on oil and non-oil exports as well as on imports of capital goods and foreign exchange facilities. The study concluded that sanctions have reduced non-oil exports and imports of capital goods, but have had no effects on oil exports. It also concluded that financial sanctions have had a greater impact on the economy and have increased lenders' expected interest rates. The effect of the above-mentioned sanctions has been estimated through measuring Iranian consumer's surplus as equal to 1.1 percent of the annual GDP of the country.

Table 1. UN security council nuclear sanctions against Iran.

Date	Resolution no.	The important issues of sanctions
31.7.2006 (A.C) 9/5/1385 (Hijri-Shamsi)	1996	The first resolution just asks Iran to stop the Nuclear program. It also threatens to boycott.
23.12.2006 3/10/1385	1737	Prohibits the sale or transfer to Iran of any materials or equipment that could have military application. Members are also bound to seize assets of 22 companies and individuals related to Iran's nuclear program.
24.3.2007 4/1/1386	1747	The banning in this resolution of purchasing offensive weapons from Iran in which countries were also demanded to be on sober and self-control to sell such equipment to Iran. Also, individuals and financial institutions around the world were asked to avoid making any new financial commitment with Iran except for humanitarian or human development cases. In this resolution, the names of 18 companies, banks and individuals associated with Iran's nuclear and missile programs were added to the blacklist.
3.3.2008 13/12/1386	1803	UN members voluntarily restrict their cooperation with Iranian banks active in their country. But the resolution obliges members to stop collaborating with Iran's national and export credit banks, because of what was called facilitating Iran's and local terrorist organizations' Nuclear and missile programs. These two banks denied the charges. According to this resolution, 13 people and 12 Iranian companies were subject to seizure of their assets and travel ban. Finally, this resolution allowed members to search air and sea cargoes to the destination of or with the origin of Iran, if they have a reasonable cause.
29.9.2008 6/7/1387	1835	No new economic or political sanctions against Iran; However, Tehran was demanded to "immediately" enforce provisions of the previous resolutions of the Security Council, most importantly to suspend uranium enrichment.
9.6.2010 19/3/1389	1929	Intensification of former penalties, and prohibition of the transfer of missile technology to Iran. The sale of nuclear equipments to Iran was banned as well. Specifically, Iranian Revolutionary Guards and the Islamic Republic of Iran Shipping Company were targets of the new sanctions. Finally, this resolution wanted the members to prevent the establishment of new branches of Iranian banks in their territory or the engagement of the banks and financial institutions active in their territory in trade with Iran.

Table 2. US major sanctions against Iran.

Date	Sanction reason	The important issues of sanctions
1358	Capture of the spy nest	Blocking all Iranian assets in America and refusing to deliver equipment and goods purchased.
1361	Alleged involvement in an explosion at the military headquarters of America	A ban on lending and facilities, export of needed spare parts, sale of aircraft and its fuel, and imports of oil products.
1369	Chemical weapons production alleged	A ban on the export of chemical and biological agents that might be used in making weapons.
1370	Manufacturing powerful military equipment by Iran	A ban on the export of any goods that might be used in making military equipment.
1373	Accused of supporting terrorism	A comprehensive ban on foreign capital and a comprehensive ban on the import and export.
1374	Financial support for Palestine	A ban on capital and exchanges of more than $40 million.
1385	Accused of supporting terrorism	Sanctions on Bank-e Sepah, bank-e Saderat, bank-e Mellt and boycott of Iran's Qods Force and Iran's 27 other organizations.
1386	Nuclear program	Sanctions of the shipping industry and intensifying aviation sanctions.
1388	Charges of violation of human rights and dealing with Seditionists	Tightening of the sanctions against Iranian Revolutionary Guards and a freeze on assets of people of the government.
1389	Nuclear program	Central Bank of Iran sanctions, freezing assets of 180 individuals and companies, a ban on international cooperation in uranium mining activities, a ban on purchasing any military equipment, refusing to cooperate in missile affairs, ceasing banking and financial transactions, sanctioning of 61 foreign companies trading with Iran and failure to provide international insurance services.
1390	Nuclear program	A ban on purchase and signing the contract in oil industry and embargo commercial bank of Iran.
1390	Support for the Syrian government and resistance	Sanction of Iran's ministry of information, Qods force and police, A ban on cooperation with companies associated with Iran's Department of Defense, Revolutionary Guards and etc.
1391	Nuclear program	Tightening sanctions on Iranian oil purchase, asset freeze on individuals and companies associating with Iran's banking and oil activities, toughening sanctions against Iran's national oil tanker company and its 27 associated companies.
1391	Supporting Islamic Awakening	Iran's Broadcasting sanctions and also applying restrictions and prohibitions for EzatollahZarghami.
1391	Missile and satellite capacity	Sanction on national space industry organization, and limitations for 50 related financial and technical companies.
1392	Nuclear program	Publishing a ban on petrochemical industry and exchanges, 19 people and companies associated with Iran, including Iran's aviation Industry Organization, Qods aviation industry and ErtebatGostarNovin Corporation.

Table 3. The European union sanctions against Iran's nuclear program.

Date	The important issues of sanctions
19.4.2007 1386 (Hijri-Shamsi)	Cooperation with Iran to import and export equipments to enrich uranium and build nuclear weapons was forbidden for members and a number of Iranian individuals and companies involved in Iran's nuclear and missile programs were doomed to the seizure of assets and a travel ban under the EU Europe.
10.2009 1388	Several Iranian officials, including Ali Akbar Salehi, head of Iran's Atomic Energy Organization were banned from traveling to EU countries due to nuclear activities. However, after the appointment of Salehi as the official Iranian Foreign Minister, this ban was canceled as a result of some criticisms in February 2011.
26.7.2010 1389	European airports were prohibited from accepting cargo flights of Iran's destination or origin.
12.8.2010 1389	European countries were banned from a joint venture with the Iranian parts in oil and gas industry of Iran. Also, Europe Union members were no longer allowed to give insurance to the Iranian government. Dealing, brokerage or assistance in the issuance of government bonds, central bank or Iranian banks is forbidden for financial institutions of the Union. Cooperating with Iran in importing and exporting of weapons and equipments for uranium enrichment or those of dual-use-civilian and military-and also sale and transfer of equipments and technology for oil refinement or natural gas condensing to the Islamic Republic was banned, too.
23.5.2011 1390	The scope of Iran's nuclear sanctions was expanded and more than a hundred people or companies including Islamic Republic of Iran Shipping Lines were subjected to sanctions against Iran's nuclear program.

Aziznejad and Seyednourani [3] investigated the effects of US sanctions on Iran's foreign trade until 2008. They have investigated the effects of sanctions on three domains of energy, goods and banking services by statistical analysis of Iran's economy data. The study concluded that Iran's energy sect has not been affected by sanctions until 2008. However, since 2007, the price of capital goods imported from Europe has increased 7 to 10 percent. Also, until 2008, Iranian banks had successfully managed sanctions by various techniques and good management so that they had not experienced much effect.

PourebadolahanQuichi, RahnamaiGharamaleki and Hojatkhah [4] investigated the effects of the costs of domestic research and development and capital and mediating goods imports on production in Iran's industry and then concluded about sanctions.

Valizadeh [5] examined approaches and theories in sanctions' effectiveness on international political economy. This study attempted to explore some new theories and approaches about the effectiveness of especially economic sanctions from an international political economy viewpoint.

ZiaieBigdeli, Gholami and TahmasbiBoldaji [6] investigated the effect of economic sanctions on Iran's trade using gravity model. The main purpose of this study was to estimate the effect of economic sanctions on Iran's bilateral trade with its 30 business partners over the period 1974-2005. The results indicate that the sanctions had negative but little effect on Iran's trade with its business partners.

Alirezaie and RajabiTanha [7] analyzed the productivity growth of regional electricity companies, considering sanction situations and the relevant policies, by using a precise mathematical model.

Department of nation's insurance economic studies [8] has analyzed the effects of economic sanctions on the country's insurance industry considering the effects of inflation due to targeting of subsidies and exchange rate appreciation in the context of the possible option and cynical form. According to this study, sanctions increase the risk of the insurance industry in the country. The first immediate effect is the outgrowing of the country's insurance market. The second indirect effect of sanctions on the insurance industry is through affecting economic growth; the reduction of economic growth in turn brings about the consequent influence on insurance industry.

Ghaffari, Jalouli, and Changi Ashtiani [9] estimated the effects of exchange rate increase and currency shocks in the framework of a macro-econometric model of small- scale structure of o the economic growth of the major sectors of Iran's economy (1976- 2012).

Torbat [10] estimated the Impact of US's trade and financial sanctions against Iran in a statistical investigation. The study has tried to estimate direct financial costs of these sanctions in three sections of foreign borrowing, financing oil projects, and costs of financial sanctions. These costs have been estimated for Iran to be 2.1% to 3.6% of GDP and 23.4 to 40.5 dollars per capita in 2000.

Cordesman and Burke [11] analyzed the effects of US sanctions on Iran's military imports costs. This study also compared Iran with some other countries of the region. It shows that Iranian military imports have increased between 2003 and 2005, but in the long term, from 1993 to 2005, they have decreased.

Hakim and Rashidian [12] estimated the effects of sanctions on Tehran stock market assets and relationship with regional markets (in period of 1998 to 2009). The model for this study was estimated in GARCH method. The results show that sanctions have had a negative impact on returns of Tehran Stock Exchange market and increased capital risk of regional capital stock markets.

Thompson [13] investigated the impact of the fourth round of US sanctions against Iran in 2010. This study has shown that sanctions pressed Iran's economy, but not enough to stop Iran's nuclear program.

Cordesman and others [14] in a study named "American-Iranian strategic competition in the game of sanctions: energy, military control, and changing system" which is part of a long-term, multi-year review of the international strategic studies center, investigated the operations of India, Japan, Korea, Russia, China, Turkey and Persian Gulf countries in context of sanctions and evaluated the effects of sanctions on oil and gas imports along with Iran's efforts to become self-sufficient and deal with sanctions.

Cordesman and others [15] updated the above-mentioned study in 2013 by adding more statistical data and more elaborate analysis. The report indicated that change in government authorities' views of sanctions and the consequent switching to talks is the result of developing sanctions' pressure and internal concerns.

Farahani and Shabani [16] have studied the effects of sanctions on Iran's tourism. They have examined data from 2003 to 2012 using descriptive statistics (some data were until 2008). In this study, data from national, civil, family and global tourism in Iran was employed. The main finding is that sanctions did not reduce tourism and its growth. Data showed that on the contrary, in certain areas, tourism growth rate has increased.

Pour international institute [17] checked the effects of sanctions on Iran's health and hygiene sects. This study was done via a survey questioning four subject groups of pharmacy owners, managers of drug manufacturing, drug importing and drug distributing companies including also 13 Aban Pharmacy. The findings of this study show that sanction via reduced availability of drug had an adverse effect on the Iranians health.

Cordesman et al. [18] updated the above-mentioned study in 2014 by adding more statistical data and further analysis along with a review of the chapter headings. This report pointed out some new data and issues discussing the consequences of developing pressures of sanctions, as well.

Moret [19] in a documentary analysis based on data from different documents attempted to investigate the anti-humanitarian effects of economic sanctions on Iran and Syria. He concludes that sanctions had many negative effects on humanitarian fields of these two countries. In addition to these studies, there have been done further studies concerning sanctions with different approaches which have little relevance to our review. So, we will not mention them.

As the review of literature suggests, there is no reliable research on sanctions' effect on Iran's economic growth so that further studies with experimental data are needed in this field.

4. DATA

Variables, except for sanctions, for the period of 1977-2012 are taken from time-series data and economic indicators of the Central Bank of the Islamic Republic of Iran, yearbooks of Statistics Center of Iran and vice president of strategic planning and monitoring.

Sanction variable: A looking at Iran's sanctions show that these sanctions are very extensive. Furthermore, sanctions have been simultaneously applied by different countries with dissimilar degrees. Hence, making these variables numeric and creating indexes for them is a very difficult task. Also, using a permanent variable as binary (0, 1) data for each sanction is difficult to the same extent. This is so because sanctions started at times close to each other and were approved and applied by three main agents that have much overlap in terms of their beginning years.

For simplicity and interoperability of inserting them into our model, we define sanction years as those years when sanctions have started and the years that followed and accordingly we assume each year that a sanction (or a set of sanctions) has started as our dummy variable so that we may pick a dummy variable for each year inserted in these three tables and allocate the zero value to years before that year and set value one for the following years. We insert each of these dummy variables separately into our model and estimate its effect. On this basis and with a look at years that these sanctions have been applied, we have 20 dummy variables for showing various sanctions; these variables will be entered into the model separately.

5. MODEL

In order to analyze direct and indirect effects of sanctions on country's economic growth, two concurrent models have been assumed; in the first model, the demand for import per capita of workers has been entered and in the second one, instead of demand for total imports, the imports of capital, intermediate and primary goods have been entered. The first model consists of three equations as follows:

$$LYL_t = \alpha_0 + \alpha_1 KL_t + \alpha_2 LH_t + \alpha_3 LXNOL_t + \alpha_4 LXOL_t + \alpha_5 LML_t + \alpha_6 SANC_t + e_t \quad (1.1)$$

$$LXL_t = \beta_0 + \beta_1 LYL_t + \beta_2 LEXCH_t + \beta_3 LFM_t X_t + \beta_4 LPXM_t + \beta_5 SANC_t + w_t \quad (1.2)$$

$$LML_t = \gamma_0 + \gamma_1 LYL_t + \gamma_2 LPD_t + \gamma_3 LPM_t + \gamma_5 VOLEX_t + \gamma_6 SANC_t + v_t \quad (1.3)$$

The second model is also formed by four equations as follows:

$$LYL_t = \alpha_0 + \alpha_1 KL_t + \alpha_2 LH_t + \alpha_3 LXNOL_t + \alpha_4 LXOL_t + \alpha_5 LMKL_t + \alpha_6 LMCL_t + \alpha_7 SANC_t + e_t \quad (2.1)$$

$$LXL_t = \beta_0 + \beta_1 LYL_t + \beta_2 LEXCH_t + \beta_3 LFM_t X_t + \beta_4 LPXM_t + \beta_5 SANC_t + w_t \quad (2.2)$$

$$LMKL_t = \gamma_0 + \gamma_1 LYL_t + \gamma_2 LPD_t + \gamma_3 LPM_t + \gamma_5 VOLEX_t + \gamma_6 SANC_t + v_t \quad (2.3)$$

$$LMCL_t = \theta_0 + \theta_1 LYL_t + \theta_2 LPD_t + \theta_3 LPM_t + \theta_5 VOLEX_t + \theta_6 SANC_t + \xi_t \quad (2.4)$$

As it can be seen in the second model, Equation (2.2) is the same as Equation (1.2) so as in both models, the exogenous variables are the same and thus these equations are common to both models.

In equations of both models, we have:

LYL: The natural logarithm of GDP per capita of the labor force (working population).

LKL: The natural logarithm of physical capital per capita of workers.

LH: The natural logarithm of human capital (workers' average years of education).

LXL: The natural logarithm of exports per capita of the employed workforce.

LML: The natural logarithm of imports per capita of the employed workforce.

LPD: The natural logarithm of the price index for domestic manufactured and consumed goods.

LPM: The natural logarithm of the price index of imported goods.

LPXM: The natural logarithm of the ratio of price index of exported goods to that of imported ones.

LPFMX: The natural logarithm of the ratio of price index of goods in foreign markets to that of Iran's exported goods.

LEXCH: The natural logarithm of the real effective exchange rate.

VOLEX: The volatility index of the real effective exchange rate (conditional variance of LEXCH variable).

LMKL: The natural logarithm of the demand for capital goods per the employed workforce.

LMKIL: The natural logarithm of the demand for the intermediate and primary goods per the workforce employed.

SANC: a Vector containing dummy variables considered as alternative variables to sanctions imposed by the United States of America, Europe Union and the United Nations (International Security Council) on Iran.

e_t، v_t، w_t، ϑ_t و ξ_t: are disturbance terms of the equations.

As shown in both equations, LYL, LXL, LML, LMKL and LMKIL are endogenous variables and other variables are exogenous.

Statistics related to research variables for the period of 1977-2012 are taken out of time-series data and economic indicators of the Central Bank of the Islamic Republic of Iran, the statistical yearbooks published by the Iran's Statistical Center, vice-president of strategic planning and monitoring and the World Bank. The two-stage least squares (2SLS) method will be used for estimating the model of the present study.

6. ANALYZING THE MODEL AND INTERPRETING THE RESULTS

Classical and conventional econometric methods for estimating model parameters using time-series data are based on the assumption that the variables are static. So, before doing any econometric analysis, it's necessary to determine whether the variables are static. KPSS unit root test results in Table 4 indicate that all variables are stable. As a result, estimations carried out via these variables will have enough credibility and the obtained relationships will not be false. The results of estimating through 2SLS method, the equations of the first model of the research, are presented in Table 5 and the similar results for the second model equations estimated by the same method are presented in Table 6.

The null hypothesis of KPSS test assumes the variables' stability and the opposite hypothesis assumes that there is a single unit root.

0, c and t represent the extended Dickey-Fuller test modes, respectively: with no intercept and time-trend, with intercept and with time trend.

Table 4. Results of KPSS unit root test.

Variable	Test mode	KPSS statistics	Critical values at risk			Results
			Percent[1]	Percent[5]	Percent[10]	
LYL	(c, 0)	0/134	0/216	0/146	0/119	Steady at 5 percent risk
LKL	(c, t)	0/144	0/216	0/146	0/119	Steady at 5 percent risk
LH	(c, 0)	0/458	0/739	0/463	0/347	Steady at 5 percent risk
LXL	(c, t)	0/088	0/216	0/146	0/119	Steady at 5 percent risk
LML	(c, t)	0/144	0/216	0/146	0/119	Steady at 5 percent risk
LMKL	(c, t)	0/138	0/216	0/146	0/119	Steady at 5 percent risk
LMIL	(c, t)	0/142	0/216	0/146	0/119	Steady at 5 percent risk
LEXCH	(c, 0)	0/302	0/739	0/463	0/347	Steady at 5 percent risk
LPD	(c, t)	0/133	0/216	0/146	0/119	Steady at 5 percent risk
LPM	(c, t)	0/108	0/216	0/146	0/119	Steady at 5 percent risk
LPXM	(c, t)	0/121	0/216	0/146	0/119	Steady at 5 percent risk
LPFMX	(c, t)	0/187	0/216	0/146	0/119	Steady at 1 percent risk
VOLEX	(c, t)	0/054	0/216	0/146	0/119	Steady at 5 percent risk

Table 5. Results of estimating the first model equations by 2SLS method.

Equation	(1.1)		(2.2) and (1.2)		(1.3)	
Dependent variable	LYL		LXNOL		LML	
Independent variable	Factor	Standard deviation	Factor	Standard deviation	Factor	Standard deviation
Intercept	0/268	0/213	*3/160	0/754	*1/284	0/465
LKL	*0/539	0/063				
LH	*0/278	0/046				
LXL	*0/363	0/034				
LML	*0/094	0/033				
LYL			*2/274	0/346	*1/691	0/173
LEXCH			*−0/219	0/065		
LPFMX			0/071	0/045		
LPXM			*0/447	0/111		
LPD					*0/801	0/255
LPM					*−0/930	0/270
VOLEX					*−5/540	1/771
US87	*−0/232	0/041				
US01			**−0/187	0/081		
US04			*−0/332	0/089		
US09					***−0/108	0/058

*, ** and *** show the significance at the probability levels of one, five, and ten percent, respectively.

Table 6. The results of estimating the second model equations by 2SLS method.

Function	(2.1)		(2.3)		(2.4)	
Dependent variable	LYL		LMKL		LMIL	
Independent variable	Factor	Standard deviation	Factor	Standard deviation	Factor	Standard deviation
Intercept	*0/331	0/207	−0/821	0/791	0/821	0/792
LKL	*0/530	0/059				
LH	0/286	0/055				
LXL	**0/360	0/030				
LMKL	***0/0045	0/023				
LMIL	*0/052	0/017				
LYL			*1/312	0/367	*1/312	0/367
LPD			**0/916	0/404	**0/916	0/404
LPM			**−0/915	0/393	**−0/915	0/393
VOLEX			−3/924	3/510	−3/924	3/510
US79			*−0/648	0/179	*−0/647	0/178
US87	*−0/243	0/037				
US01			**−0/362	0/138	**−0/362	0/139
US06			*−0/183	0/065	*−0/183	0/065
US07			**−0/129	0/055	**−0/129	0/055
US09					−0/103	0/089

*, ** and *** shows the probability level of 1%, 5%, and 10%, respectively.

It should be noted that in all equations estimated, dummy variables of SANC are entered in step-forward way for all the sanctions. Finally, dummy variable or variables which were statistically significant have been preserved in the model and the remaining ones were removed. Also, since the relations (1.2) and (1.4) in the first model are the same as relations (2.2) and (2.5) in the second model, the results of these estimations have been reported only in Table 5.

Based on estimated results of Equation (1.1), we may say that:

- By a one percent increase in the physical capital per capita of the working force, GDP per capita of that force will have a 0.539% increase.
- By a one percent increase in human capital (average years of schooling of employees), GDP per capita of the labor force will increase by 0.278 percent.
- By a one percent increase in the country's exports per capita, GDP per capita of the labor will increase by 0.363 percent.

- By a one percent increase in imports per capita, GDP per capita of the labor will increase by 0.094 percent.
- But significant negative coefficient of 1987 sanction of US against Iran shows that after this sanction, Iran's economic growth has been declined by 0.232 percent. This is normal because this sanction was concurrent with the year 1366 when Iran was at the height of the war , and the country's infrastructures were damaged; on the other hand, this sanction beside restricting the export of technology to Iran, banned import of all goods and services from Iran to United States of America, too. Since at that time Iran was heavily involved in war and its exports was severely restricted and did not either have significant business relationship with the United States, it can be concluded that this negative impact much beyond indicating the effects of US sanction against Iran shows the impact of the war on the economic growth variable. As a result, it can be stated that the United States sanctions have not directly affected Iran's economic growth.

Based on the estimated coefficients of Equation (1.2) in the first model and the Equation (2.2) in the second model, we have:

- By one percent increase in the real effective exchange rate, non-oil exports of Iran per the workforce declines by 0.219 percent. This coefficient is negative due to the fact that the export industry's dependence on importing capital, intermediate and primary goods is rooted in the very production process so that as exchange rate appreciates, the costs of importing these industries increase more than their exporting earnings and consequently, industrial production and exporting react negatively to exchange rate appreciation.
- Ÿ Faced with a one percent increase in GDP per capita of the employed people, the country's non-oil exports increase by 2.274 percent.
- With one-percent increase in the ratio of the price index of the goods in foreign markets to the index of export goods, the country's exports per capita increases by 1.149 percent.

- By a one-percent increase in the ratio of the exported goods' price index to imported goods' price index, exports per capita of the country will increase by 0.447 percent.
- The negative significant coefficient of 2001 and 2004 US sanctions against Iran suggests that after these sanctions, Iran's non-oil exports were reduced by 0.186 and 0.332 percent, respectively.
- According to the coefficients of the Equation (1.3), we can state that:
- By a one percent increase in GDP per capita of the employees, the demand for imports per capita increases by 1.691 percent.
- With a one percent increase in produced and consumed goods inside the country, country's demands for imports rises by 0.801 percent.
- With a one percent increase in the price index of imported goods, the demand for imports decreases by 0.930 percent.
- The significant negative coefficient of exchange rate fluctuation index indicates the negative effects of uncertainty in the exchange rate market on the demand per capita of imports.
- But significant negative coefficient of 2009 US sanction against Iran indicates that after this sanction, Iran's import demand faced a 0.108 percent reduction.
- Coefficients of equation (2.1) for common variables are close to coefficients of equation (1.1); thus, only two new variables will be discussed here:
- By a one percent increase in the imports of capital goods, the employed people's GDP per capita increases by 0.045 percent.
- By a one percent increase in the imports of intermediate and primary goods, GPD per worker will increase by 0.052 percent.
- Based on coefficients of Equation (2.3), we have:
- By a one percent increase in GPD per capita of the employed people, the country's demand for imports of capital goods increases by 1.318 percent.
- By a one percent increase in price index of the goods manufactured and consumed inside the country, demands for imports of capital goods increases by 0.916 percent.
- By a one percent increase in price index of imported goods, the demand for capital goods imports decreases by 0.915 percent.

- Exchange rate volatility index is negative. However, this effect is not significant here.
- But significant negative coefficient of dummy variables of US sanction against Iran in 1979, 2001, 2006, 2007 shows that Iran's imports demand for capital goods has been reduced.
- Based on the coefficients of the Equation (2.4), we have:
- By a one percent increase in GPD per capita of employees, import demands for intermediate and primary goods will increase by 1.581 percent.
- By a one percent increase in the price index of country's manufactured and consumption goods, import demands for intermediate and primary goods will increase by 1.446 percent.
- By a one percent increase in the price index of imported goods, country's demand for imported intermediate and primary goods is reduced by 1.557 percent.
- The significant negative coefficient of the exchange rate variations suggests the negative effects of uncertainty in the exchange market rate on the demand value for imports of intermediate and primary goods of the country.
- But significant negative coefficient of dummy variables of US sanctions against Iran in 1979 and 2009 indicates that after these sanctions, demands for imports of primary and intermediate goods has been reduced.

7. CONCLUSIONS

In this study, the direct and indirect effects of sanctions on the Iranian economy were examined with an emphasis on the external sector of the economy. In this regard, two models were developed at the same time; in the first model, total imports were considered and in the second model instead of total imports, imports of capital, intermediate and primary goods used in producing jobs have been considered, and were entered into model separately. Estimates from both models simultaneously using two-stage least squares (2 sls) method for the period 1355-1391 indicated that the sanctions has no considerable direct impact on economic growth of Iran; rather, sanctions have affected economic growth indirectly by restricting the total imports, imports of capital goods, intermediate goods, primary goods, and exports leading to slowing down of the country's economic growth. In general, imports of capital goods were more sensitive to the issue of sanctions compared to other variables. Speaking more specifically, 2012 sanction led to a reduction in the country's oil export revenues, 2001 and 2003 sanctions led to a reduction in export revenues, 1979 and 2009 sanctions limited the country's imports of intermediate and primary goods, 1979, 2001, 2006, and 2007 sanctions limited the country's imports of capital goods and 2009 sanction limited the country's total import demand.

Also, based on the estimated coefficients of these models, it can be said that the determinants of economic growth in order of importance are physical capital per capita of the workers, exports per capita of the employees, human capital and imports per capita. Also, in exports per capita of workers, variables in order of importance are the workforce revenue per capita, the ratio of price index of export goods to that of import goods, the real effective exchange rate, and the ratio of price index of the goods of foreign markets to Iran's export goods' prices index.

In imports field, workers' income per capita, the prices of import goods, the prices of domestic manufactured and consumed goods are respective determinant factors.

Also, fluctuations in exchange rates limit the demand for total imports, intermediate goods, and capital goods, but these fluctuations have not any significant effect on capital goods import.

REFERENCES

1. Zarif, M.J. and Sadjadpour, S.M.K. (2008) Multilateral Diplomacy: Theory and Practice of Regional and International Organizations. Faculty of International Relations, Ministry of Foreign Affairs, Sofia, Vol. 2, 562-560.

2. Yavari, K. and Mohseni, R. (1388) The Effects of Trade and Financial Sanctions on Iranian Economy: A Historical Analysis. Majles & Rahbord Quarterly, 61, 9-53.

3. Aziznezhad, S. and Seyednourani, S.M. (1388) Analyzing the Effects of Sanctions on Iran's Economy Focusing on Foreign Business. Majles & Rahbord Quarterly, 61,165-210.

4. Porebadolahan Kovich, M. and Rahnamay Ghavamaleki, G. and HojjatKhah, R. (2010) The Role of Internal R & D and Imports of Capital and Intermediate Goods on Industries Production in I. R. Iran. Journal of Economic Research, 95, 1-30.

5. Valizadeh, A. (1389) Approaches and Theories of the Sanction Effectiveness in International Political Economy. Politics Quarterly, 17, 349.

6. Zia-eeBigdeli, M.T., Gholami, E. and TahmasbiBoldaji, F. (1391) The Analysis of the Economic Sanctions on Iran's Trade: Applying the Gravity Model Framework. Economic Research, 48, 109.

7. Alirezaee, M. and RajabiTanha, M. (1392) Assessing the Productivity Growth of the Regional Electricity Companies Regarding the Sanction Situation and Associated Policies. Journal of Quality and Productivity of Iran's Electricity Industry, 3, 1-9.

8. Nation's Security Economic Studies Organization (1392) The Effects of Economic Sanctions on Iran's Insurance Industry (Considering the Inflating Effect of Targeting Subsidies and Exchange Rate Appreciation). Research and Development Management, Report No. 47.

9. Ghaffari, H., Mahdi, J. and Ali, C.A. (2013) Forecasting Effects of Increasing, Exchange Rate on Economic Growth in Iran's Important Economic Sectors (1976-2014). Journal of Economic Growth and Development, 10, 41-58.

10. Torbat, A.E. (2005) Impacts of the US Trade and Financial Sanctions on Iran. Blackwell Publishing Ltd., Oxford.

11. Cordesman, A.H. and Burke, A.A. (2007) UN Sanctions and Iranian Arms Imports. Center for Strategic and International Studies, Washington DC.

12. Hakim, S. R. and Rashidian, M. (2009) Properties, Linkages, and the Impact of Sanctions on the Tehran Stock Exchange, June 2009.

13. Tampson, R. (2011) The Effectiveness of the Fourth Round of Sanctions against Iran. Stanford Journal of International Relations, 13, 13-1. https://web.stanford.edu/group/sjir/13-1/iran.pdf

14. Cordesman, A.H., Bosserman, B., D'Amato, J. and Gagel, A.C. (2011) US and Iranian Strategic Competitition, The Sanctions Game: Energy, Arms Control, and Regime Change. Center for Strategic and International Studies, Washington DC, 6 October 2011.

15. Cordesman, A.H., Gold, B., Khazai, S. and Bosserman, B. (2013) US and Iranian Strategic Competition: Sanctions, Energy, Arms Control, and Regime Change. Center for Strategic and International Studies, Washington DC, 22 January 2013

16. Farahani, B.M. and Shabani, M. (2013) The Impact of Sanctions on Iran's Tourism. The Open Access Journal of Resistive Economics (OAJRE)/Economic & Sanctions, 1. http://oajre.ir/wp-content/uploads/2014/07/Farahani-and-Shabani-Journal.pdf

17. Pour Institute International (2013) The Impact of Sanctions on Iranian People Healthcare. September 2013, Version 1.1.

18. Cordesman, A.H., Gold, B. and Coughlin-Schultz, C. (2014) IRAN—Sanctions, Energy, Arms Control, and Regime Change. Center for Strategic and International Studies, Washington DC, January 2014

19. Moret, E.S. (2014) Humanitarian Impacts of Economic Sanctions on Iran and Syria. European Security. http://dx.doi.org/10.1080/09662839.2014.893427 [Citation Time(s):1]

3

CHAPTER

The Impact of Competitive Devaluation on the Foreign Trade of Turkey

Parisa Fathi* and Mustafa Ersungur S

International Economy, IIBF Economics Department Ataturk University, Erzurum, Turkey

ABSTRACT

Exchange rate system, although it is an important factor in determining the real value of the currency of a country, economy, inflation, devaluation, interest rates vs. foreign trade, such as the affect in many ways. In the study, competitive devaluations and trade relationship is investigating in Turkey. The relationship between foreign trade and competitive devaluations, cumulative method ARDL approach to study is to investigate where there is a long-term relationship between the variables and factors related to long-term model and error correction is estimated between 1965-2014 periods for TB. The results indicate that positive and significant correlation between TB and RER and also between TB and GDP there is, and significant and negative correlation between TB and P, as well as between TB and G there is. Long-term variable coefficient equals 0.80.

Keywords: Devaluation; Foreign trade; ARDL

INTRODUCTION

In this study, we determine the impact of competitive devaluations in Turkey's foreign trade with econometric analysis. Competitive devaluation is usually a mover to close the current account deficit of a fiscal policy. While devaluation, decreases the export prices of currency and increases the price of imported goods of national currency. The purpose of devaluations on one hand by encouraging exports is to increase foreign exchange earnings and on the other by reducing domestic demand for imported goods is to save foreign exchange. To make a good result of devaluations in improving the current account balance, it depends on the Marshall-Lerner condition, $e_m + e_x \geq 1$. This situation by assuming an infinite traction of supply, means that the total domestic demand for imported goods(e_m) and foreign demand for exports(e_x) is greater than one. The bigger the total traction than one, the larger the impact of exchange rate adjustment in the external balance will be. The success of devaluations to keep domestic prices depends on no changing in the price of domestic goods in foreign countries as well as consumer habits. However, if the trade deficit depends on structural factors such as low productivity in the national economy, the lack of production and technology and lag of management, the success of the devaluation of national currency in foreign balance will be limited [1]. After the devaluation of the domestic currency, being the total value of traction less than one in the short term, lead the effect of J curve to be one. According to this approach, immediately after the devaluations, first the balance of foreign trade distorted more and the improvement occurs with a certain delay. In the context of summarized theoretical explanations above, it is believed that changes in the variable exchange rate affect the trade balance.

THEORETICAL FOUNDATIONS

For the first time Maggie interpreted this phenomenon based on Marshall-Lerner condition Because of the weakening national currency, the real value of import and export volume does not change, but imports more expensive than before, and thus the trade balance worsens the situation. Because by weakening the national currency, the real value of import and export volume does not change, but imports get more expensive than before thus the trade balance situation get worse. Over time, both the suppliers and consumers reacted to the weakening of the national currency and import and export values based on the relative price of domestic goods began to modulate and the trade balance situation improve. In other words, weakening the national currency with intervals affect the trade balance. The Chart of reaction trade balance delay to weaken the national currency, which resembles the letter J, called J-curve effect."

National currency devaluation has two quantity and value effects. The effects of devaluation, represents the exports increasing and imports decreasing. And the impact of its value represents an increasing in import costs according to the domestic currency. In practice it is found that the effect of value which causes deterioration in the trade balance may occur before the quantity effects which improve the trade balance. As mentioned above, this situation is known as the J-curve effect. Because in this case, the trade surplus curve will be drawn as J-curve.

LITERATURE REVIEW

Rezaei Abyaneh Bahareh [2], studied on the asymmetric effects of exchange rate fluctuations on export prices in Iran. And reached the conclusion that export prices reaction is asymmetric to increase and decrease the value of money. So the reaction of export prices according to the negative shock of exchange rate (devaluation) is more than positive shocks (increasing the value of money).

Kazerouni Ali and Mojiri Hadi [3] studied the effect of National currency devaluation on Iran's trade balance with six selected business partner. According to the experimental results between Iran, China and the United Arab Emirates in the short term, the effect of J curve has been confirmed, while it doesn't apply in the other countries (France, Germany, South Korea and Switzerland). In addition to that, J Curve only has been confirmed between Iran and the Emirates in the longer term and rejected in order to the other studied countries.

In this study Carmen and Reinhat [4] has examined the relationship between currency devaluation, relative prices and international trade.

According to the obtained results, relative prices play an important role in determining trade flows, but sometimes there is no systematic relationship between trade balance and relative prices.

Mahesh Kumar and Chaulagai [5] has tested j-curve hypothesis for Nepal and concluded that devaluation is ineffective in correcting the lack of business in Nepal.

Tirsit Genye [6] has studied the impact of devaluation on Ethiopia's economic growth. And according to these studies it is conducted that devaluation has a negative effect on gross domestic product (GDP) of Ethiopia.

DATA AND EMPIRICAL FINDINGS

Reveals the laws of economics as digital and a variety of economic issues to be examined numerically, the econometric methods are needed to assist in obtaining the correct economic decision. In the study, to establish a close relationship between theory and practice is applied econometric analysis. The results achieved by the results of the econometric analysis of the results achieved in other studies in the literature to assess whether it is in the same direction. In the study, to examine the impact of competitive devaluations in Turkey's foreign trade, it covers the years 1965-2014 data for the period between [7]. Data were taken from the World Bank and the model is as follows:

$$\ln TB_t = \beta_0 + \beta_1 \ln GDP_t + \beta_2 RER_t + \beta_3 \ln G + \beta_4 P + u_t$$

Variables used are as follows:

LNTB: was defined as the logarithm of the ratio between exports of goods (X) to imports of goods (M).

RER: the official exchange rate (official market) US dollar at the beginning of the domestic currency (ER), the US wholesale price index (WPIUS) and i in the country's consumer price index (CPI).

LN GDP_t: was defined as logarithm of the national output,

P: was defined as the inflation.

LNG: was defined as logarithm of the government expenses.

In order to evaluate the reliability of variables Dickey Fuller test is used (**TABLE 1**).

TABLE 1: Unit root test.

Variables	GDP	RER	G	P	TB
	1. difference	1. difference	1. difference	1. difference	1. difference
Test statistics	-3.753	-4.392	-2.217	-7.915	-7.057
Critical values					
1% level	-4.262	-4.356	-2.636	-3.646	-3.653
5% level	-3.552	-3.595	-1.951	-2.954	-2.951
10% level	-3.209	-3.233	-1.610	-2.615	-2.617

Regression analysis results of all data according to the level of significance of 5% is statistically significant.

DYNAMIC MODEL

Our model for dynamic pattern is as follows:

$$LTB = \alpha + \sum_{j=1}^{q} \mu_j LGDP_{t-j} + \sum_{j=0}^{p_1} \beta_{1t} LG_{t-j} + \sum_{j=0}^{p_2} \beta_{2j} RER_{t-j} + \sum_{j=0}^{p_3} \beta_{3j} P_{t-j} + T + V_t$$

Dynamic model is based on the results (**TABLE 2**), while RER and GDP positive and significant, G is negative and significant. So the reduction of the nominal value of the Turkish currency increased exports and reduced imports to Turkey, this also increase the trade balance is Turkey. Turkey's GDP increased that is an increase in both export and import, since the increase in exports greater than imports increase the country's trade balance [8]. Fiscal policy that is more in the form of increased government spending, investment and private consumption increased, leading to an increase in aggregate demand and this increased demand for imports and the trade balance will worsen (**TABLE 2**).

TABLE 2: The results dynamic pattern model.

Variable name	factor	T-statistics
LTB (-1)	0.53013	2.8826 (0.008)
LTB (-2)	-0.32962	-2.5686 (0.017)
LG	-0.65572	-3.9296 (0.001)
LG (-1)	0.59085	3.7892 (0.001)
LG (-2)	-0.34608	-3.3516 (0.003)
LGDP	0.32093	2.4428 (0.023)
P	-0.0012543	-1.9652 (0.062)
RER	0.84758	2.5371 (0.018)
C	0.68968	1.8696 (0.674)
T	-0.011980	-2.3989 (0.025)
R^2=0.72		

CONVERGENCE TEST

Dynamic model, to understand the long-term convergence is considered T-statistical model.

According to Schwarz Byzn criteria for being considered the optimum number of delays, the dependent variable (TB) is a pause, so we have:

$$t = \frac{\sum_{j=1}^{q} \lambda_j - 1}{\sum_{j=1}^{q} S_{\lambda_j}} = \frac{.53013-1}{.18391} = -2.56$$

Where t is calculated absolute values from the absolute value provided by benerje (Associated with the process, the 90% confidence level, are for 2.042) is large. H0 hypothesis is rejected, and the results show that the 90% confidence levels between the variables of the model are thought to be stable long-term relationship [9].

ESTIMATES OF LONG-TERM RELATIONSHIPS

TABLE 3, shows ARDL provide a long-term model with coefficient calculated. According to the obtained results, RER variable factors, has a positive and significant effect on the balance of payments. Assuming all other variables remain constant, if RER one percent increase, TB, 0.10601 percent increase. Just the same, the GDP variable, on TB, there is a significant and positive effect, if a percent of GDP is increase, 0.40142 percent increase in TB. G variable factors, has a negative and significant impact on the balance of payments. So if G one percent increase, TB, 0.51402 per cent decrease because when government spending increases and this will lead to an increase in aggregate demand and this increased demand for imports and the trade balance will worsen. Inflation (P) in the long term significant negative impact on trade balance (TB) Because when a country's domestic prices rise this increase imports and decrease exports, the trade balance is reduced as a result [10].

TABLE 3: Results of a long-term review model.

Variable name	Factor	T-istatistik
LG	-0.51402	-2.9224 (0.008)
LGDP	0.40142	2.2727 (0.033)
P	-0.00157	-2.1382 (0.043)
RER	0.10601	2.4596 (0.022)
C	0.86264	2.0066 (0.057)
T	-0.01498	-2.5077 (0.020)

ESTIMATION OF ERROR CORRECTION MODEL (ECM)

Error correction model, the relationship between the dependent variable and independent variables represent in the short term. ECM (-1) factor estimate for the model, -0.80 were obtained and show that each year 80 percent of short-term ımbalance TB close to the long-term stability [11].

TESTS: The estimated model, to investigate abuses and violations of Tests: The estimated model, to investigate abuses and violations of non-classical assumption is need for the implementation of some of the tests in this study and the results are brought to the **TABLE 4**.

TABLE 4: Test classic assumptions in the model search.

`Test statistic	Lagrange coefficients	Prob.	F statistic	Prob.
Autocorrelation test	0.64244	0.725	0.20847	0.813
Heterogeneity of variance test	3.5934	0.1661	1.2831	0.298

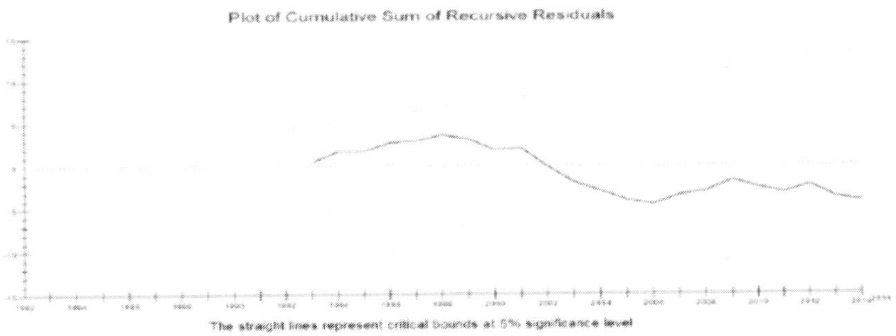

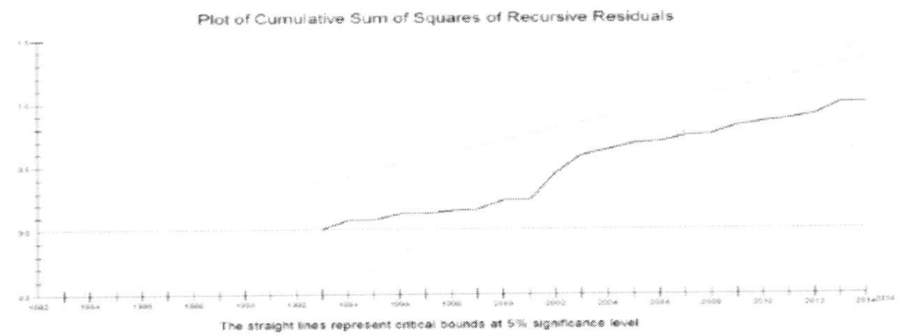

FIGURE 1: Chi-cumulative and cumulative residual waste Charts.

According to the obtained results at the level of 10%, no serial autocorrelation and variance heterogeneity deficiency hypothesis is not detectable. As a result, the model is valid classical assumptions.

STABILITY TESTING OF THE COEFFICIENT: CUSUM and CUSUMQ tests: If the cumulative residual and cumulative residual square diagrams are between two straight lines (95% confidence interval) are, the null hypothesis that there is no structural breaks will be accepted and if figures are from outside the confidence interval, presence of structural breaks will be accepted [12].

According to **FIGURE 1**, the coefficients of both models has been stable over the period examined.

RESULTS

In this paper, the impact of competitive devaluation on the trade balance of Turkey, using co-integration ARDL approach for the longterm relationship between variables is used and factor related to longterm models and error correction on the trade balance for the period 1965-2014 have been estimated. The estimated model is considered five variables: 1-Logarithm of the trade balance 2-Real exchange rate 3-Inflation 4-Logarithm of GDP 5-Logarithm of government spending. The results of long-term relationships indicates that log of governments expenditure, log of GDP, inflation and real exchange rate are factors affecting the logarithm of Turkey's trade balance. As government spending leads to an increase in aggregate demand and increase aggregate demand is also increasing import demand, and increase in import demand led to a deterioration of the trade balance of country [13]. On the other hand there is inflation reduces the effect of devaluation on the trade balance, because inflation is an increase in export prices and this led to a decline in exports and increased imports, and the trade deficit will eventually be. As well as an increase in the real exchange rate is an increase in the price of foreign goods, and this will reduce imports and raise exports, and ultimately lead to an increase in the trade balance. Increase in GDP also due to an increase in exports as well as imports, but in Turkey's exports increased more than imports, that the trade balance would be better. Here is the GDP effect on the trade balance is more than the actual exchange rate.

In the short-term analysis of a causal relationship between the model variables from short-term to long-term joint was observed.

REFERENCES

1. Seyidoglu H (2009) Uluslararas Iktisat, Istanbul: Guzem Can Yayinlari 24.

2. Bahareh RA (2011) Asymmetric effects of exchange rate fluctuations on export prices, pp. 14-20.

3. Ali K, Hadi M (2011) The effect of devaluation on the trade balance of trade with six selected partner (Auto Regressive Distributed Lag), Iran Journal of Economic Research Winter 13: 77-102.

4. Reinhat CM (1995) Devaluation, Relative Prices, and International Trade: Evidence from Developing Countries. MPRA Paper No. 6974.

5. Chaulagai MK (2015) Testing the J-Curve Hypothesis:A Case of Nepal. NRB economic review 17-36.

6. Genye T (2011) Currency Devaluation and Economic Growth, The case of Ethiopia, Stockholm University.

7. Bahmani-Oskooee M, Alse J (1994) Short-run versus longrun effects of devaluation: error correction modeling and cointegration. Eastern Economic Journal 20: 453-464.

8. Bahmani-Oskooee M, Kandil M (2009) Are Devaluations Contractionary in MENA countries? Applied Economics 41: 39-150.

9. Barson WH (1983) Economic Structure and Policy for External Balance. IMF Staff Papers.

10. Diaz-Alejando CF (1963) A Note on the Impact of Devaluation and Redistribution and the Redistributive Effect. Journal of Political Economy 71: 577-580.

11. Krugman P (1999) Balance sheets, the transfer problem, and financial crises. IT.

12. Anne DK (1983) Exchange Rate Determination, Cambridge University Press.

13. Dominic S (1987) International Economics, Macmillan.

4

CHAPTER

ECONOMIC POLICIES AND DEVELOPMENT IN SUDAN (2000-2013)

Dr. Badreldin Mohamed Ahmed Abdulrahman

Department of Economics, University of Zalingei, Sudan

ABSTRACT

Economic policies have been played a vital role on development in Less Developed countries (LDCs). This study investigates from an empirical point of view the impact of economic policies on development in Sudan during the period 2000-2013. Economic policies represent by (Money supply, Interest rate, Taxation and government expenditure) variables while gross domestic product (GDP) represents economic development. For this purpose data were collected from various sources namely Central Bank of Sudan, Central Bureau of Statistics, Taxation Chamber and ministry of Finance. By using e-views and applying ordinary less squares method to a linear form of the model, the obtained results showed that economic policies have significant impact and effect on development in Sudan during the period (2000-2013).

Keywords: *economic, policies, development, gross domestic product, data*

INTRODUCTION

Economic policy refers to the actions that governments take in the economic field. It covers the systems for setting level of taxation, government budgets, the money supply and interest rate as well as labor market, national ownership, and many of the areas of government intervention into the economy. Most factors of economic policy can be divided into either fiscal policy or monetary policy. Fiscal policy deals with government actions regarding taxation and spending, on the other hand monetary policy deals with central banking actions regarding the money supply and interest rates. Such policies are often influenced by international institutions like international monetary fund (IMF) or World Bank (WB) as well as political beliefs and the consequent policies of parties.

It is increasingly recognized that the financial system plays a crucial role in process of economic development. The government helps make this possible by adopting sound macroeconomic policies, including a sound fiscal as well as monetary policy, acting to establish financial markets where they do not yet exist, and providing prudential regulation of the financial system (Todaro and Smith, 2011).

OBJECTIVE OF THE STUDY

The objective of this study is to show the impact of economic policies on development in Sudan during the period 2000-2013. The paper falls into five sections. Section two reviews literature, while section three discusses economic development in Sudan. The empirical model and methodology as well as results and conclusion remarks are in section four and five respectively.

LITERATURE REVIEW

In developed nations monetary and financial policy play a major direct and indirect role in government efforts designed to expand economic activity in times of unemployment and excess capacity (economic recession) and to contrast that activity in times of excess demand and inflation. Basically monetary policy works on two principle economic variables: the aggregate supply of money in circulation and the level of interest rate. The supply of money (basically currency in circulation plus commercial bank deposits) is thought to be directly related to the level of economic activity in the sense that a greater money supply induces expanded economic activity by enabling people to purchase more goods and services. This in essence is the so-called (Monetary Theory of Economic Activity). Its advocates argue that by controlling the growth of money supply through central bank operations, governments can regulate their nation's economic activity. On the other side of the monetary issue are the so-called Keynesian economists who argue that an expanded supply of money in circulation increases the availability of loanable funds. A supply of loanable funds in excess of demand leads to lower interest rates. Since private investment is assumed to be inversely related to prevailing interest rates, businessmen will expand their investment as interest rate falls (Todaro, 1977).

The Less Developed Countries (LDCs) encounter greater limitations than Developed Countries in using monetary and fiscal policies to achieve macroeconomic goals. The banking system, often limited in its ability to regulate the money supply to influence output and prices in developed countries, is even more ineffective in LDCs. Usually the money market in developing countries is externally dependent, poorly organized fragmented and cartelized (Khalil, 1993). Also he said that, the most important taxation goal in LDCs is to mobilize resources for public expenditure.

According to the IMF, the amount of these resources is determined by GNP per-capita, the share of the mining sector in GNP, the share of exports in GNP and tax policy. It is describe to look at how tax policies affect public spending and the impact of taxes on stability of income and prices. However, achieving these crucial taxation goals must be viewed in light of other goals such as improved income distribution, efficient resources allocation, increased capital and enterprise and administrative feasibility. The LDCs governments must consider all of these goals when designing tax schemes to achieve rapid economic growth to improve the lot of the poor and to stabilize prices.

A widely spread belief among economists is that monetary policy has relatively short-lived effect on real variables such as unemployment. Previous studies indicate that monetary policy affects the output gap only at business cycle frequencies, but the effect on unemployment may be more persistent in countries with highly regulated labour markets (Alexius and Holmlund, 2007).

ECONOMIC DEVELOPMENT IN SUDAN

The Sudan's economy has witnessed major transformations during the last three decades. Full government control over economic activities characterized the period of the 1960s, while an inward-looking strategy dominated development policy during the early 1970s and mid-1980s. Economic difficulties assumed crisis proportions during the second half of the 1970s, following the ambitious development program launched at early 1970s. The failure of the investment boom to increase the economy's productive capacity has accelerated the crisis (Ali, 1985).

In 1979 Sudan became one of the first countries to adopt International Monetary Fund and World Bank macro-economic stabilization and structural adjustment programs. However, the economy continued to slide further through the 1978-84, which witnessed very active adjustment operations. Growth collapsed during this period to an average annual rate of -1.7% per capita, while macroeconomic policies continued to worsen. Inflation shot to more than 27% and for the first time inflation tax (at 6.2% of GDP) exceeded seigniorage revenue by more than 1% age point, indicating the increasing inefficiency of monetary policy. The reforms emphasized two central policies: successive devaluation and trade liberalization measures that shifted imports (and to some extend exports) from the official market to the free market. These reforms were also motivated by the emerging role of Sudan as a major labor-exporting country to the oil- surplus economies of the Middle-East. Remittance from Sudanese nationals working abroad averages more than three times the Dollar value of official export during 1983-84. These huge foreign exchange resources promoted the government to adopt reforms to unify the exchange rate. Having failed to attract further investment from the oil surplus economies in the Arab region, these reforms are aimed to mobilizing the resources of the remittances from these countries. However, these efforts were largely unsuccessful, and Sudanese nationals have continued to send the bulk of their remittances through the parallel foreign exchange market, attracted by its more depreciated exchange rate (Elbadawi, 1992).

The fiscal performance of the economy for 1978/79-1984/85 was weak. The share of total revenue to GDP remained stagnant with an annual average rate of 12%, while the share of expenditure to GDP increased from 15% in 1978/79 to 23% in 1883/84, mainly due to the increasing costs of the civil war in the southern part of the country. The poor fiscal performance resulted in large budgetary deficits. External finance and use of foreign aid counterpart funds covered about 60% of the overall deficit, leading to more dependency on foreign aid. There was a considerable increase in money supply, with the annual rate of monetary expansion reaching about 40% during 1981/82-

1984/85. The average inflation rate for the same period was 27 %.(Hag Elamin and Elmak, 1997). They argued that in term of fiscal performance, the ratio of domestic revenue to GDP was about 8% in 1990-1992, but rose to 11% in 1993. There was a considerable improvement in the contribution of tax revenue, while rose from 122% in 1991/92 to 214% in 1992/93. The total expenditure as a share of GDP increased from 10% in 1990/92 to 17% in 1992/93. Despite these improvements, the budget deficit remains high and was mainly financed internally by Central Bank borrowing with no or little external finance. Money supply during the National Economic Salvation Program (NESP) increased fourfold, from (Sudan pound) Ls31.6 billion in 1990/91 to Ls55.5 billion in 1991/92 and an estimated Ls133 billion at the end of the program. The money supply grew at an average annual rate of 83%. This led to a high level of inflation, estimated at 114% in 1991/92, 106% in 1991/92 and 112% in 1992/93.

During the first half of the 1990s, a massive fiscal expansion financed chiefly through domestic borrowing, led to sharp increases in money supply and a three-digit inflation rate as well as an unprecedented deterioration in the exchange rate. To address mounting macroeconomic imbalances and instability, a program of economic reform was designed in 1997 and more seriously implemented since then. Among other measures, the programs involved tightening and reorienting monetary policy to lower the rate of inflation, elimination of most credit controls, and the introduction of new instruments for indirect monetary control. The program initiated a process of economic recovery that resulted in the unification and relative stability of the exchange rate, declining inflation rate and a doubled real output growth rate by 2001. Budget deficit was reduced from 3.8% of GDP in 1996 to 0.7% in 1998, due to cuts in government spending. Annual inflation was brought down to 8% by 2000, where excess liquidity in the market created in the period of high inflation was absorbed through two instruments: Government Musharaka Certificates (GMC) and Central Bank Musharaka certificates (CMC). In addition Sudan's balance of payments constraint was relaxed significantly, when its oil exports began in 1998, turning a 300$ million annual bill for petroleum product into a sources of revenue that could earn more than 3.7$ billion a year. Overall, the Sudanese economic fundamentals have improved, with the average real GDP growth of 4.7% in 1990 – 2000 compared to 1.2% in 1985

– 1990. In fact, over the past six years, with an average of 6.5%, the Sudanese GDP growth rate is among the highest rates in developing countries. However, Sudan still confronts some serious economic problems. Foreign dept still stands at 24$ billion, a huge figure for Sudan that has a GDP about 9$ billion. Furthermore, the armed conflict in Darfur and eastern Sudan mean that military spending remains high deposit the end of civil war in the South. In adequate infrastructure and limited sources of investment financing are major obstacles to the development of the Sudan economy (Elhiraika and Abu Ismail, 2005).

In Sudan, total deposits are dominated by demand deposits with a share of over 70%, whereas saving and investment deposits remain relatively small. Kireyev (2001) argues that this phenomenon a reflection of the cash nature of the Sudanese economy where individual prefer to have instant access to their funds. This phenomenon also reflects the failure of the banking sector to offer investment opportunities that suit potential depositors. Deteriorating investment climate and creeping inflation led to highly negative profits rates on deposits in the 1990s, encouraging savers to invest heavily in property and other real assets. Even banks used to invest in the property sector until 1995 when the BOS prevented such practice.

The IMF (1977) diagnosed the causes of the crisis by noting that "over past few years a number of external developments affecting budgetary operations, credit expansion and cost-price relationships have resulted in structural disequilibria in the Sudanese economy; these are clearly indicated by the several imbalance in the budget and the balance of payments. In addition to taking steps to eliminate the causes of the imbalances, it has become necessary to take corrective action through depreciation of the Sudanese pound. A principal aim of such a reform is to accelerate the rate of growth by rationalizing the allocation of the resources so as to best utilize the Sudan's present and potential comparative advantage particularly in agriculture and agro- industries" (quoted in Ali, 1984).

Sudan was able to achieve and sustain high growth rates in the 1990s and 2000s within a framework of very tough self-imposed Structural Adjustment Programs (SAPs). The real gross domestic product (GDP) growth rate, on average, for the period 2000-2008, amounted to 7.7% annually, varying between 10.2% in 2007 and 6.1% in 2003. Growth is estimated at 4.9% in 2009 and projected to be around 5% in 2010. The sustained growth rates of GDP for the period 2000-2008 were achieved. Within a context of stable macroeconomic policies and relative controlled and carefully guided inflationary pressures (Ahmed, 2010). Also he continued saying that the government was able to stabilize prices and sharply reduce inflation from a record high of 130.6% in 1996 to a single digit by the end of the 1990s. Since 2000, oil and related sectors have been driving GDP growth, despite their relatively smaller shares in GDP composition. Agriculture (composed of irrigated, traditional rain-fed and mechanized crops, livestock and forestry sub-sectors) contributed more than 40% of GDP in the 1960s, 1970s and 1980s but declined to more than 36.2% and 35.9% in 2007 and 2008, respectively.

RESEARCH MODEL, DATA AND METHODOLOGY

Our model takes the following form:

$$Y = fi(G, T, M, R) \quad (1)$$

$$fi > 0 \quad (2)$$

(i) Is G, T, M, R)

Where:

Y is gross domestic product (GDP), G is government expenditure, and T is taxation as percentage from GDP. M is money supply defined as M2 and R is margin of profit represents interest rate (because of Islamic financial system in Sudan. In economic theory, economic policies impact positively on economic development, so that we expect positive signs of parameters. Taxation (T), government expenditure (G), money supply (M) and interest rate (R) represent economic policies variables used. The former two variables indicate to fiscal policy while latter two represent monetary policy. Economic development (Y) is measured by gross domestic product (GDP) and this is the dependent variable in the model. Data of the study is collected from various sources, namely the Taxation Chamber, Central Bureau of Statistic, Central Bank of Sudan and Ministry of Finance and National Economy.

Table 1: Taxation (T), Interest rate (R) (2000- 2013)

Year	T (as share of GDP)	R (%)
2000	3.0	20
2001	3.9	12
2002	4.0	12
2003	3.8	12
2004	3.9	10
2005	3.4	10
2006	3.6	10
2007	4	10
2008	3.3	10
2009	3.9	10
2010	4.0	10
2011	3.5	10
2012	6.2	12
2013	2.8	11

Source: Central Bureau of statistics, Central Bank of Sudan and Taxation Chamber

Table 2: Gross Domestic Product (Y), Government Expenditure (G), Money Supply (M) in Thousands SDG, 2000-2013

Year	Y	G	M
2000	33662.7	1845.1	3466.7
2001	40658.6	2615.1	4322.1
2002	47756.1	2915.6	5632.7
2003	55733.8	3334.0	7340.9
2004	68721.4	5736.9	9604.5
2005	85707.1	7916.9	14031.4
2006	98718.8	9906.5	17871.8
2007	114017.6	9635.2	19714.6
2008	127746.9	10810.8	22933.2
2009	135659.0	12102.1	28314.5
2010	162203.9	28324.0	35497.9
2011	186689.9	32193.0	41853.0
2012	243412.8	29821.5	58663.3
2013	267898.6	31195.2	65663.3

Source: Own Calculated based on data from table Central Bureau of Statistics and Central Bank of Sudan

Note: the data of 2013 for table 1 and 2 are own estimation

RESEARCH RESULTS AND CONCLUSIONS

By using E-views and applying ordinary least squares (OLS) technique to the data covering the period (2000- 2013) on the variables mentioned above, we estimated the linear form of equation (1), The regression results are given in equation (3), where the figures inside the brackets are the t-ratios of the estimated parameters:

$$Y = 0.2G + 6212.1T + 3.6M + 514.5R$$

(0.3) (2.4) (8.9) (0.7)

$R2 = 0.99$ $F = 659.2$ $DW = 1.28$ (3)

Equation (3) is statistically significant at the 5% level of confidence as indicated by the (F) ratio. The value of R2 suggests that 99% of the variation in development (Y) is explained by variations in the government expenditure (G), taxation (T), money supply (M), interest rate (R) which represents economic policies.

The Durbin-Watson statistic indicates the absence of serial correlation in the model at the 5% level.

From above findings, the study concludes that economic policies have significant impact and effect on development in Sudan during the period (2000-2013).

REFERENCES

1. Ahmed, M. M (2010): Global Financial Crisis Discussion series Paper 19: Sudan Phase 2. Overseas Development Institute 111 Westminster Bridge Road, London. SE17JD.

2. Alexius, A and Holmlund, B. (2007): "Monetary Policy and Swedish Unemployment Fluctuation". CESIFO working paper No.2044.

3. Ali, A.A. (1984): "Some Aspects of Sudan Economy", postgraduate teaching Material series No.1. Development Studies and Research Centre, Faculty of Economics and Social Studies University of Khartoum.

4. Ali, A.A. (1985): The Sudan Economy in Disarray: Essays on the IMF Model, Khartoum, Sudan.

5. Elhiraika, A.B. and K. Abu Ismail.(2005): " Financial Sector Policy and Poverty Reduction in Sudan", working

paper,0411, Economic Research Forum. Cairo, Egypt.

6. Hag Elamin, N.A and Elmak, E. M. (1997): "Adjustment Programmes and Agricultural Incentives in Sudan: A comparative study", AERC Research paper 63. African Economic Research Consortium, Nairobi. March 1997.

7. IMF Reports on Sudan "Various Issues".

8. Khalil, S. (1993): "Monetary and Fiscal Policies in LDCs: Limitations and Constraints". Economic Review. Finalarticle.com. 04 May, 2011.

9. Kireyev, A. (2001):"Financial Reform in Sudan: Streaming Bank Intermediation", IMF working wp/01/53.

10. Todaro, M. P. (1977): "Economics for developing world", Sheck Wah Tong Press, Hong Kong. Todaro, M. P and S, C. Smith (2011): "Economic Development", Eleventh Edition, Pearson Education Limited. England.

5
CHAPTER

Analysis of the recent Sudanese Industrial Policy in the New Structural Economics Framework: The Way towards Economic Transformation

Yagoub Elryah

Economic Studies Department, Industrial Research and Consultancy Center IRCC

Abstract Economic growth and per capita income in Sudan have substantially declined in the past five years. Major reason for this is the failure of the economy to grow because of absence of proper economic policies to manage the structural endowments. In this study I would like to address the following research questions, why is structural change and industrial upgrading becoming increasingly important as a determinant of country's economic transformation, and how should these components be linked for a New Structural Economics framework. I have argued that the most of the recent developed economies have achieved the potential economic development lie in the politics of the different societies that adopted these policies. In contrast, the failure industry policies in the recent lower middle-income countries, in the case of Sudan that the economic policies were generally very bad, this can be devoted to the fact that the policies were driven by the desire to maintain political power and this will not support economic growth. Furthermore, I found evidence that a proper industrial policy and steadily economic growth in Sudan, the political equilibrium is necessary to change political institutions.

Keywords: economic policy, structural change, comparative advantage, New Structural Economics

1 INTRODUCTION

If some or most developed countries have succeed in managing their endowment structures, and attaining high income growth, by adapting proper industrial policies, then least and lower middle-incomes have opportunity to advance their economies and thereby catch-up the developed world. Following [1] large theoretical and empirical literatures have developed during the past ten years, which have analyzed why the recent least and lower middle-incomes developing countries with natural resources are not developed, although are qualified to achieve the potential economic development. Up to this point, however, fewer has been achieved the economic prosperity through industrialization.

We contribute to the literature with this macroeconomic analysis of industrial policy in Sudan in the context of New Structural Economics framework. By comparing the industrial policies in Sudan with those in Korea and China during the first stage of development, we have created benchmark on how industrial policy should be designed. This allows me to test a variety of hypotheses derived from economic development theories.

Since Sudan gets its independence, most industrial policies fail to achieve the potential economic development due to the fact these policies are not related to Sudan's endowment structure and comparative advantages. We consider the new structural economics framework to analyze the recent industrial policy towards economic transformation.

The facilitated and committed governments on achieving economic development have been attracting for economists. The field of economic development has been addressing issues such as these and much of technology and innovation for transfer poor countries has been working out to a considerable degree. Nevertheless there continues to be in developing countries failure, particularly on the least developing countries, to recognize the true importance of structural change for these countries. This can be achieved through the Growth Identification and Facilitation Framework (GIFF) and targeting latent comparative-advantage industries and support economic growth

Sudan's economy has been struggling to rrecover from its economic shock, which requires stabilization and structural policies that complement one another. As general known, stabilization policies lay the foundation for economic growth to achieve lower inflation and reduce government deficits. Then the structural policies attain its effect after resolving the macroeconomic imbalances. Likewise, the structural policies intensify the effectiveness of many stabilization measures: promoting competition, for instance, this may lead to lower prices and, consequently, lower inflation.

In this research, our main purpose is to add to existing empirical studies by examining impacts of stabilization policies on declining Sudan's economy.

The sustainability of growing economic growth can be achieved through combination of stabilization and structural policies. The main goal of stabilization policies is to achieve lower prices and lower inflation and thereby reduce budget deficits. However, over the past few years, Sudan has experienced external trade deficit, continued a depreciation of exchange rate and higher inflation and unemployment rates, which results higher inflation of 53%, unemployment of 43% and budget deficit [1].

The new conditions in Sudan, particularly with regard to economic stabilization and economic policies, are acknowledged to be necessary but not of themselves sufficient for sustaining economic development in the both long and short terms, which require growth andnew forms of specialization.

Economic policy is based into two concepts, the first concept defines the economic policy as a generic name relating to industries, the second one is rather narrow and it includes policies that restrict or eliminate competition among firms to achieve particular goals, for instance, protecting and promoting industries.

There is generally broad agreement in economists thinking and practice that economic sector is an engine of economic growth, and offers an effective way to create employment, incomes, and prosperity. This study seeks to rethink the conceptual framework needed for formulating economic policy in the conditions currently facing the majority of the countries of the region. The problems we will be addressing are not exclusive to them, however, and the debate has very similar features both in the more highly industrialized countries and in those at an intermediate level of economic development.

In this study I would like to address the following research questions. Why is comparative advantage becoming increasingly important as a determinant of country's economic transformation, and how should be sustained for achieving a higher economic growth? Whether the government policies will be sufficiently strong to cause the growth of agricultural sector? And What is the main drivers' growth of the agricultural sector in Sudan?

The remained paper organizes as follows. In the next section I present related literature review and discusses the new structural economics approach to industrial policy. Section three answers the research questions why is structural change and Industrial upgrading becoming increasingly important as a determinant of country's economic transformation, and how should these components be linked for a New Structural Economics approach. Section four analyzes the recent development of sustainability of comparative advantages. Final section concludes.

2 LITERATURE REVIEW

In this section, I review related literature and try to shed some lights on how the new structural economics can be the best framework to transform the economy and thereby achieve a higher income growth. If we carefully examined the current developed countries and its experiences and how they advanced their economy we will have a good lesson to transfer Sudan economy to upper-middle income, the best way to achieve this is to rethink again on our development policies as proposed by [1].

New Structural Economics (NSE), which proposed by [1] argues that the development path of lagging economies should start with identification of their endowment structure and search for growing tradable industries in fast growing countries with similar endowment structure but several times higher per capita income. Further step in this direction is identification of existing private domestic firms in those industries and the removal of constraints to quality upgrading or further firm entry. Moreover, in industries without domestic firms FDI or firm incubation programs should be employed together with measures to scale up successful private innovation. In this context, [1] identifies special economic zones and industrial parks as important measures. Finally, the role of government is needed to compensate pioneer firms through temporary tax incentives, direct credits for investments and access to foreign exchange.

The NSE framework suggests following industrial policy in order the countries achieve higher economic growth and thereby transfer the economy into high development income. By another words, if a particular country manages its endowment structure and its industrial policy based on its comparative advantage, in one generation the economy will catch-up the developed world.

The international trade theories illustrate that the comparative advantage is an important concept for explaining trade patterns. Which was was first developed by the classical economist [2] building on [3] principle of absolute advantages.

Smith and Ricardo has explained the occurrence of absolute and comparative advantages as the result of differences in labor productivity. [4] and [5] developed the idea of comparative advantages in a model based on differences in factors endowments. However, it is well known that measuring comparative advantage and testing the Hecksher-Ohlin theory have some difficulties [6] since relative prices under autarky are not observable. Given this fact, [7] proposes that it may not be necessary to include all constituents effecting country's comparative advantage. Instead, he suggests that comparative advantage is "revealed" by observed trade patterns, and in line with the theory, one needs pre-trade relative prices which are not observable.

Most recent literature has recognized the importance of developing comparative advantages to transform a country to higher income growth [8]. However, the vital role of the sustainability of comparative advantages in Sudan has not been empirically investigated thereby creating a research gap in this area. This study is undertaken to develop a practical framework for sustainability and priorities of comparative advantages of agro-industry commodities in Sudan.

The absence of proper strategies, economic reform and lack of economic policies have now resulted in low levels of per capita income, where a majority of labor force either to immigrate abroad and working in temporary and non-productive activities [1]. Addressing these require structural transformation to high productivity levels and focusing on long-term sustainable sources for economic growth and inclusive development, and move towards agro-processing industries.

As [9] argue "if we can learn about government policy options that have even small effects on long-term growth rates, we can contribute much more to improvements in standards of living than has been provided by the entire history of macroeconomic analysis of countercyclical policy and fine tuning". To promote this transformation, the fundamental question arises from how policy makers in Sudan design effective development policies.

Further studies related to agricultural trade have found that Sudan has lost its market shares of most of agricultural products, for instance, the production cotton and Gum Arabic has decreased by 30% and 60% in 1999 and 2007 respectively.

[10] studied the performance of Sudan exports over the period from 1970-93, the author found that the impact of price incentives on export earning was a minimal and the programs adopted by the policy makers have not created improvement in the price incentives.

In their research, [11] measured the competitiveness of Gum Arabic at Sudan crops market; they employed participatory learning and action (PLA). The authors conclude that the Gum Arabic showed varying comparative advantages and despite adopting the liberalization measures the market is predominating.

Using the Policy Analysis Matrix (PAM), [12] evaluated the Sheep production market in Sudan. The study found that the high taxes on sheep's production have affected negatively on the export and the value added has a positive relation with foreign exchange.

The theoretical implications of this study may fill the above mentioned gap related literature by analyzing the priorities of comparative advantages of agro-industrial products. However, in Sudan attempts have not been made to link the comparative advantages to agro-industrial products.

Sudan is considered have abundance in resources, usually most of economic activities are based on labor-intensive (agriculture, animal husbandry and fishery). However, without exploit all the economic endowments, especially the human capital, which witnessed improvement in human capital index, the availability of land and natural resources, electricity grids, perfect regulations, port facilities, airports, telecommunication systems, attractive investment environment, basic facilities such as ports in most of Sudanese provinces, trains, roads. Besides that, Sudan locates in the central of the world with costal for connecting with other world.

3.NEW STRUCTURAL ECONOMICS FRAMEWORK TO SUDAN'S INDUSTRIAL POLICY

This section also devoted to address the following research question. Why is structural change and industrial upgrading becoming increasingly important as a determinant of country's economic transformation, and how should these components be linked for a New Structural Economics approach.

In this context, Sudan has many opportunities to catch-up the upper-middle income or even higher-income economies. Starting from its economic endowments or factor of production, such as natural resources, labor, and capital, this can be used in production process. We can also ad infrastructure as one of endowment components, which includes soft infrastructure and hard infrastructure as cited in [8].

3.1. Why is Structural Change and Industrial Upgrading Increasingly Important?

The first answer to the question is simple, through manufacturing. Advanced and emerging economies are becoming more dependent upon industry because they are increasingly involved in advanced technology, innovation, economic parks and free trade areas.

What all these means for Sudan is that these countries cannot achieve economic development, cannot sustain its economic growth. Instead, they find itself increasingly have to adapt and initiate stabilization policies and struggling to recover from it economic shocks.

The second reason why structural change and industrial upgrading will become more central and increasingly is that adapting economic products that Sudan has comparative advantages in will transfer it to higher economic growth. There are several kinds of research findings and observations which illustrates this point.

First, research shows that the East Asian newly economicized economies have steadily sustained its annual GDP growth between 8% and 10% for more than a decade. In 2012 the year followed the secession of South Sudan; Sudan adapted stabilization policies, with the aim of recovering from the economic shock by the year 2019 with an average growth rate of at least 7.1% per annum [13].

Second, research evidence is beginning to accumulate that economic transformation and achieved economic diversification is not a life-long process and the economic development could be happen if the country builds a proper model to transfer it to high income growth. Sudan will have to be much more of what these issues are how to initiate policies to transfer the labor from traditional sector into the economic one?

3.2. What are the Major Components of Stabilization Policies and Economic Recovery?

The field of economic development has been addressing issues such as these and much of technology and innovation for transfer poor countries has been working out to a considerable degree. Nevertheless there continues to be in developing countries failure, particularly on the least developing countries, to recognize the true importance of structural change for these countries. In this research, our main purpose is to add to existing empirical studies by examining impacts of stabilization policies on declining Sudan's economy.

Since late 2011, Sudan has observed remarkable decrease in economic growth, which increased inflation and unemployment rates. Since then, Sudan underwent economic reforms that favored adopt stabilization policies. Considering that the ongoing five-year economic reform plan (2015-2019) for growth and poverty reduction cannot be achieved unless stabilized the macroeconomic indicators.

The absence of proper strategies, economic reform and lack of fiscal and monetary policies have now resulted in low levels of per capita income, where a majority of labor force involved in agricultural activities [14]. Addressing these require structural transformation to high productivity levels and focusing on long-term sustainable sources for economic growth and inclusive development, and move towards agro-processing industries.

As [15] argue "if we can learn about government policy options that have even small effects on long-term growth rates, we can contribute much more to improvements in standards of living than has been provided by the entire history of macroeconomic analysis of countercyclical policy and fine tuning". To promote this transformation, the fundamental question arises from how policy makers in Sudan design effective development policies.

Economic policy becomes one of the major issues in developing countries. The sustainability of Sudan's economic growth is extremely difficult without transformation from agriculture to industrialization process. A well planned economic policy gives the country to set up many industries and convert it into modern areas and transfer the economy into developed economies. There is a need a country to involve in a number of structural changes, for instance production techniques and economic output. In this section we will give a historical review as related to economic development in Sudan.

This study is expected to add several primary contributions to the existing literature. First, it extends the theoretical and empirical literature by analyzing the priorities of comparative advantages of Sudan's commodities under the context of new structural economics. Starting from 2000, Sudanese economy entered a novel era with the rapid economic growth and, it has undergone significant regulatory and structural changes in the aftermath of the 2011 South Sudan secession. Second, this study will apply three different methods, which may provide insight for the existing literature if the analysis is sensitive to the methods employed.

I believe this study is an important contribution to economic transformation and development in Sudan. There is clearly stated for academic and practitioners to pay attention to the impacts on Sudan's economic growth, as it has received little or no academic attention. However, the main aim of this study is to make an empirical contribution to the ongoing debate on economic policy.

We tend to analyze the priorities of comparative advantage of Sudan's commodities. To this end, the research applies a variety of econometric models to identify the relationship between the endogenous and exogenous variables for the recent period from 2005 to 2015.

4.QUALITATIVE EEVIDENCE FROM SURVEYS AND INTERVIEWS

[1] has examined why some Asian countries, such as four tigers and new industrialized economies of South east Asia were successfully achieved higher economic growth by adapting industrial policies and attracted FDI to finance the economic development. While Sub-Sahran African countries still struggling in least developing countries and failed to achieve economic progress.

The first key result is evidence on despite the huge natural resources, location and higher skilled labor, Sudan has not benefited from these resources. The country is dominant by agriculture where it contributes around 34% to the GDP, while industry contributes 35% of the GDP. Sudan has opportunity to adapt industrial policies related to its comparative and competitive advantages in agricultural commodities.

The second is the existing industrial policies is that the Sudan's economy is fragile and relies on agricultural products that do not have comparative advantage in. The implication is that for sustained economic growth to occur, Sudan basically needs two things: concentrating on the extractive industries and develop particular products that Sudan may have comparative advantage in.

Finally, in order for Sudan to have the capacity to perform effectively over a period of time it must be plan for transferring the economy into higher growth. But economic and economic development are difficult undertakings that pose complex problems and for the firms that operate in Sudan. One of the requirements for success in such endeavor is ability to adapt structural reforms and identify the products that have comparative advantage in.

5.THE INDUSTRIALIZATION PROCESS IN SUDAN

The industrialization process and strategic plan of industrial sector can be distinguished to eight distinct periods are as follows.

The first attempt design industrial policy goes back to the pre-independence period until the 1956. During this period, Sudan has exported raw and primary products and public sector was responsible indirect from production and distribution.

The second period started from 1960-1969, the private sector has invested and entered the market and started to play its role.

The third period was from 1956-1960, the modern manufacturing was started.

The fourth period from 1969-1973, the socialist orientation shapes the business environment, where many firms were become a public sector.

The fifth period, from 1973-1978, the public sector was controlled the agro-industrial investments.

The sixth period from 1978-1989, the industrial sector has suffered from the lack policies.

The seventh period started from 1990-2000, which witnessed the entering of new technology to the existent industries. Many industrial firms were established and started to contribute to the economic growth. It's the years witnessed the economic reform and privatization, where may public firms were converted to private firms, due to the fact that the productivity in the public sector are less and non-profitable compared to the private sector.

The eighth period started from 2000-2010, which witnessed the oil production, where many private firms were successfully established.

The ongoing industrial policy started from 2015 to 2019, with aims is to promote industrialization and allows the industry to lead the economic growth.

In this context, I concentrate on the recent industrial policy as related to the New Structural Economics as it taken into account the specific industries to achieve economic development in Sudan.

6.CONCLUSION

In this paper I have tried to shed light on the role of comparative advantages of agro-industry in transforming the economic development in Sudan. The economic theory pointed that a well planned industrial policy, committed and facilitated government and concentrated on the industries that country's has comparative advantages in, no matter how country in any development stage will transformed stimulate economic growth and development to higher income growth.

There are many countries successfully transformed its economies into advanced economies and others were not. I have argued that the most of the recent developed economies have achieved the potential economic development lie in the politics of the different societies that adopted the policies. In contrast, the failure industry policies in the recent lower middle-income countries, in the case of Sudan that the economic policies were generally very bad, this can be devoted to the fact that the policies were driven by the desire to maintain political power and this will not support economic growth.

The author suggests for having a proper industrial and trade polices based on Sudan endowment structure will enhance economic growth, the political equilibrium is necessary to change political institutions. We may have much to learn from the successes and failures of development attempts.

REFERENCES

1. Lin, J. Y. (2012). New structural economics : a framework for rethinking development. Washington, DC: The World Bank.
2. David Ricardo (1817) Principles of Political Economy and Taxation, John Murray, London.
3. Adam Smith(1776) The Wealth of Nations London: Methuen & Co., Ltd.
4. Heckscher, E. (1919). The Effect of Foreign Trade on the Distribution of Income. Ekonomisk Tidskrift, 497-512. Reprinted as Chapter 13 in A.E.A. (1949). Readings in the Theory of International Trade, 272-300 (Philadelphia: Blakiston) with a Translation in H. Flam and M. J. Flanders (Eds.). 1991. Heckscher-Ohlin Trade Theory, 43-69. Cambridge: MIT Press.
5. *Ohlin, Bertil, 1933, Interregional and International Trade (Cambridge: Harvard University Press*
6. Balassa, B. (1989), ' "Revealed" comparative advantage revisited', in: B. Balassa (ed.), Comparative Advantage, Trade Policy and Economic Development, New York University Press, New York, pp. 63–79.

7. Stiglitz, J., J. Lin, C. Monga, and E. Patel. (2013). 'Economic Policy in the African Context'. *Policy Research Working Paper. Washington, DC: World Bank*.
8. Yagoub Elryah (2015) "Back to the Agriculture - the Development of the Comparative Advantage of Sudan's Commodities. Journal of Finance and Economics, 3(1), 1-5.
9. Robinson, J. A. (June 22-24, 2009). Economic Policy and Development: A Political Economy Perspective. *World Bank ABCDE conference* (pp. 15-47). Seoul : World Bank.
10. Alamin Hag Nasedin (1997), Export Performance in Sudan: Recent Trends and Policy Impact. Journal of Economic Cooperation among Islamic Countries 18, 4, 57-76.
11. Tarig E. Mahmoud, Maruod E. Maruod, Manal A. Khiery Ahmed M. El Naim, Moayad B. Zaied. (2014), Competitiveness of Gum Arabic Marketing System at Elobeid Crops Market, North Kordofan State, Sudan. World Journal of Agricultural Research, 2 (5), 252.
12. Elsedig Elbadawi, Fatimah Mohamed Arshad, Zainalabdin Mohammed and Mohd Mansor Ismail. (2012). Assessing the Competitiveness of Sheep Production in Selected States in Sudan.
13. Sudan Central Bank (2014) "annual financial reports (2005, 2010, 2011, 2012, 2013 and 2014), Khartoum, Sudan: Central Bank of Sudan.
14. Yagoub Elryah (2016) Sudan's Economic Decline and the Role of Fiscal and Monetary Policies in Sustaining Recovery, Pyrex Journal of Economics and International Finance, vol. 1, issue 1, p 14-19.
15. Gisselquist, R. M. (2015). State capability and prospects for close coordination Considerations for economic policy in Africa. *WIDER Working Paper 2015/035 World Institute for Development Economics Research* , 1-16.

6
CHAPTER
Institutional Development, Governance, and Ethnic Politics in South Sudan

Madut Kon*

The TAOS Institute, York University, Ottawa, Canada

ABSTRACT

This article discusses **ETHNICITY** and socio-cultural complexity in governance, political systems, and bureaucratic institutions in South Sudan. Using the partially thematic and content analysis of the grounded theory analysis, the major themes and categories outline patterns of cultural norms and values in the absence of national identity that affects the pace of sustainable peace, **ECONOMIC DEVELOPMENT**, good governance, and **DEMOCRATIC** transformation in the country. The outcome suggests that South Sudan continues to face multi-faceted socio-cultural, political, and economic challenges in its transition from ethno-centric system to viable democratic governance. This includes a genuine quest for nation-building transformation to a viable state, establishment of functional system, security, and rule of law and order in the country. The outcomes suggest that South Sudan Policymakers has paid minimum attention in eradication of poverty, high illiteracy rate and dogmatic ethnic values. Nonetheless, the country is in a dire need for traditional and cultural peace-building process among various ethnic-groups and communities as a corner stone for a sustainable socio-economic and political development.

Keywords: Ethnic politics; Governance; Indigenous society; Conflicts; Ethno-centrism

INTRODUCTION

Contemporary politics of South Sudan started with the Anglo-Egyptian Condominium form1898 to 1955. During this time, Britain and Egypt occupied Sudan, with separate **BUREAUCRATIC** arrangements for the north and south. Sudan became independent at the beginning of 1956 and faced long civil wars in the decades that followed [1]. From 1955 and 2005, northern and South Sudan experienced everlasting conflict and war. On 9 January 2005, the Comprehensive Peace Agreement (CPA) was signed by the SPLA/M and the NCP led government in Khartoum [2]. The CPA has granted semi-autonomy government to South Sudanese with a new Interim Constitution. Under the stipulations of the peace settlement, the SPLM leader John Garang was made the First Vice-President of the Republic of Sudan, and President of the Government of South Sudan. Three weeks only after being sworn into office in July 2005, John Garang died in an aircraft crashed and succeeded by SalvaKiirMayardit according to his seniority in the SPLM/A movement (ibid).

On 9 January 2011, Southerners voted on whether to become an independent nation or to remain part of greater Sudan. South Sudanese decided to separate from the north by more than 98 percent of the vote. On 9 July, 2011, the Republic of South Sudan was declared a sovereign country (ibid).

However, the process of building a cohesive national identity and new nation have yet to materialize in South Sudan due to the persistence of competing social and cultural factors, a high illiteracy rate among the populace, and the lack of well-trained political leaders (World Bank, 2010).

With the signing of the Comprehensive Peace Agreement (CPA) January 9th, 2005, many South Sudanese thought the absence of war would automatically bring about sustainable peace and development in their newly established country.

As such, it is noticeable that armed **CONFLICTS** in many parts of the South Sudan can be attributed to lack of cohesive and coherent national agenda and policies for a sustainable development and livelihood exacerbated by politics of an identity deep-rooted in historic ethnic feuds [3]. Historically, South Sudan, like most countries in Africa, was a colonial invention during the European scramble for Africa when the European powers arbitrarily divided up Africa based on their interests with no regard to the geo-ethnic and cultural realities of the people [1]. As such, ethnic groups who were at some point traditional enemies found themselves within common boundaries defined as a region, province, or a township. Matters were further worsened when other ethnic groups, at the dawn of independence, started using ethnocentric divide-and-rule politics to settle scores under the excuse of law and order [4]. Since its independence, the South Sudan embraced ethnic rule, supported by the military, thereby weakening the establishment of the rule of law and order, as well as peace and security (ibid). This has delayed the creation and development of strong and credible state institutions in the country. The military systems of governance in South Sudan have undermined the concepts of civil society, multiparty democracy, and freedom of speech and movement due to lack of a permanent constitutional stipulations that safeguard these values(ibid). Nonetheless, the unresolved post separation issues with Sudan have led South Sudan to adopt profligate military spending. Hence, instead of social services and developmentprojects, the Government of South Sudan spent about 42 percent ($555 million) of its budgets on military procurements [5]. These figures may be higher as both SPLM-Juba and SPLM-IO continue to engage in an arms race and still have a complicated unresolved political dispute.

Apparently, investments in the arms race and worldwide oil crisis have led to divestment from other sectors of the economy, thereby affecting economic development and growth as the government deemed spending on programs such as education, agriculture, healthcare, and infrastructure as nonessential(ibid). These spending sprees not only restrained development projects but also held the **SOCIOECONOMIC** developments of South Sudan hostage to military manipulations and created the conditions for what is currently known as a failed state (**FIGURE 1**) [6].

The Fragile States Index 2014, also Placed South Sudan on the top of high risk countries of which highest points of measured factors that constituted such condition was placed on issues of Refugees and Internally Displaced Person (IDP), group grievances, fictionalized elite, human rights, human flight and legitimacy of the state. Other factors included quality of public services, poverty and economic declines, security apparatus, uneven development and external interventions. In total, South Sudan earned the highest points (112.9) making the country the most fragile state in the world.

Nonetheless, ethnic tensions like those in many African countries such as Somalia, Rwanda, Congo, etc., have become major challenges affecting the pace of peace and development in South Sudan. This is because communities and social groups identify themselves with tribes, cultures, villages, and regions as mechanisms of resistance and preservation of ethnic identity [7].

The Construction of Ethnicity

Decades of civil war between North and South Sudan helped to produce a collective perception of social, cultural, and political identity - known as "South Sudanese" – where the population thought of themselves as a homogenous society. Ethnic variations, cultural diversity, and ethnic divides along 65 ethno-tribal groups were not considered to be a ticking time bomb if not managed carefully in the nation building plan. This is because the construction of the South Sudanese identity was shaped by peoples' shared history of a common struggle to survive, and the preservation of African cultures from the eras of slavery; Turko-Egyptian rule in 1822, and British-Egyptian Condominium rule in 1898 to 1955. This struggle continued through independence to the era of Arabization and Islamization adopted by successive central governments in Khartoum after the independence of Sudan in 1956 [8].

Several attempts were made during these foreign interferences to maintain **ETHNO-CULTURAL** and tribal identities, one of which was manifested in the rebellion of Nuer and Azande ethnic groups against the colonial rule which resulted in the killing of British officers and Governor of Bahr El Ghazal in 1901 [9]. In 1930, the colonialists acknowledged southern Sudan as an ethnically and culturally distinct society, a concept that led to the total elimination of Arab influences and interests in South Sudan by 1940. This paradigm shift in the colonial politics and policies has lasted up to 1946, when it was then revised due to growing Arabs and Northern Sudanese influence in South Sudan and their resistance against the colonial policy of treating South Sudan as a distinct society [1]. However, the South Sudanese devoted many efforts to forming a country of their own in the Juba Conference in 1947, which was aimed to discuss the fate of South Sudan between unity with then Sudan or separation, the formation of the Liberal Party in 1955 with a renewed call for Federation in Sudan, and the Torit resistance which sparked the Anya-Nya civil war movement in 1963-1972 that ended with a semi-autonomous government in Southern Sudan. The last final push was that of the SPLM movement 1983-2005 which led to the settlement and successful independence in 2011 with signing of the Comprehensive Peace Agreement (CPA) in 2006 [10].

These synopses of historical events meant to provide a background on geopolitical factors that fostered unity of propose, and constructed common identity adopted by mostly by all African **INDIGENOUS** ethnic groups who are now known as South Sudanese. However, among these ethnic groups, the psycho-social prediction of peoples' interactions, identity, sense of belonging, and political thoughts are shaped by ethnic norms, clan and tribal affiliations, followed by region and individual's villages. For these reasons, ethnic feuds at local or communal level are easily transformed to the dynamics of power-sharing, political disagreement and ethno-tribal conflicts at the national level.

With all the ethno-cultural and political challenges, South Sudan gained its independence on July 9, 2011 after decades of war with Sudan in which about two million people perished, and an estimated four to five million people were internally displaced, while others took refuge in neighboring African countries, Europe, Australia, USA, and Canada. The independence of South Sudan, however, did not put an end to internal ethno-tribal clashes, rebellion, or the external border conflicts with Sudan [1].

Consequently, South Sudan continue to experience cycles of violence in forms of political rivalry, ethnic tensions, distrust between the government and the people, fueled by undisciplined ethnosized national army or better classified as armed militias [11]. The ten states in the country have at least experienced some of inter-communal violence, human rights issues, as well as dire economic condition and psycho-social well-being.

Ethnographic Map of Ethnic Groups

The people of South Sudan, as per an **ETHNOGRAPHIC** map, have been classified as Nilo-Saharan of Eastern-Sudanic, with few identifying themselves as *Bantus* [8]. The people of South Sudanese were united by their determination to end policies of assimilation and divide-and-rule introduced by the Arabized Muslims of old Sudan since independence in 1956.

However, the missing narrative in the literature of ethnicity and ethnic grouping in South Sudan is that anthropologists and biologists assert that South Sudanese of the Nilo-Saharan origin are categorically kin by race and ethnic linkages [12]. Even so, it remains a challenge to promote such assertions even among the Nilotic themselves, or even creating an agreed upon national identity with a collective sense of cultural, ethnic, political, and common history of nation building. The perception of a self and group as a distinct ethno-tribal entity is much greater within the larger South Sudanese society, than any national symbols that may identify them as one nation.

South Sudan is home to 64 different ethnic groups. As per the census, there are still some disputes over the accuracy and reliability of the statistical data, especially the data gathered under the successive governments of Sudan before the independence of South Sudan. The first census that included South Sudan for the first time was conducted in 2008, of which its results was announced unilaterally by the Government of National Unity (GONU) in Khartoum, and rejected by the Government of South Sudan (GOSS). The named **CENSUS** sets the number of people in South at 8,260,490, about 21.10 % of the national average, of which about 520,000 of the South Sudanese population were cited living in North Sudan. The same census estimated population growth from 5,329,267 in 1983, to 8 260 490 in 2008. No mention was made of the internally displaced peoples (IDPs), refugees, and migrants in surrounding countries and abroad(National Bureau of Statistics, 2014). Authorities in South Sudan thought the number reported by the government did not reflect the exact number of people in South Sudan and their demographic characteristics. This was because government of then Sudan had no plans for any socio-political or economic development for the people or the region [13]. The Old Sudan policies were rather placed on social engineering and reconstruction of peoples' cultures and communities, through introduction of Arabic and Islam culture and religion to build(what was thought at the time by Northern Sudanese) a more homogeneous identity and society [14].

The ethnic distribution of South Sudanese groups can be better understood in the context of ethnic profile within the three regions of Greater Bahr el Ghazal, Greater Upper Nile, and Greater Equatoria. These three regions were established by colonial administration since 1920s and later redistributed into ten States by the Khartoum regime. Such clustering, coupled with the colonial policies of divide and rule have constructed sense of regionalized socio-political identity which in many aspect delayed conducive environment for a peaceful coexistence and socio-cultural and economic development, and most importantly contributed in cycles of regional political tensions in the politics of representation nationally. **TABLE 1** below shows the ethnic variation in South Sudan, clustered by number of ethnic groups as per overall regional percentages and region of inhabitants (**TABLE 1**).

TABLE 1: Profile of Ethnic Variation by Regions.

Greater Bahr el Ghazal	Greater Equatoria	Greater Upper Nile
Aja, Atuot (Reel), Balanda-Boor, Balanda-Bviri, Banda, Bongo,Dinka (Jieng), Feroghe, GolloJur (Beli and Modo), (Luo) Mananger (Luo), Ndogo, Ngulngule, Sere, Shatt, Yulu Kara, Binga, Indri, Mangayat	Adio (Makaraka), Acholi, Avukaya, Azande, Bai, Baka Bari, Dongotona, Didinga, Ifoto, Kakwa, Lokoya, Lopit, Lotuka (Otuho), Larim (Boya), Kuku, Lango, Logir, Lulubo, Madi, Moro, Mundari, Pari, Pojulu Nyangwara, Suri (Kachipo), Toposa, Imatong, Keliku, Lugbwara, MoruMundu, Nyangatom, Tenet, Tid, Woro	Murle, **Nuer** (Naath), **Dinka** Shilluk (Chollo), Anyuak (Anyuaa), Jiye, Maban, Uduk
Total: 21 (32%) Ethnic groups	**Total: 36 (55%) Ethnic groups**	**Total: 8 (13%) Ethnic Groups**

As illustrated, the number of ethnic groups in South Sudan varies by region. The three regions of South Sudan account for 65(100%) of the nation's ethnic groups. The Greater Equatoria Region accommodates 36 different ethnic groups, which account for 55% of total ethnic groups in the country. The Greater Bahr el Ghazal Region accommodates 21ethnic groups, 32% of the total ethnic groups, and the Greater Upper Nile Region accommodates only 8 ethnic groups, 13% of the total ethnic group in the country.

Within these ethnic variations, the 55% of ethnic and tribal communities within Greater Equatoria have managed to re-construct their multi-ethnic-group identities to a cluster of regionally based identity to be known as "Equatorian" socio-political arena rather than their ethnic or tribes of particulars. Apparently, the constructed regional identity of "Equatorians" is being mistaken to a tribe, rather than a monocular for a group of ethnic groups. The concept of *Equatorians* as an identity is based on a cluster of 36 tribes that managed to construct a region of inhabitant as a common identity rather than ethnic affiliations. Bahr el Ghazal and Upper Nile regions have failed to recognize and adopt such regionalized identity over ethnic and tribal identity. However, a similar concept of groups identity and clustering has been also adopted among the *Fertit* groups of Western Bahr El Ghazal, a cluster of 14 ethnic groups that have managed to socially, culturally, and politically adopt a communal constructed identity known as "*Fertits*" rather than tribes of origins. The rest of Western Bahr el Ghazal ethic groups of Luo, Bongo, and Dinka remained distinct ethnic groups in the region.

In this context, the challenges of equitable ethnic representation in politics, **GOVERNANCE**, peace-building, harmony, and peaceful coexistence among ethnic groups have become major hindrances for nation building and conflict resolution in South Sudan. Highlighting the concept of clustering is quite useful for a better understanding of ethnic structure of the South Sudanese society and their perception of political and socio-cultural identity. **FIGURE 1** below shows the ethnic groups variation by regions (**FIGURE 2**).

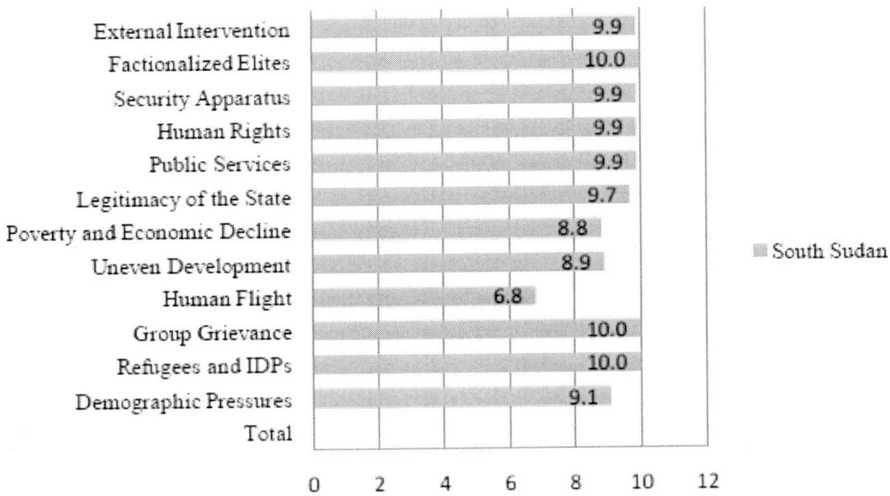

FIGURE 1: Fragile States Index 2014[1].

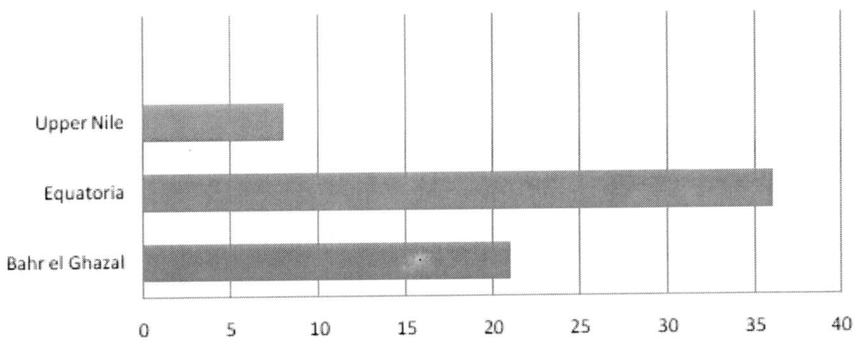

	Bahr el Ghazal	Equatoria	Upper Nile	
Ethnic Groups	21	36	8	

FIGURE 2: Ethnic representation by region.

By examining the ethnic variation as shown (**FIGURE 1**) above, the Greater Equatorial region appeared to hosts the majority of the ethnic groups in South Sudan and have a better record of peaceful co-existence and mutually agreed upon clustered sense of identity [15]. However, it is worth noting that this majority is based on ethnic distribution, not the total population in the region per national capita. The Greater Bahr el Ghazal came second in numberof diverse ethnic groups hosted in the region, aswell, it hosts the majority of the Dinka ethnic groups in the country. The Greater Upper Nile hosts only eight ethnic groups and a home to the majority of Nuer ethnic group in the country.

THE POLITICS OF IDENTITY

After its independence in July 2011, the SPLM ruling party and its leadership slipped into an ethno-centric approach of governance which depended heavily on nepotism and **POLITICAL** appointments over skills and qualification of potential candidates. Such practice has led to a weak system of governance, political party and bureaucratic functions in the country. The adoption of ethnic-based practice also led to multi-faceted challenges and problems such as corruption, lack of rule of law, violation of human rights, ethnic exclusions, and ineffective mechanism of conflict resolutions and prevention [16].

Major cycles of this state of insecurity were witnessed in Jonglei State, Unity, Upper Nile, and some pockets in Greater Bahr El Ghazal and Greater Equatoria states. Many affected groups are the ethnic minority tribes who lack influence and equal representation in SPLM political party, government, and the military. It is equally true that the government, political parties, and the armed forces are ethnically dominated and structured along tribal alliances under an umbrella of (SPLM/SPLA) political party [11]. The mentioned systemic domination has been shaped by the history of tribal contributions and loyalty to the movement during the civil war between SPLA/M and the central government in Khartoum since 1983. In this scenario, other minority ethnic groups, who were used in counter-insurgency tactics on the Khartoum old Sudan side, have managed to join the new Independent South Sudan government through negotiated peace settlements with the SPLM ruling party. Those minority ethnic groups, who have totally rejected the new system, either formed opposition parties, or took up arm against the centralized SPLM/A led government in Juba.

The term *politics of identity* is used here in reference to ethno politics and other policies that are designed to be exclusionary and aimed to further the objectives of a selected few usually at the expense of the majority [17]. In South Sudan, the politics of identity has been adopted from successive regimes in the old Sudan which has successfully use it as means to divide and rule the country by creating a competing ideology tainted with a concept of us vs. them identity paradigm. In this context, religious sectarianism created frictions not only between Muslims and Christians and also between Muslims who claim to be more Islamic than others in Sudan. Nonetheless, Arabism- an ideology that sought to promote Arab nationalism at the expense of the African identity was introduced as yet another racial divide mechanism that widened the gap between Sudanese Arabs and Africans in the South East and Western Sudan. In its genesis, these politics of identity have fractured Sudanese society so deeply that it resulted in conflicts between the central and marginalized ethnic groups in Darfur, Southern Kordofan, Blue Nile, Red Sea Hills, and South Sudan [1]. Therefore, it is fair to say that South Sudan has modeled the politics of identity adopted from Sudan after its independence and after deviating from the SPLM vision of rebuilding just and free democratic society. South Sudan is a country of over sixty tribes but only two ethnicities, Dinka and Nuer, dominated the government until the outbreak of December 15th civil war and the subsequent massacre of the Nuers in Juba.

As a result, hiring practices now made on ethnic and tribal allegiances. Additionally, some in the SPLA/M claim to be more "SPLA/M Proper" than others because they claimed not to have rebelled against it and to have sacrificed more for the cause of freedom than others and as such feel entitled to government privilege [18]. Such ideas have not only led to rampant tribalism in the public sector but also incompetence and massive corruption that has interfered with development and service delivery thereby fuelling a growing discontent, unrest, insecurity, and instability in South Sudan(ibid).

The politics of identity and tribalism are becoming challenges to South Sudan as both constitute triggers for potential divisions and undermining the fabric of the South Sudanese society. The politics of identity not only favor certain groups in South Sudan but also redefines the composition of South Sudan's society and construct the image of the country as being made up only of the two competing tribes (Dinka-Nuer). Nonetheless, these localized ethnocentric policies created suspicions, resentments and conflicts making it difficult to promote a national identity and socio-political cohesion.

Equity, Representation, and Feud

Due to the disputed numbers and conflicted views on projection of population in South Sudan, it is imperative that the government of South Sudan conduct its own census to obtain an accurate projection of the population in the ten states of the country. This will help create better plans for allocation of better services, **EQUITY**, and fair distribution of resources. It will also eliminate the fallacies of communities' sense of entitlements because of being the largest as per their ethnicity, not over the national average of South Sudan population. The Dinka ethnic group has self-proclaimed their ethnic group to be the majority, and Nuer as the second majority against non-Dinka, and non-Nuer in South Sudan. Such perceptions led to a second era of marginalization and secondary citizenship of which the rest of 63 ethnic groups in South Sudan complained of power abuse, nepotism and discrimination.

The continuation of ethnic violence, political disputes, insecurity, corruption, marginalization and tribalism are in most cases associated with the two-dominant ethnic communities in South Sudan (Dinka- Nuer), otherwise known as the tribes of majority. Should the country adopt the working statistical figure of 2008 in Sudan, Dinka constitutes about 26% of the national average, Nuer with 24% and about 46% of South Sudanese ethnic groups are neither Dink nor Nuer. Therefore, in a fair democratic process, it would be difficult for the two tribes to claim a majority, or vote in members of their tribes based on their ethnic identities. However, the two ethnic groups have dominated of socio-political and economic affairs including the military powers in South Sudan.

In an equitable governance system, the fair share of the two ethnic majorities should have been 54% of the national average. The last Kiir- Machar's government was a clear example of political and economic power sharing and domination based on ethnicity and their historical rivalry to maintain peaceful co-existence between the two tribes (Dinka- Nuer). As a result, South Sudan slipped into its current conflict and has remained a volatile and fragile state. After the December 15th crisis, the government has set its priorities on ethnic groups competing interest of tribal alliances to win the war, and not that of nation-building and socio-economic developments. In practice, South Sudan categorically adopted the same model of Arabized system of governance in the then-united Sudan of which only 35% of Arabized Sudanese claimed ownership of the country, and marginalized 65% of its population. In this context, about 63 ethnic groups of South Sudan lives under the clemency of the two ethnic tribes of Dinka and Nuer, with the Dinka being the most dominant militarily, politically and economically. Many argue that the leverage of domination was brought into the play through over-representation of the Dinka ethnic group within the SPLM/A movement, and the negotiated peace settlements with the Dinka's traditional rivals, the Nuer who were over-represented in the counter-insurgencies and oppositions in Khartoum-led government(s).

Lack of socio-cultural and political will to address these competing tribal, regional, and ethnic interests has fuelled ethno-tribal conflicts which remained a major factor that hinders the nation's socioeconomic and political development.

New Section in here such as- Ethno-Political Rivalry in Localised Conflicts (**FIGURE 2**) below shows the framing of Grounded Theory (GT) and Situational Analysis (SA) to further illustrate perceived politics of identity and incidents of conflict among South Sudanese ethnic groups usually reported nationally and internationally. Among the 64 tribes of South Sudan, **FIGURE 2** focused only on tribes that came into contact with other tribes in some form of ethno-political rivalry, land disputes or revenges reported on current active or inactive conflict within the regions of Greater Bahr el Ghazal, Upper Nile and Equatoria. According to Charmaz [19], grounded theory analysis is a process of naming each line of written data. With that coding process, I have also acknowledged Charmaz's statement that coding every line may seem like an arbitrary exercise because not every line contains a complete sentence and not every sentence may appear to be important. The thematic and content analysis of the grounded theory provided an opportunity for analysis of common incidents in similar situations, or different incidents in similar situations within the ten states of South Sudan. The process of analysis continued till all incidents were exhausted, or reached what is known as theoretical saturation in grounded theory, which is the stage where there is no further emergence of new themes from the data being analyzed [20]. The narrative was supported by statements from data collected to eliminate forced data analysis and bring the process closer to the stories reported. The Situational Analysis Matrix (SAM) was thereafter used in the form of Mind Map and Smart diagrams, which further facilitated analysis of the main themes and categories (**FIGURE 3**) [21].

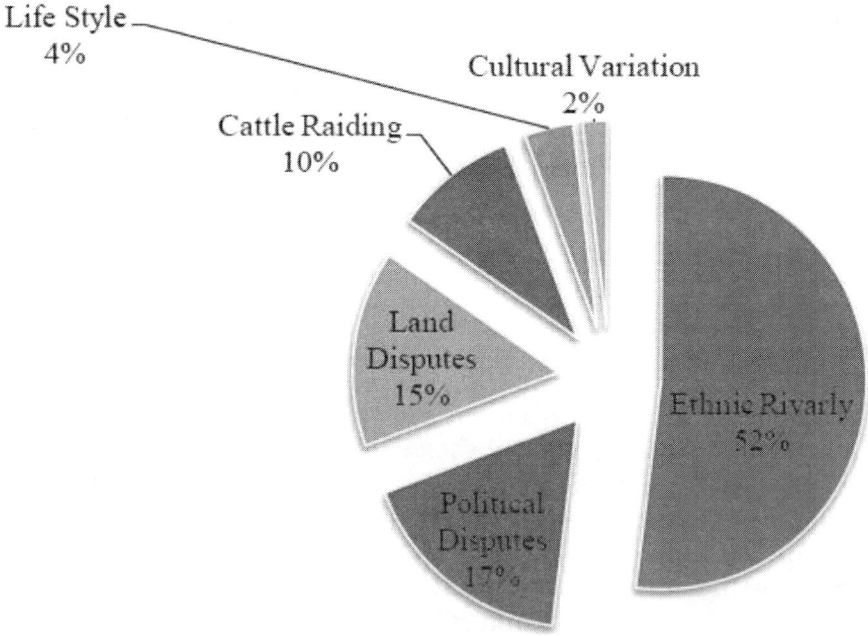

FIGURE 3: Reported incidents by causes of conflicts.

Ethnicity and tribal affiliation have been cited as an underlying cause of the ongoing inter-ethnic and political conflicts in the country. Major ethnic clashes reported in South Sudan since its independence were influenced by ethno-tribal, group cultures and their life style. The characteristics and mechanism of any conflicts reported in Bahr el Ghazal and Upper Nile regions involved some forms of ethnic factor. These ethnic factors are thereafter transformed to political and sociocultural conflicts in a form of wealth acquisitions (Cattle raiding), lands grabbing and displacements of rival ethnic groups.

Some of these conflicts were later transformed and understood as political rivalry due to the fact that large segment of the population are illiterate and do not meaningfully engage in political process nor understands it. Political rivalries were followed by land disputes due to wide spread of displacement within the country and resettlement of IDPs fleeing ethnic altercations, or military confrontation and counterinsurgency [3]. Other conflict has been attributed to ethnic and tribal groups who have adopted cattle raiding as a cultural practices or way of life.

Leadership and Governance

At the national level, it is noted that independence of South Sudan did not affect anticipated change in citizens' welfare nor strengthen political will to eradicate discrimination, marginalization and injustice. In addition to winning the title of a fail state, South Sudan track record for the last ten years has proven dismal in terms of tribalism, human rights abuses, corruption, as well as social disorder in all of its ten states [6].

Further, the adoption of ethnic identity among the rulers in South Sudan was interpreted by the minority ethnic groups as a divisive and exclusionary political tool and is designed to control and keep others away from centers of power [18]. Those powers should have been used to advance the common good or address the dire socio-economic development. In addition, such ideologies have fostered corruption, lack of accountability and self-centered ruling elites that elevate their interests above that of their countries.

In 2009, an estimated 47-51% of South Sudanese were under the national poverty line (World Bank, 2013). This high percentage of poverty is likely due to lack of sustainable development and limited livelihood opportunities after the independence [6]. Nonetheless, at the leadership's level, poverty eradication will require vision, planning, commitment and equitable investment.

To date, over 90% of the citizens of the South Sudan live in rural areas and made their livelihood directly from agriculture through forestry, farming, hunting and fishing thereby making it the single largest source of food supply and manpower [22]. However, lack of direct investment in agriculture and basic infrastructure of the South Sudan has ensured that this sector remains poorly serviced and rudimentary. As such, South Sudan face challenges in the provision of food security for a growing population within its newly created towns and localities. Lack of investment in agriculture and other private sectors of the economy have affected not only service delivery but also a potential to develop and improve the standard of living and export of local agricultural produce. Therefore, to improve the standard of living in South Sudan, there is a need for the governments not only to adopt the Millennium Development Goals [23] but also to move beyond poverty reduction and develop long-term plans and set goals for sustainable development and industrialization to expand their economic base.

In addition to inequality, maladministration, poverty, and underdevelopment also fuel cultures of corruption, insecurity, unrest, instability, and constant **MIGRATION** of an unskilled workforce from rural areas to urban centers. According to African Development Bank Group [24] interim country strategy paper, the South Sudan governments has no genuine strategies to eradicate poverty and underdevelopment, but are rather forced to deal with the consequences such as corruption, insecurity, unrest, and instability repressively without providing solutions to the problem in the first place. Therefore, to address the poverty and underdevelopment, the government of South Sudan need to divert spending from militaries to education, healthcare, infrastructure, food security and all or any services essential for basic needs. This will ameliorate the pressures on government in the short term as it will help increase employment and decrease discontent. The investment will also have an added advantage of increasing the tax base of the government giving the governments other means of generating more revenues.

As for justice system, there are no independent parliaments or judiciaries thereby severely limiting the roles these institutions play in enacting and enforcing law and order. The executive branches have overshadowed the legislative and judiciary and indeed seized the roles of the other two branches of governments. Consequently, then, presidential decrees have replaced legislations as sources of law and order thereby creating climates of uncertainties, limitations in law enforcements, and contradictions in governance. As well, South Sudan has yet to promulgate permanent constitutions. The absence of permanent constitutions has encouraged despotism, impunity, repression, misrule, and corruption thereby making it harder for the country to attract long-term investments (with exception of oil industries) because of the risk of instability. In short, the lack of a permanent constitution in South Sudan is detrimental to its political stability and economic development [25].

CONCLUSION

In conclusion, after the independence of South Sudan on July 9, 2011 from the Sudan, politicians within the SPM ruling party diverted their attention from the core issues that triggered the rebellion against the successive governments in Khartoum and demand for separation. Even so, many Western nations, lead by the United States, have contributed massive financial, logistical, and technical supports to help with the efforts of rebuilding governance system and rehabilitations of basic infrastructures in country. These Western contributions yielded little in terms of moving South Sudan towards a viable country due to the long and unresolved history of ethnic conflicts, and its influences in socio-cultural, bureaucratic, and political institutions. It is therefore time for the policymakers and international community to shift their efforts from monitoring and reporting on government performance, to investment in human capital through skills development, peace building and peaceful co-existence, reconciliations and socio-cultural and economic development of people. The current style of ethno-centric governance in South Sudan that built on **ETHNIC POLITICS,** dominations and representation based on tribal alliances continues to drag the country into an endless cycle of violence. This form of governance system in South Sudan will not foster process of nation-buildings, peaceful co-existence, or economic development in the country. As such, government priority should be place on eliminating cycles of tribal counter-insurgency, inter-clans disputes, cattle raiding and ethno-political rivalry. This can be done through ethnic reconciliations and social inclusions in all aspects of socio-economic development, genuine grass-root inter-ethnic reconciliations and promotion of peaceful co-existence. South Sudan will need to seriously transform these complicated barriers to cohesive social well-being and nation building through peace and social economic development. All efforts and resources should be invested in promotion of education, grassroot inter-ethnic and tribal reconciliations. Without addressing these divisive ideologies, South Sudan will continue to wallow in misrule mired by corruption, insecurity, underdevelopment, and poverty for decades to come.

REFERENCES

1. Idris A (2013) Identity, citizenship, and violence in two Sudans: Reimagining a common future. Political and International studies collection.

2. About south sudan(2014) Malinume development Goal. UNDP.

3. (2010) Negotiating Sudan's north-south future. The International Crisis Group.

4. Odwar H, Gai S (2015) In Committee from the House of Commons - Subcommittee on International Human Rights.

5. The World Bank (2007) Sudan public expenditure review synthesis report. Open knowledge repository.

6. Patricia T (2014) Statehood or Bust: The Case of South Sudan. Fund for Peace.

7. Roy WG (2001) Making societies: The historical construction of our world. Pine Forge Press.California.

8. Beshir MO (1984) Ethnicity, regionalism, and the national cohesion in Sudan. Thousand Oaks. CA.

9. David de C (1995) South Sudan claims right of self-determination. University of Pennsylvania-African Studies Center.

10. Rolandsen ØH (2009) Land, Security and Peace Building in the Southern Sudan. Oslo: International Peace Research Institute. The International Relations and Security Network.

11. UNMISS (2012) Incidences of inter-communal violence in Jonglei State. United Nations Missions in South Sudan South Sudan.

12. Robertshaw P (1987) Prehistory in the up per Nile Basin. The Journal of African History 28: 177-189.

13. Deng FM, Gifford P (1987) The search for peace and unity in the Sudan. The Wilson Center Press,USA.

14. Markakis J (1987) National and class conflict in the horn of Africa. Cambridge University Press, Cambridge.

15. Gurtong (2015) South Sudan Peoples' profiles. Bringing south Sudan together.

16. (2015) South Sudan Seen as One of World's Most Corrupt Nations. Voice of America.

17. Gracia JE (2005) Surviving race, ethnicity, and nationality: A challenge for the twenty-first century. Rowman& Littlefield.

18. Madut J (2012) Diversity, Unity, and Nation Building in South Sudan. Washington, DC.

19. Charmaz K (2006) Constructing grounded theory: A practical guide through qualitative analysis. Sage Publications, California.

20. Clarke AE, Friese C (2007) Grounded theorizing using situational analysis. Sage Publications, UK.

21. Denzin NK (2007) Grounded theory and the politics of interpretation.Sage publications, UK.

22. Yongo-Bure B (2007) Economic development of southern Sudan. University Press of America, UK.

23. Hulme D (2009)The millennium development goals (MDGs): A short history of the world's biggest promise. Social science research network.

24. (2012-2014) South Sudan interim country strategy paper. African Development Bank Group.

25. (2015) Overview of corruption and anti-corruption in South Sudan. Transparency International.

7

CHAPTER

Popular Rentierism and Tourism Development in Kuwait

CodyParis, Simon Rubin

SchoolofLaw Middlesex University Dubai

ABSTRACT

The purpose of this paper is to explore the challenges facing tourism development in Kuwait due to the particularly unique political-economic system of 'popular' rentierism. Kuwait's tourism industry is relatively underdeveloped in comparison to other GCC countries and has not received much attention in the academic tourism literature. While insights of from this study will be useful for understanding the role of tourism in the rentier economies, this paper will also help to further theorize tourism within the field of political science and international political economy. This study provides both a macro-level analysis of the political economic obstacles to tourism development in Kuwait and the more micro-level challenges that have resulted, particularly in relation to mega-development projects, such as the $3.3 billion dollar Failaka Island development.

Keywords: *political economy, Rentier Theory, Arabian Gulf, tourism development, oil-economy*

INTRODUCTION

The purpose of this paper is to explore the challenges facing tourism development in Kuwait due to the particularly unique political-economic system of 'popular' rentierism. Kuwait's tourism industry is relatively underdeveloped in comparison to other GCC countries and has not received much attention in the academic tourism literature. The paper is based upon field work in Kuwait and the examination of secondary resources including academic literature, media, and government documents. While insights of from this study will be useful for understanding the role of tourism in the rentier economies, this paper will also help to further theorize tourism within the field of political science and international political economy. Additionally this paper attempts to address a deficit in the literature, as noted by Bianchi (2004) , "What many of these...Political economy analyses of international tourism had in common was their overly generalized view of macro-structural processes... whilst crucial aspects of local/regional economic development were certainly overlooked and under-theorized" (p. 271). This study provides both a macro-level analysis of the political economic obstacles to tourism development in Kuwait and the more micro-level challenges that have resulted, particularly in relation to mega-development projects, such as the $3.3 billion dollar Failaka Island development.

CURRENT STATE OF TOURISM IN KUWAIT

There are many obstacles facing the future development of tourism in Kuwait including the lack of tourism infrastructure, attractions, and a challenging environment for private industry. Recently, there has been renewed focus on developing the tourism industry in Kuwait as part of a wider economic diversification strategy meant to reduce the dependence on the oil revenue that makes up the majority of the GDP. This new focus on tourism, however, is met with certain challenges and opportunities. Perhaps the most pressing obstacles related to the revitalization of tourism in Kuwait are the country's relationship and proximity to Iraq. Although the 1990 Gulf War is long over, tension between the countries is still high, especially with Iraq's current political instability (Alsdirawi & Faraj, 2004). This, in addition to a heavily guarded demilitarized zone along the 240 km border, gives potential visitors a negative perception of safety in Kuwait. Another obstacle for Kuwait's tourism industry is the lack of attractions for tourists. The visitation to Kuwait has been relatively low over the past decades due to inaction by the government to promote international tourism (Alhemoud & Armstrong, 1996). In one of the only academic tourism papers on tourism in Kuwait, Alhemoud & Armstrong (1996) concluded, in a study of university students and English-speaking foreigners in Kuwait, that neither group was very impressed by the country's tourist attractions, man-made or natural.

Kuwait's tourism is relatively underdeveloped in comparison to other GCC countries. In 2011, Kuwait ranked 61st globally with 362,000 tourists, which is expected to grow to about 639,000 by 2021. Some government officials have actually stated that the aim is to attract one million visitors within five years (Kiesnoski, 2011). In 2009, Tourism contributed USD 535 Million, accounting for 0.88% of the country's exports. While the total tourism receipts have increased, the percentage of the country's exports represented by the tourism industry has decreased from 4% in 1998, likely a result of the September 11th attacks and subsequent war in Iraq. While the number of international tourists are quite low in comparison to other top destinations in the region, there are a large number of international day 'visitors'. According to Kuwait Tourism, about 82% of the nearly 3.8 million International visitors only stay for the day and spend less than $100 per person (Kiesnoski, 2011). The international inbound tourist arrival numbers are in stark contrast to the outgoing tourism market. In 2007 there were 2.7 million outbound tourists from Kuwait. The outbound tourists spent USD 8.2 billion, which accounted for nearly 27% of the country's imports. The scale of this outbound market suggests that there is a huge amount of untapped potential for growth in the domestic tourism industry. There is a long tradition of domestic leisure and recreational activities in Kuwait. Many Kuwaiti families construct short-term tents in large camping communities in the desert during the winter months. During these cooler months, many Kuwaiti's spend weekends or evenings in these tents, many of which are furnished with all the comforts of home. Additionally, there is large number of beach chalets, where Kuwaiti's spend time pursuing leisure activities. Recreational activities including four-wheeling, jet skiing, boating, fishing, horseback riding, falconry, are all quite popular. The traditional pursuit of these activities combined with the large number of outbound tourism from Kuwait suggest that there is a huge potential for capturing the domestic tourism industry.

Since 2004, there has been a large development push in the tourism and hospitality industry. Twenty-five hotels and resorts have been built or are planned by international brands including Hilton, Four Seasons, Jumeirah and Intercontinental. The massive increase in hotel beds combined with the planned hotel and resort components of the mega-developments ($85 billion City of Silk, $3.3 billion Failaka Island) will provide the need for the development of attractions to draw leisure tourists to Kuwait. Currently the market is largely made up of business tourists, most of whom are connected to the US military operations in Iraq and the energy sector. While Kuwait has relaxed visa procedures for certain regions (e.g., GCC, North America, Australia, and most of Western Europe) (Stensgaard, 2004), visitors from other regions still have to deal with often complicated and tedious procedures (al-Shamari, 2011).

The country's accessibility and mild climate during the spring and winter months provide some of the necessary draw for international tourists. There are also some unique attractions for visitors including the iconic Kuwait Towers, the Liberation Tower, Old Souk and Grand Mosque, the waterfront Corniche, and an array of beautiful beaches. Kuwait's Tourism website also includes several other attractions for visitors go to including amusement parks, ice skating rink, swimming pool complex, resorts, yacht clubs, parks, and Green Island, the first artificial island in the Gulf region (Touristic Enterprises Company, http://www.kuwaittourism.com). Kuwait also offers visitors a unique and arguably better opportunity for experiencing authentic cultural experiences and interactions with the local population. As one travel agent in

California stated, "every single time we've ended the Persian Gulf route and our clients reminisce, they mention Kuwait as a highlight. It may not have all the glitz and glamour, but they were so glad they visited" (Kiesnoski, 2011). The relative lack of tourism development in Kuwait can create the perception of being a more authentic destination, that is off-the-beaten track or exotic. As a tour operator quoted by Kenneth Kiesnoski (2011) suggests, "Kuwait has something different to offer. Sometimes the lack of development is an attraction unto itself and the lesser-known regions often end up being the highlights of one's travels." While the lack of attractions provide some visitors with a positive feeling, it leaves very little for the tourism industry in Kuwait to work with to market or brand the destination, particularly to international long-haul tourists. Kuwait lacks the iconic attractions from antiquity as in Jordan and Egypt, the modern attractions of Dubai and Abu Dhabi, or the natural beauty of destinations like Oman.

Additionally, the ban on alcohol means that Kuwait lacks the nightlife that other destinations in the Gulf have, a potential disincentive for many leisure tourists. On the other hand, some in the tourist industry point to the lack of coordinated marketing initiatives and lack of governmental support of the tourism industry as the main obstacles for increasing the number of international tourists and keeping domestic tourists in Kuwait (Kiesnoski, 2011; al-Shamari, 2011). The tourism sector in Kuwait is handled by a small division in the Ministry of Commerce and Industry, and not by a separate ministry or board. This means that any international promotional activity and campaigns, such as the ITB in Berlin or the World Travel Market in London are supported by the private sector entities such as Kuwait Airways, the tourism operator Kuwait Tourism Services, and the Kuwait Hotel Owners Association. Essentially, many in the private sector feel that the tourism industry is treated with indifference by the government. As one CEO and hotel owner stated, "In the government no one listens to us or gives us feedback. For 25 years, we've been fighting for recognition, but they're not supporting us. We just want the government to recognize us as an industry" (Kiesnoski, 2011). This lack of support reflects the ongoing challenges for private businesses in Kuwait, and the general lack of support for non- oil related economic activities during the last few decades. The National Assembly non-support for the private sector, and specifically tourism, can be seen as a reflection of the wider indifference of Kuwaitis. This is arguably changing, as many Kuwaitis have recognized the need for economic reforms and diversification of the economy, and thus the recent expansion of the hospitality industry and the recent general economic reforms suggest that there is a shift in the perception of the tourism industry's role in securing the economic future of the country.

In March of 2011, the Kuwaiti Ministry of Commerce drafted a tourist strategy to stimulate tourism so that it can provide a viable source of income to the country. The strategy includes the implementation of an external marketing plan and a detailed map of all tourist facilities in Kuwait (al-Shamari, 2011). A former under-secretary for tourism suggests that Kuwait "needs to offer more touristic and recreational facilities than what is has now and a comprehensive marketing plan that begins by informing citizens and residents of Kuwait about what is available in Kuwait before marketing it abroad" (al-Shamari, 2011). . This emphasis on creating awareness domestically can have two important impacts on the future of the industry. First, it can help to, according to the current under-secretary of tourism in the Ministry of Tourism, "build awareness about domestic tourism to Kuwatis who travel abroad every week. We want to encourage them to go to Kuwait Islands, which could be a tourist attraction" (al- Shamari, 2011). Second, by creating awareness among the population, there might be larger support for pro-tourism activity by the elected officials in the National Assembly. The next sections explore the political economy of Kuwait and the current economic reforms and development plans in Kuwait in more detail. These provide a foundation for understanding the context of future tourism development in Kuwait.

POLITICAL ECONOMY OF KUWAIT

Rentier theory emerged from analysis of the political economy of the oil-dependent GCC countries. A *rentier state* can be defined as a state in which the government is a primary economic player and uses its 'legitimate' monopoly over a geographic area to extract significant rents from international transactions (Beblawi & Luciani, 1987). Since a significant share of the rentier state's revenue is derived from the rents imposed on international transactions, the state is freed from the need to extract internal revenues through taxation on the domestic economy (Jenkins, Meyer, Costello, & Aly, 2011). While rents derived from energy resources are the most commonly examined, rents can be derived from other sources including: other natural resources, foreign grants/soft loans, and worker remittances. Additionally, income from international tourism based on the use of unique natural or cultural attractions are also examples (Richter & Steiner, 2008). The relationship between tourism and rentierism has only just recently been explored, and none of which have explored the unique relationship between 'popular rentierism' (Yom, 2011) and tourism as is the case in Kuwait. Mansfeld and Winckler have examined the overall challenges of tourism development as a long-term economic alternative to oil-based rentier economies in the GCC using the example of Dubai (2007) and Bahrain (2008). Additionally, Richter and Steiner (2008) examined the neo-patrimonial rentier state of Egypt and argued that the transformations that occurred over the last few decades have resulted in a diversification of external rents instead of an overall downsizing of the rentier character of the Egyptian economy.

After the oil crisis in the 1990s, many of the GCC nations started to move towards diversification, privatization, liberalization and deregulation in order to support long-term economic growth, and the development of the tourism industry is a central component to these strategies. Within the GCC, tourism has been a main focal point of economic diversification strategies. Dubai, Abu Dhabi, and Qatar are good examples of this strategy in action. Overall the development of the tourism industry in Kuwait can be seen as a failure in comparison. While there have been several attempts expand international and domestic tourism in Kuwait, mostly from the private sector, the overall political and economic landscape in Kuwait has resulted in several major challenges for the future development of tourism industry. In particular, there is a lack of public-private partnerships (Hvidt, 2007) and state owned enterprises (Hertog, 2010), which have been instrumental for the development of the tourism industry (and in particular infrastructure) in places like Dubai.

The need for these wide ranging economic reforms have been recognized by policy and business leaders, it has been particularly slow among the oil-rich Gulf States and the Middle East more generally, when compared to other parts of the world (Hvidt, 2007). While some places like Dubai have seen recent 'booms' in development resulting from economic diversification and an efficient form of state-sponsored capitalism, Kuwait has not. Herb (2009) suggests that Kuwait has developed a reputation as a challenging place for business. Inward foreign direct investment in Kuwait lags way behind the rest of the GCC. During the last 50 years the increase oil revenues have led to the development of an 'allocation state' (Luciani, 1990) in Kuwait, where oil revenues are redistributed to citizens thus decreasing the interdependence of the private sector and government (Hvidt, 2007).

Kuwait's economy can be considered an extreme form of rentierism, in which the majority of the economic activity is based on the oil industry. While other rentier states in the region have been able to successfully adopt economic diversification strategies, the unique form of 'popular' rentierism (Yom, 2011) has created challenging conditions for economic development and diversification. Kuwait's popular rentier system combines characteristics of other Gulf rentier states with the uniquely participatory political system that is responsive to internal social forces and the vulnerability and influence of external relations (Gray, 2011). Formal and informal political participation in Kuwait is tied to unique historical roots that differentiate from other Gulf States, and thus the relatively democratic political system has been stained despite the rentier system (Segal, 2012).

Kuwait has the strongest parliament in the GCC, whereby the parliament is able to vote no confidence in individual ministers. The parliament is made up of individuals elected through free and fair elections and there is nearly universal adult suffrage[17]. The parliament's power thus results in the ruling family appointing ministers who are responsive to the parliament and avoid offending the majority within parliament. As a result the structure of the Kuwaiti political system tends to support political deadlock. Thus, many of the large scale economic reforms or infrastructure projects are held up by the political system.

The private sector in Kuwait often places the blame for the economic problems at the country on the National Assembly. As one Kuwaiti economist said, "Kuwait has adopted the worst of democracy and the worst of dictatorship, the country lives on oil revenues, which makes it a temporary country" (Herb, 2009: 381). Different from other democratic capitalist political economic systems, the extreme rentier economy in Kuwait produces a situation where the large level of natural resource wealth weakens the 'threads of mutual interest' that often tie together wage labor and capital (Herb, 2009). The Kuwaiti parliament does what it is supposed to, it represents the interests of the large number of citizens who rely on public sector jobs.

Another issue related to large scale developments is land ownership. Challenges that arise during tourism planning are often related to land ownership issues. In Kuwait, about 90 percent off the country's real estate is owned by the government (not the ruling family), thus any private sector developments that require land, must secure it through government channels. Due to questionable development agreements in the past, the land has become "highly politicized" (Herb, 2009: 386). The Kuwait Government's reluctance to sell land has lead to a bureaucratic system that restricted access for prospective developers and in some cases, halted approved BOT projects as a result of changing legislature and "bureaucratic inaction" (Herb, 2008: 389). In Kuwait, the majority of projects are developed under build, operate, transfer (BOT) mechanisms, in which the private sector finances, builds, and operates the developments for a specified time period. After this period the entire development is transferred back to the government, and the government retains the land title. While in most countries BOT are employed mostly for infrastructure projects, in Kuwait, they are used for almost all large scale projects. More on current BOT projects are discussed later in this paper. While some non-infrastructure BOT projects have been completed, many others have failed to see any movement because of bureaucratic differences. While the private sector wants the government to use oil revenue for development projects, the majority of Kuwaitis want to see the government distribute the revenues directly to the citizens (Herb, 2009).

One illustration of the impact of these political challenges to development can be seen in the turmoil over the Failaka and Bubyian island projects (discussed more later). In 2005 the government entity overseeing the development projects, the Dividend Zone Agreements & Kuwaiti Islands & Mega Projects Development Team (Dizart), was dissolved and replaced with the Mega Projects Agency. The newly formed MPA answers directly to the Ministry of Public Works. The dissolution occurred amidst criticism by the nine prequalified investor groups, and the lack of necessary political clout to move the projects forward. The MPA, however, is made up of the same staff with the same duties, with just a name change (MEED, 2005).

In addition to the issues related directly to the development of major projects and the business climate, the parliamentary instability during the last decade has also hampered economic reforms and progress on major projects. As a consequence the more economically progressive and liberal voices have been marginalized by the election of more conservative representatives and the overall popular support for the current system that redistributes the oil wealth directly to the citizens. Since 2006, the Emir has used his constitutional power to dissolve parliament and call for new elections four times. According to one newspaper editorial (Gulf News Editorials, 2008), much of the instability can be attributed to allegations of corruption and a continual lack of cooperation between ministers and the opposition-dominated parliament. Many in the private sector see the constant political logjams and the 'snap' elections as being detrimental to the ongoing development projects (Kerr, 2011). The most recent elections in February 2012 resulted in the opposition bloc, made up of Sunni Islamist and tribal candidates, winning 34 of the 50 seats in parliament. There are fears that the increased power of the Islamist- Tribal coalition could further destabilize the sectarian harmony. The country's tribal structure and growing Islamism have largely sidelined the more liberal and socially progressive political movements in the country and represent two distinct threads of opposition to the Shia ruling elite (IISS, 2012). The result of the parliamentary instability has been that the majority of members of the opposition, fueled by the public allegations of corruption and lack of transparency by the executive branch, could continue to appease popular opinion, and thus interfere with the development process including many of the urgently needed infrastructure projects. Additionally, mega development projects and economic diversification/liberalization policies have been sidetracked due to the infighting between government, parliament, the public and other bureaucratic interests groups due to the uniquely democratic political system (Hertog, 2010)

Amidst this political turmoil, the executive branch has spearheaded a series of economic reforms in the country, as part of the "Kuwait Vision 2035" plan. These reforms include new capital markets, labor and privatization laws, and $115 billion investment undertaken by public and private sectors (IISS, 2012). The reform agenda includes several key reforms. The plan includes the reduction of the 'red tape' surrounding staring and operating a business, and increased access to land and capital for startups. Additionally, the plan supports the auctioning of government land and to engage the private sector in the development of public land. The plan also calls for increased privatization to reduce public sector employment growth, salaries, and expenditures (UK Trade & Investment, 2011).

ECONOMIC REFORMS AND DEVELOPMENT PROJECTS

With oil comprising a majority of the GDP and a climate that does not support much agriculture, the diversification of Kuwait's economy is an important step for future stability. While some GCC countries have taken different approaches (i.e., government or private funding), all GCC countries have a shared vision of regional growth through economic diversification (e.g., manufacturing, health care, education, and tourism) (Rice & Mahmoud, 1996).

The Kuwait Vision 2035 is a series of 5-year plans through 2035 with the goal of transforming "Kuwait into a financial and trade hub for investment, in which the private sector leads economic activity, fueled by the spirit of competition, and raising the efficiency of production in under a supporting institutional State agency, establishes values, preserves the social identity, achieves balanced human development and provides appropriate infrastructure, improved legislation and encouraging business environment" (Zawya, 2011). This plan will attempt to remove bureaucratic barriers to the private sector, increase government agency effectiveness, and increase access to land, among other high impact reforms (Al-Jazzaf & Al- Mutairi, 2009).

To accomplish this, Kuwait has proposed several developments in line with the government's 3rd Master Plans. The purpose of Kuwait's 3rd Master Plan is to define the goals and policies for future developments and describe the use of land during the next 30 years (Helmy, 2011). The 3rd Master Plan is considered the first phase of the Kuwait Vision 2035 because it enables legislation and policies to accomplish the vision's goals. The new policies aim to attract more private sector participation, especially in housing development. For example, in the past private investors and contractors were not supportive of governmental contracts for welfare housing, citing low financial return and government legislation that decreases private investments by providing units to welfare participants for free (Helmy, 2011). The 3rd Master Plan and sub phases aim to increase private sector participation "by reducing the ownership and supervision from the public sector in many economic sectors" (Helmy, 2011: 15). These reforms will have a large impact on future tourism developments, as many of the mega projects include mix-use facilities combining housing, retail, leisure, and tourism projects.

The most recent phase of the 3rd Master Plan, Kuwait's Five-Year Plan (2010) includes 1,100 oil and non-oil economic projects with an estimated cost of $125 billion. These projects include hospitals, housing, a highway system, airport improvements, and tourist attractions. To balance the high costs and retain ownership, the government will employ, in most cases, the "build, operate, transfer" (BOT) mechanism to complete these projects developments. Dictated by Kuwait law, BOTs rely on private Kuwait corporations to construct and operate projects with an understanding that the infrastructure and operations will be turned over to the government after a period of time. BOTs provide a revenue opportunity for private businesses and the government benefits from gaining infrastructure and delaying operational costs for 30 to 40 years. This law is mutually beneficial in some respects, however the ultimate beneficiary is the Kuwait government. Despite the inevitable transfer of operations and infrastructure to the government, some private companies (e.g., Injazzat Real Estate Development Company K.S.C.) take pride in public good BOT developments. Injazzat believes BOT projects are "advantageous, as the private sector clearly possesses the knowledge and ability to deliver projects on time and budget" (Injazzat, 2007). One example of a successful BOT development is the Sulaibiya wastewater treatment and reclamation facility; a 30 year contract in operation since 2004, this facility secures untreated water provided by the government, treats the wastewater, and then sells the treated water back to the government (Al-Otaibi & Abdel-Jawad, 2007). Projects such as the Sulaibiya Treatment facility, however, were under criticism in 2006 when "financial and administrative violations" (Al-Qaheri & Al-Mejren, 2009: 330) surfaced and the government responded by enacting new regulations on BOT developments in 2008. The past legislature on BOT developments led to the private sector's misuse of public funds and lack of sufficient public revenue from projects (Al-Qaheri & Al-Mejren, 2009). There are several issues and obstacles that BOT developments face (Helmy, 2011); including, delays due to long documentation cycles, lack of human resources with project implementation skills, and lack of vacant land due to governmental regulations. In order for Kuwait's 3rd master plan to become successful, the government must consider these challenges and respond with attractive BOT regulations that streamline procedures and provides transparency (Helmy, 2011). Without consideration of the previous challenges to the BOT mechanisms, current and future reforms of the economic system might fall short of the goals laid out in Kuwait Vision 2035.

To enhance Kuwait's economy, appearance, and citizen well being the government has approved projects such as, the Bubiyan Island Development, the Jaber Al-Ahmad Al-Sabah bridge expressway, the Jaber Al Ahmed Al Sabah Hospital, and Khairan Residential City. Bubiyan Island is Kuwait's largest island and poised to become a trading hub with the development of an international port, a harbor, and residential areas. The new bridge is a 750 million KD endeavor to connect the developing Silk City with smaller cities on the fringe of Kuwait City via an overwater expressway. More citizen-oriented projects include a new hospital in Surra with advanced diagnostic and treatment capabilities and the space to accommodate 1,268 beds. In addition, residential projects such as the Khairan Residential City will provide housing for Kuwait's growing population. This particular residential city is one of the largest with 35,844 expected residential units. These developments and others, such as a new university campus capable of accommodating 40,000 students, will provide Kuwait and its people with the economic tools to compete in the global arena.

Planned Development Projects and the Tourism Industry of Kuwait

The Kuwaiti National Assembly passed a five year development plan that includes a total of 1,100 projects, including numerous Mega Projects, totaling an estimated US$125 billion in spending (Kuwait Five Year Plan, 2010). The plans main aim is to address economic pressures felt since the start of the global economic recession in 2008 by decreasing the country's dependence on oil. Among these projects are several that are aimed at increasing the economic revenues of international and domestic tourism.

Within Kuwait's new Five-Year Plan, there are several large projects that will contribute to the country's growing tourism industry. These developments include, Failaka Island, Madinat Al Hareer (or the Silk City), Kuwait International Airport expansions, and projects to beautify downtown Kuwait City and Sulaibikhat Beach through developments such as, greening projects, a new metro rail system, and "cultural and educational services and facilities, which [will help] stimulate both tourism and the economy in the country" (KMC Holding, 2007). The beautification projects of downtown Kuwait City and Sulaibikhat Beach have expected values of 20 million KD and 35 million KD, respectfully. One key tourism development is Madinat Al Hareer; a city that will be built from the ground up and projected to be complete by the mid 2020's. The other key development is the addition of a new terminal at the Kuwait International Airport with construction expected in 2012; the project is planned to be completed in phases over the next 30 years (International Airport Review, 2008).

Madinat Al Hareer or the Silk City is an ambitious urban development in Subiya expected to take around 25 years to construct. Approved in 2008, construction of highways, roads, and support infrastructure has already begun. This $94 billion (USD) development will provide 430,000 new jobs and will be home to 750,000 residents, a National Wildlife Sanctuary with an eco-tourist resort, a financial center, a duty-free trade zone, a new airport, convention facilities, an Olympic stadium and other sports facilities, and the Mubarak Al Kabir Tower (which upon completion will be the tallest building in the world with over 200 floors). This project also incorporates the Bubiyan port development and the Jaber Al-Ahmad Al-Sabah Bridge connecting the Silk City with Kuwait City via two man-made islands. The city will support four major districts know as, Finance City, Leisure City, Culture City, and Ecological City. According to the firm spearheading the Silk City project, these four city centers "match the demands of [Kuwait's] contemporary society for new places to work, relax, learn, and preserve the natural heritage of [the] land" (Civic Arts, 2011). Finance City will become a new global business, commerce, and trade center. This will be accomplished by its proximity to the planned international airport and bridge to Kuwait City, giving global investors easy access to the district. Leisure City is located near the estuary of two major rivers providing beaches and waterways for leisure pursuits. In addition to vacation attractions such as, resorts, hotels, and rental properties, Leisure City will include an athletic center, academies of sports and sports medicine, and sporting complexes designed for large-scale international events. Cultural City will rest on the tip of the Subiyan peninsula and will give citizens a place for cultural knowledge and academic, diplomatic, and policy research, as well as centers for performing arts. Lastly, Ecological City will feature the region's nature preserve, in addition to an ecological research facility. This district will also become an ecotourism destination providing views of the desert preserve and educational information about the wildlife. Silk City and its surroundings will attract international tourists with its innovation and excitement, similar to Abu Dhabi and other Middle East destinations.

The completion of the new terminal at Kuwait International Airport outside of Kuwait City is expected in 2016. This terminal will have the capacity to service 50 million passengers annually, with the first development phase set to accommodate 13 to 25 million annual passengers. Due to the structure's location and arching design, there will be enough space to operate between 30 and 51 gates and jet ways after the first phase of construction. In subsequent phases a second passenger terminal will be constructed and the capacity is expected to increase to 100 gates and jet ways. To service the new terminals, infrastructure projects such as, new roads and access points, two parallel runways, maintenance facilities, hangers, fuel depots, a rail system, and an installation of the Kuwaiti Al Mubarak Air Force Base. This terminal will not only be flexible enough to accommodate millions of travelers and larger aircraft (i.e., Airbus A380), but will also be one of the most environmentally friendly terminals in the world with the goal of a "Gold" LEED certification upon completion. With concrete construction, the terminal structure will have thermal mass and the roof will utilize photovoltaic cells for terminal operations. The terminal will offer lush landscaping to provide aesthetics and comfortable microclimates. Curtain buildings such as the parking structure will be incorporated into the landscape, adding to the terminal's natural appearance. The new terminal at Kuwait International Airport will also act as a symbol of economic security and pride for Kuwait's citizens. This project will provide employment opportunities as well as a culturally inspired icon for the State of Kuwait.

CONCLUSION

All of these developments will provide a huge expansion of the necessary infrastructure for growth of the tourism industry in Kuwait. However, the planned development of Failaka Island will be the centerpiece in the strategy for Kuwait to emerge as a competitive tourism destination. The development plan for Failaka is to create an 'iconic' destination that will move Kuwait onto a competitive alternative to Dubai, Abu Dhabi, and Qatar as a leading destination for international long-haul, regional, and domestic tourists.

The development of Failaka Island is an integral part of Kuwait's future tourism development plans. Recent economic reforms provide hope for the success of the Failaka Island development, which has been stifled in the past. There have been several development plans for the island dating back to the 1960s which have been hampered by the political and economic landscape of Kuwait. The magnitude of the current development also poses a challenge of balancing the large-scale development of the island and the preservation of the natural and historical richness of the island. When examined within the context of the overall political and economic landscape of Kuwait, the feasibility of these proposed mega projects is questionable, as is the future expansion of the tourism industry in Kuwait.

REFERENCES

1. Alhemoud, A. & Armstrong, E. (1996). Image of Tourism Attractions in Kuwait. *Journal of Travel Research*, 34(4), 76-80.

2. Al-Jazzaf, M. & Al-Mutairi, E. (2009). Kuwait Team's Report. *DevelopingKnowledge Economy Strategies to Improve Competitiveness*. Alexandria: World Bank Institute.

3. Al-Otaibi, A. & Abdel-Jawad, M. (2007). Water security for Kuwait. *Desalination*, 214, 1-3.

4. Al-Qaheri, H. & Al-Mejren, A. (2009). A decision support system for plot pricing of BOT projects in the State of Kuwait. *International Journal of Computer Information Systems and Industrial Management Applications,* 1, 329-340.

5. Alsdirawi, F. & Faraj, M. (2004). Establishing a Transboundary Peace Park in the Demilitarized Zone (DMZ) on the Kuwait/Iraqi Borders. *Parks,* 14(1), 48-55.

6. al-Shamari, K. (2011). Kuwait seeks methods to boost tourism. *Al-Shofra*, April 22, 2011. . http://al- shorfa.com/cocoon/meii/xhtml/en_GB/features/meii/features/business/2011/04/22/feature -03

7. Beblawi, H. & Luciani, G. (1987). *The rentier state: Nation, state, and Integration in the Arab World.* London: Croom Helm.

8. Bianchi, R. (2004). Towards a new political economy of global tourism. In R. Sharpley & D. Telfer (eds), *Tourism and Development: Concepts and Issues*, p 271. Clevedon: Channel view.

9. Civic Arts (2011). *Madinat Al Hareer (City of Silk).* http://www.civicarts.com/madinat-al- hareer.php

10. Gray, M. (2011). A theory of "late rentierism" in the Arab states of the Gulf. *Occasional Paper No. 7.* Georgetown University School of Foreign Service, Qatar.

11. Gulf News Editorials (2008). Political schism is Kuwait's Bane. *Gulf News,* March 19, 2008. http://gulfnews.com/opinions/editorials/political-schism-is-kuwait-s-bane-1.92068

12. Helmy, M. (2011). Ivestigating the critical success factors for PPP projects in Kuwait. KTH Royal Institute of Technology, Sweden. Master's Thesis.

13. Herb, M. (2009). A nation of bureaucrats: Political participation and economic diversification in Kuwait and

the United Arab Emirates. *International Journal of Middle East Studies,* 41,

14. Hertog, S. (2010). Defying the resource curse: Explaining successful state-owned enterprises in rentier states. *World Politics,* 62(2), 261-301.

15. Hvidt, M. (2007). Public-private ties and their contribution to Development: The case of Dubai. *Middle Easter Studies,* 43(4), 557-577.

16. IISS (2012). Kuwait's political turmoil threatens progress. *Strategic Comments,* 18(3). Jenkins, J., Meyer, K., Costello, M., & Aly, H. (2011). International rentierism In the Middle

17. East and North Africa, 1971-2008. *International Area Studies Review,* 14(3), 3-31. Kerr, S. (2011). Emir dissolves Kuwait's parliament. *Financial Times,* December 6, 2011.

18. http://www.ft.com/cms/s/0/ef834dc4-201d-11e1-8462-00144feabdc0.html#axzz1uNYlxhbo

19. Kiesnoski, K. (2011). Kuwait plays catch-up. *Travel Weekly: The National Newspaper of the Travel Industy,* October 18, 2011. http://www.travelweekly.com/Middle-East-Africa-Travel/Kuwait-plays-catch-up/

20. KMC Holding (2007). KMC Management projects. http://www.kmcholding.com/en/p/management_projects.aspx.

21. Kuwait Five Year Plan (2010). http://kuwait-embassy.or.jp/pdf/kuwait-five-year-plan.pdf\ Luciani, G. (1990). Allocation vs Production states: A theoretical framework. In G. Luciani (ed),

22. *The Arab State,* p 65-84, London: Routledge.

23. Mansfeld, Y. & Winckler, O. (2007). The tourism industry as

an alternative for the GCC oil- based rentier economies. *Tourism Economics*, 13(3), 333-360.

24. Mansfeld, Y. & Winckler, O. (2008). The role of the tourism industry in transforming a rentier to a long-term viable economy: The case of Bahrain. *Current Issues in Tourism*, 11(3), 237-

25. MEED (2005). Agents of fortune: The newly formed public body will be pulling out all the stops this summer in an effort to get the giant Failaka and Bubiyan projects underway. *Middle East Economic Digest*, 49(26).

26. Richter, T. & Steiner, C. (2008). Politics, economics and tourism develoipment in Egypt: Insights into the sectoral transformations of a neo-patrimonial rentier state. *Third World Quarterly*, 29(5), 939-959.

27. Rice, G. & Mahmoud, E. (1996). Trends in international business thought and literature: The Arabian Gulf Countries. *Thunderbird International Business Review*, 38(5). 715-730.

28. Segal, E. (2012). Political participation in Kuwait: Diwaniyya, Majlis, and Parliament. *Journal of Arabian Studies*, 2(3), 127-141.

29. Stensgaard, A. (2004). Kuwait unveils new tourism era. *AMEinfo.com: The Ultimate Middle East Business Resource*, May 5, 2004. http://www.ameinfo.com/pdfdocs /38996.pdf

30. UK Trade & Investment (2011). Working together to support Kuwait's Development Plan. http://www. thedukeofyork.org/DOYResources/PDFs/UKTI_Kuwait%20 Opportunities_J une%202011.pdf

31. Yom, S. (2011). Oil, coalitions and regime durability: The origins and persistence of popular rentierism in Kuwait. *Studies in Comparative International Development*, 46(2), 217-241.

32. Zawya (2011). Kuwait Development Plan. *Zawya: Business Intelligence for you on the Middle East and North Africa,* April 26, 2011. http://www.zawya.com/story/pdf/ Kuwait_Development_Plan-ZAWYA20110426052757/

8
CHAPTER

The International Experience in Private Sector Development: Lessons for Kuwait

Mohammad Ramadhan, Marwa Al-Musallam

Kuwait Institute for Scientific Research Techno Economic Division, Kuwait City, Kuwait

ABSTRACT

The State of Kuwait is a small rich oil-based economy characterized by dominance of the large public sector in major economic activities. Such imbalanced structure has limited the role of the private sector in economic activities and has adversely affected economic growth. Based on the review of international experience in private sector development, this paper aimed to substantiate the impact of both private and public sectors growth on economic performance. Analysis of Kuwait's public expenditures verified the public sector dependency on oil revenues and inefficient utilization of resources. The theoretical review revealed a positive direct relationship between high GDP growth rate and the increased role of the private sector in the economy. Moreover, the review of recent transitional economies experiences in constructive economic transformation can be considered as an evidence of a rapid effective private sector growth. Finally, the analysis also demonstrated that Kuwait's public sector expenditures depict a rent seeking behaviour that has negatively impacted the society welfare.

Keywords: Private Sector Development, Public Sector, Economic Growth, Transitional Economies, Rent Seeking, Kuwait

1 INTRODUCTION

Kuwait is a small rich economy with abundance in crude oil that is entirely owned by the state. The economy depends heavily on oil exports with an estimated GDP of US$ 166.5 bn in 2011. Oil revenues accounted for 65% of GDP, 95% of exports, and 94% of government income, CSB [1] . The government of Kuwait in its efforts to share the oil wealth with its citizens has adopted an extensive welfare-oriented approach toward development. The development of Kuwait has overwhelmingly depended on public policies geared toward heavy government spending. Escalating government expenditures have resulted in high standards of living and one of the highest per capita in the world estimated at $48,900 in 2011, CSB [1] . Accordingly, such public policies have led to the dependence on the government for the provision of employment and most social services (e.g., education, healthcare, housing, electricity and water). Such dependence has created prolonged structural imbalances that include among others: dominance of public sector over the private sector; heavy dependence of national income, public budget, and aggregate exports on oil revenues; and dichotomy in the labor market with high concentrations of the national labor in the public sector and soaring concentrations of expatriate labor in the private sector.

More importantly these policies have adversely limited the role and the contribution of the private sector in economic activities. This fact has detrimental impact on the sustainability of long-term economic growth. Over the period 2002-2011, the share of the private sector in GDP has averaged around 31.5%, CSB [1] . This small share indicates the limited role of the private sector in Kuwait's economy. It is a fact that the private sector controls the majority of the non-oil activities. However, the contribution of most of these activities to the GDP and non-oil GDP may be said to be minimal, except for the two main activities of transport, storage and communications; and finance, insurance, real estate and business services.

In response to these structural imbalances and pressures on the public budget, and in order to energize the role of the private sector companies in economic activities, the government of Kuwait embarked on a privatization plan. The most important step in Kuwait's privatization initiative was the declaration of the law 37/2010 for regulating the privatization program and operations. Subsequently, the Supreme Council for Privatization (SCP) was established in May 2012 by the Amiri Decree 106/2012 for the purpose of executing and implementing the law. In April 2013, the government has passed the law 98/2013 for the purpose of establishing a national fund for the development of small and medium companies. Prior to that, the law 10/2007 was passed for the protection of competition in Kuwait. While the initiation of these laws is a positive step in private sector development, the government is very slow in establishing the administrative and operational structure of these organizations. Moreover, by reviewing the theoretical background for the role of the public sector in economic development, this paper intends to emphasize the importance of the reducing the public sector size in the Kuwaiti economy.

The main argument to be raised in this regard: will the growth and the expansion of the private sector have a positive impact on the economy in terms of long-run output and employment? In other words, to overcome the public sector inefficient utilization of resources, the government should reduce its share in economic activities in favour for a more vibrant role of the private sector. This paper intends to address this issue by substantiating the impact of both private and public sectors role on economic growth, based on evidence from the theoretical review and the experience of transitional economies in private sector development. The paper will proceed in the following structure. Section 2 highlights the role of Kuwait's government expenditures in the economy by analyzing the components of public finance. Section 3 reviews the theoretical relation between public/private sectors development and economic growth. Section 4 will shed the light on the concept of transitional economies. Section 5 analyzes the experiences of transitional economies in private sector development. Section 6 discusses the issue of public sector role in deepening rent seeking behaviour in Kuwait. Finally, recommendations and lessons for Kuwait are summarized in Section 7.

2. KUWAIT'S PUBLIC FINANCE

Kuwait's economy is characterized by the dominance of the public sector and heavy dependence on oil exports both in terms of the generated value added and revenues. Due to soaring oil revenues in 2011, total nominal GDP grew substantially by 32.9% from US$ 125.3 bn in 2010 to US$ 166.5 bn in 2011. Kuwait's oil and nonoil GDP accounted for 59.9% and 40.1% of total nominal GDP in 2011, respectively. Table 1 presents the main components of public budget for the last four fiscal years FY 2009/2010 - FY 2012/2013. Government Spending in FY 2012/2013 reached a historical high level at US$ 68.3 bn, around 74.1% increase from the FY 2009/2010 budget of US$ 39.2 bn (around 18.5 % growth rate per annum). The massive rise in spending was forced by the hikes in salaries, grants, and transfer payments. Total government revenues were estimated at US$ 113.3 bn, with oil income constituting 93.6% of total revenues.

More importantly, the primary budget surplus peaked at US$ 44.9 bn in 2012. In fact, the last 13 public budgets have all posted surpluses in public budgets. Expenditures in Kuwait's public budget are classified into five chapters (categories). For FY 2012/2013, the expenditures were as follows, salaries US$ 17.1 bn—commodities and services US$ 12.9 bn—transports, machinery and equipment US$ 0.5 bn—construction, maintenance and public acquisitions US$ 5.9 bn—miscellaneous expenditures and transferable payments US$ 31.9 bn. Expendi tures on chapters one and five, i.e., salaries and miscellaneous expenditures (subsidies for electric and water, health, education) constituted around 72% of total public spending. In contrast, the high spending on wages and subsidies overshadows spending on capital investment and developmental projects. i.e., investments on construction projects and maintenance constituted only 9.3% of the total expenditures.

Table 1. Kuwait public budgets for (FY 2009/2010-2012/2013).

Value in Billion US Dollar				
Description	**2009/2010**	**2010/2011**	**2011/2012**	**2012/2013**
Expenditures	39.24	58.76	60.75	68.33
Salaries	11.14	12.40	14.66	17.10
Commodities and Services	7.58	10.11	9.86	12.88
Transport, Machinery and Equipment	0.79	0.55	0.52	0.56
Const., Main. and Public Acquisitions	3.77	6.11	5.90	5.85
Miscellaneous Exp. and Transfer Payments	15.96	29.58	29.81	31.94
Revenue	61.70	77.89	108.00	113.27
Oil Income	57.85	72.26	102.05	106.06
Nonoil Income	3.85	5.63	5.95	7.22
Primary Surplus/(Deficit)	22.45	19.13	47.25	44.95
Reserve for Future Generations	6.17	7.79	10.80	28.32
Final Surplus/(Deficit)	16.28	11.34	36.45	16.63

Source: Ministry of Finance, General Accounting Affairs Guidance & System Department, State of Kuwait, 2009-2010, 2010-2011, 2011-2012, 2012-2013.

While one can look favorably at the surpluses of Kuwait's public budget, trade balance, current account balance, and absence of public debt; the fact that the budget revenues are heavily dependent on oil income emphasizes its high sensitivity to fluctuation in oil prices. Hence, sustaining a balanced budget in the absence of other sources of income (no tax income) requires high oil prices at all times. The dependency on oil revenues also raises the concern on the future strains that these expenditures will have on the public budget in the light of government lack of efforts to diversify its sources of income. Moreover, it should be emphasized that expenditures on capital formation has lagged behind over the years. Within the context of previous underinvestment, it is necessary that capital spending increases considerably in order to energize the private sector role in the economy. Hertog (2102) has shown that members of the Gulf Cooperation Council (GCC), including Kuwait, were successful in the creation of many efficient State Owned Enterprises (SOEs) within the public sector. These SOEs adhere, to an extent, to some good corporate governance. While one can view these SOEs as a positive effort within the bureaucratic public sector in the state of Kuwait. The government of Kuwait should energize the role of the private sector in the economy by reducing its role, which include privatization of some of these SOEs.

3. THE ROLE OF PUBLIC AND PRIVATE SECTORS IN ECONOMIC GROWTH

In the pursuit of reviewing the international experience on private sector development (PSD), it should be noted that economic theory does not address the issue of PSD per se. However, microeconomic theories have developed in reference to market competition and equilibrium (perfect competition-monopoly-oligopoly). Economic theories focused on how firms in different markets can utilize resources efficiently (capital and labor) in the production of goods and services at lower costs, and the role of prices, wages, and other economic variable in determining equilibrium between demand and supply. Economic theory postulates that efficiency in allocating resources and production can lead to economic growth regardless of the nature of the firm, Hall and Papell [2] . It is also a fact that most of the capitalistic economies adopt the principles of "free market", where production of most goods and services lies within the private firms. The right of private ownership of resources and production is a fundamental concept in capitalistic markets. The role of the public sector in most developed economies is limited to the principles of supervision, regulations, and management of the overall economy. The role of the government is not extended to compete in production with private firms. This is related to the basic assumption that the private firms are more efficient and competitive than public entities; also, to the fundamental fact that the private firm cannot compete against a public entity that simultaneously owns both the resources and the regulatory power (such as the case in Kuwait).

A study conducted by the World Bank [3] indicated that the private sector plays an important role in promoting economic development and growth, in addition to reducing poverty. It contributes directly to enhancing the quality and the standards of living, and achieves integration with the public sector by providing the products and services needed by the society. Dabbah [4] indicated that the allocation of many activities to the private sector reduces the burden of providing such services by the public sector. In turn, the public sector can focus on regulating, supervising, and monitoring these activities through appropriate public policies. Furthermore, the allocation of economic activities to the private sector could foster a competitive business environment that could increase quality and/or reduce cost of the output (products and services). It could also create an enabling environment that might attract foreign investment leading to more competiveness and gradual removal of monopolistic practices. In a nutshell, reducing the role of public sector in economic activities could minimize inefficient public spending and enhance allocation of resources.

There are limited studies on the impact of private sector development on growth. This is probably due to the fact that in most developed economies the share of the private sector in GDP does not vary to a great extent. Bennett [5] examined the effects of PSD on economic performance, using a panel data on 26 transition economies for the period (1991-2003). The methodology was aimed at examining the effect of growth in factor inputs (capital market and private sector development) on GDP growth. The econometric results revealed that private sector development enhances growth, and it was found that the elasticity of the private sector share on economic growth was around 0.18 percentage point. In other words, a one percent increase in the share of the private sector in GDP would increase the growth rate by 0.18 percentage points.

On the contrary, there is an extensive theoretical and applied literature regarding the relationship between the size of the public sector (share of government expenditure in GDP) and the rate of economic growth. Historically, governments in developed economies have played an important role in achieving high level of economic growth. Most elected governments in developed economies have aspired to regulate the economy properly, implement the laws, and protect property rights. Their efforts to a certain degree have resulted in high level of economic development. On the other hand, the international experience shows that economies controlled entirely by governments (public sector) have witnessed relatively low level of economic growth. This is due to the fact that most economic decisions are controlled entirely by governments with the absence of the private sector interest, Mavrov [6] . This argument leads to this important question, i.e., what is the appropriate size of the public sector that insures optimal economic growth?

Empirical literature has addressed this issue with conflicting results. Ram [7] , among others, indicated that economic growth can be stimulated by large government size. On the other hand, Barro [8] and many others contradicted the aforesaid assumption and indicated that as the size of government increases, in the relative term, it reduces the growth of per capita income, Bairam [9] ; Grossman [10] . Therefore, these contrasting findings showed that large government size can affect economic growth both positively and negatively. However, Husnain [11] pointed out that within these mixed findings, a consensus emerges that up to a certain level, government activities can stimulate growth, but beyond this level, the size of government may reduce economic growth. Husnain's findings regarding the optimal size of government in Pakistan were among the few studies within the developing countries. The study attempted to determine the optimal size of government in Pakistan using Scully model [12] for the period 1975-2008. The econometric analysis revealed that government size is optimized when public expenditures reach 21.5% of GDP. The estimated threshold size is lower than the current size of government in Pakistan. However, the difference between current and optimal size is very small. The author suggested that enhancing efficiency of public sector expenditures is more important than large fiscal adjustments to improve level of economic growth.

Barro [13] presented an endogenous growth framework that allows government expenditure to increase economic growth through the provision of public services that can be used as an input to private sector production. However, he noted that government expenditure crowds out more productive private investment, and hence, can affect the growth rate negatively in the long run. Barro demonstrated that the growth rate has an inverted U shape with respect to the size of government expenditure as share of GDP. The U shape indicates that the growth rates increase initially with the rise in share of government expenditure in GDP and then decline. Within this growth framework, Barro [8] addressed the issue of the optimal share of public sector in the economy by examining the public share of 98 countries. He identified a significant inverse relationship between the share of public sector in GDP and GDP growth. He concluded that the average share of public sector in these economies was around 20%. He assumed that this rate is relatively high and indicated that growth rate would increase if public expenditures were to be reduced. Within this context, both Barro and Husnain findings emphasize the fact that the 20% average public share in GDP is extremely low in relation to Kuwait's high public sector share (70% of GDP).

4. PRIVATE SECTOR DEVELOPMENT IN TRANSITIONAL ECONOMIES

Based on the aforementioned introduction and in order to evaluate the international experience in expanding the role of the private sector, a good starting point is to review the experience of the transitional economies that have taken major strides in moving away from publicly controlled economies toward dynamic role of the private sector. A transitional economy is an economy which adopts combined mechanisms of liberalization, macroeconomic stabilization, privatization, and legal and institutional reform in order to transform itself from a centrally planned economy to a free market. Falke [14] showed that the elements for the transition process to a free market include among many, allowing market forces to set prices rather than a central planning organization, removal of trade barriers, the need to privatize state-owned businesses and resources, and the creation of a financial sector to accommodate the requirements of private capital. The transitional process has been implemented to a varying degree in China, the former Soviet Union and Communist bloc countries of Europe, and in many third world countries. In a wider sense, the definition of transition economy refers to all countries which attempt to change their basic constitutional elements towards market-style fundamentals. This includes heavily regulated Asian-style economies, post-dictatorship Latin American and underdeveloped African countries.

In essence, the transition process can be viewed as the functional restructuring of the role of public entities from being a provider to a regulator and an enabler, with emphasis on the private sector as an engine of growth. The existence of private property rights may be the most basic element of a market economy, and therefore implementation of these rights is the key indicator of transition process, IMF [15] . The European Bank for Reconstruction and Development (EBRD) [16] , developed a set of indicators to measure the progress in transition. The main elements of the transition process can be summarized in the following:

1) Liberalization: the process of allowing most prices to be determined in free markets and lowering trade barriers that distort the world market price structure.

2) Macroeconomic stabilization: aiming to control and lower the expected rise in inflation that resulting from liberalization and the release of restricted demand. This process requires discipline over the government budget and the growth of money and credit (i.e. fiscal and monetary

policy) and advancement toward sustainable balance of payments.

3) Restructuring and privatization: the creation of a viable financial sector and reforming public enterprises to enhance their capabilities of producing competitive goods and transferring the public ownership to the private sector.

4) Legal and institutional reforms: redefining the role of the state in these economies from being a provider to a regulator by establishing the rule of law and introducing appropriate competition policies.

5. THE EXPERIENCE OF TRANSITIONAL ECONOMIES

This section analyzes the private sector development process of the transitional economies as an evidence of extremely speedy and effective private sector growth. Table 2 presents the share and average growth rate of private sector in GDP for countries classified as transitional economies according to the EBRD reports for the period 1991-2010. The results in the table indicate clearly that the private sector had increased its share in the GDP to substantial levels in all the listed countries by 2010. The average share of the private sector (output) in GDP increased from 20% in 1991 to 67% in 2010. Detailed examination of the results revealed that at the initial stages of the transition process, the average private sector share in GDP during the 1990s almost tripled from 20% in 1991 to 58% in 2000. The average private sector's share grew modestly during the last decade to 67% in 2010. It can also be seen that 23 out of the 30 countries listed in the table reached an outstanding 67% and more private share in GDP in 2010. The rapid growth of the private sector in the 1990s coincided with the transfer of assets from the public sector to the private sector. This could be attributed to the aggressive privatization policies adopted by these economies along with removal of constraints that inhibited private sector development. Once the average private sector share approaches around 60% of GDP, the increment in the share depicts a less dynamic pattern.

Table 2. Share and average growth rate of the private sector in GDP for transitional economies.

Countries	Private Sector Share of GDP					Average Growth Rate			
	1991	1995	2000	2005	2010	(1991-1995)	(1996-2000)	(2001-2005)	(2006-2010)
Albania	24	60	75	75	75	53	8	7	6
Armenia	N.A	45	60	75	75	70	9	13	5
Azerbaijan	N.A	25	45	60	75	120	11	13	16
Belarus	7	15	20	25	30	191	77	27	14
Bosnia and Herzegovina	N.A	N.A	35	55	60	N.A	17	8	6
Bulgaria	17	50	70	75	75	37	54	9	6
Croatia	25	40	60	60	70	113	7	7	3
Czech Republic	17	70	80	80	N.A	13	5	5	4
Estonia	18	65	75	80	80	63	11	9	2
FYR Macedonia	N.A	40	55	65	70	12	6	4	7
Georgia	27	30	60	65	75	−35	9	11	7
Hungary	33	60	80	80	80	17	13	7	2
Kazakhstan	12	25	60	65	65	175	12	17	12
Kyrgyzstan	N.A	40	60	75	75	103	21	6	12
Latvia	N.A	55	65	70	70	56	8	11	2
Lithuania	15	65	70	75	75	83	7	8	2
Moldova	N.A	30	50	60	65	N.A	14	14	7
Mongolia	N.A	N.A	N.A	N.A	75	70	9	15	13
Montenegro	N.A	N.A	N.A	N.A	65	−12	−27	7	7
Poland	45	60	70	75	75	28	11	5	6
Romania	24	45	60	70	70	70	40	18	8
Russia	10	55	70	65	65	139	26	18	11
Serbia and Mont	N.A	N.A	N.A	55	60	N.A	10	16	9
Slovak Republic	N.A	60	75	80	80	12	−61	8	4
Slovenia	16	50	55	65	70	39	9	7	3
Tajikistan	N.A	25	40	50	55	125	35	21	18
Turkey	N.A	N.A	N.A	N.A	70	50	48	20	6
Turkmenistan	N.A	15	25	25	25	73	24	19	−152
Ukraine	8	45	60	65	60	−34	15	15	13
Uzbekistan	N.A	30	45	45	45	32	35	23	18
Average Growth Rate	**20**	**44**	**58**	**64**	**67**	**62**	**16**	**12**	**3**

Source: The European Bank for Reconstruction and Development (EBRD) Transition Report (1991, 1995, 2000, 2005, 2010), The European Bank for Reconstruction and Development.

The question to be raised in this regard is whether there was any positive impact of increasing the private sector share in these countries on the overall economy. Examination of the GDP average growth rate over the four sub periods listed in Table 2 indicated clearly that GDP grew at a very high rate as these economies shifted toward more private sector share in the economy. The average GDP growth rate in the first sub period (1991-1995) was the highest at 62% per annum. Even though the average growth rate declined in the following sub periods (1996-2000) and (2001-2005), it was still high at 16% and 12%, respectively. Finally, as the transitional economies moved toward an average of 67% private sector share in the GDP in the fourth sub period (2006-2010), the average GDP growth rate declined to an acceptable moderate rate of 3%. The results seemed to verify the positive direct relationship between GDP growth and a more active role of private sector in the economy. Moreover, the early years of transition witnessed a notable rise in the number of firms, a fundamental shift in the size distribution toward smaller enterprises and the creation of a service sector, largely comprising of numerous small enterprises, Brixiova and Kiyotaki [17] .

Private Sector Development in UAE and China

To emphasize the notion of private sector development, this section reviews the experience of United Arab Emirates (UAE) and Republic of China in promoting the role of the private sector. The experience of the UAE, as a regional Gulf country, in diversifying sources of income is very important and suitable to Kuwait future development. The UAE is a prime success case in its ability to diversify sources of income and lessen dependency on oil. This was achieved by effective attraction of foreign investment and increase of the investments opportunities for the private sector in all economic sectors, in particular, the financial, real estate and services sectors. By adopting and implementing aggressive development plans and strategies that focus on PSD, the share of nonoil GDP in total GDP had increased from 46.8% in 2005 to 56.2% in 2010. Considering also that the GDP had increased by more than one third from US$ 180.6 bil in 2005 to

US$ 297.6 bil in 2010, it could be verified that UAE has maintained high growth during this period while increasing the share of nonoil activities in the economy. The importance of strategic development plans and PSD can be seen in the case of The Emirate of Dubai, where the previous Strategic Development Plan (SDP) for the period 2000-2010 was aimed at to increase GDP to US$ 30 Billion by 2010. However, due to effective implementation of the plan, Dubai achieved that objective in 2005 (five years prior to the target date). During the plan period, the share of oil revenues in the Emirate government total revenues had declined from 52% in 2000 to 24% in 2008. The recent SDP was formulated around five main guiding principles, including economic development which focuses on the unique partnership between the public and private sector and the ability to adopt free market economy principles to enhance innovation and initiatives, Financial Division [18] .

Economic reform in China has resulted in unprecedented economic expansion since 1978, and paved the way for China to become the second largest economy by 2010. According to Kanamori and Zhao [19] the economic reform plan can be categorized into two main components; the development of necessary regulatory laws and policies, and the formation of China economic model. First, in 1987 "The Provisional Act of Private Enterprise of People Republic of China (PRC)" was formed. This law legitimized for the first time the existence of a private enterprise to be fully protected under the PRC law. Second, the development of the Chinese Model based on economic and the political reform. The economic aspect adopted an open door policy, which allows the foreign investors under the provisional act full ownership with no conditional requirements for local partners. The foreign ownership facilitated the transfer of capital, technology, and managerial skills into China and enabled the investors to capitalize on the country domestic resources. This process induced a positive spell over China's privet sector. During the economic growth process, China engaged with global markets by competing with the best manufactures and service providers, leading to the development of modern China today.

On the other hand, the political part was handled by the ruling party who have full control over the government, courts, laws, and flow of information. Callick [20] stated that the combination between China's model and the mass population, gave the country a manufacturing competitive advantage in terms of cheap labour and low production costs. All of the aforementioned elements have contributed in increasing the GDP from $356 billion US in the 1990 to $5926 billion US in 2010, with an average growth rate of 10% per annum, Zheng and Yang [21] . Moreover, the economic growth is significantly related to private sector expansion in China. Chandrashekahr [22] showed that since the induction of "The Provisional Act of Private Enterprise of PRC", 80% of the state owned enterprises and entities were privatized, leading to an increase of the private sector share in the GDP from almost zero contribution in 1990 to 50% and 65% share by 1998 and 2005 respectively.

6. THE RENT SEEKING BEHAVIOR AND LARGE PUBLIC SECTOR IN KUWAIT

The rationale behind the argument that economic growth would be reduced as the size of government (share in GDP) increases can be justified and attributed to political factors, Scully [23] . In most political systems, elected governments try to benefit their constituencies by providing opportunities for them (jobs/business contracts) within the public sector. The behaviour of the government and its constituencies is a classical rent-seeking problem. In economics, rent-seeking is defined as an attempt to obtain economic rent by exploiting the social or political environment in which economic activities occur, rather than by increasing the social welfare, or creating new wealth. The spending of money by a political lobbyist in order to be given a share of wealth that has already been created is an example of rent-seeking behavior. A famous example of rent-seeking is the effort to gain various monopoly privileges due to government regulation of free enterprise competition. Tullock [24] indicated that since resources are expended but no new wealth is created, the net effect of rent-seeking is to reduce the sum of social wealth. The origin of the term refers to the gaining control of land or other pre-existing natural resources. Therefore, while profit-seeking implies the creation of wealth, rent-seeking implies the use of the power of the state or government to distribute wealth between different groups of individuals.

In most cases, the expansion of the public sector could affect the economy negatively. In the case of the State of Kuwait (a political systems with nonelected government), the ruling government uses its ownership of resources to satisfy its constituencies through three main mechanisms:

- Continuous Employment of Kuwaitis in the Public Sector: The government justifies its employment process as part of its responsibilities according to the Kuwaiti constitution, which states that government is responsible to provide jobs for all Kuwaiti. Article 41 in the 1960 Kuwaiti constitution implies that "Each Kuwaiti has the right to work in a suitable job, and the State has to insure equal provision of jobs to all Kuwaitis". In 2010, around 280,088 Kuwaitis were employed in the public sector representing around 76.6% of the total public sector labor force. The heavy employment of Kuwaitis exerts pressure on the public budget with no apparent value addition, leading to what is known as "disguised unemployment". However, the social justification of using public resources for employing nationals in unproductive jobs does not prevent the process of being classified as a rent-seeking phenomenon. In other words, the addition of more Kuwaitis to the public sector will not increase the society's level of wealth.
- Lucrative Governmental Posts: The rent-seeking behavior becomes more apparent when it comes to high paid managerial and governmental posts, where different interest

and political groups lobby the government to maintain their share in these lucrative positions that carries vast benefits. Hence, the escalating inefficiency can be attributed to the fact that public sector resources are not allocated and utilized based on productivity criteria.• Procurement of Business Contracts: Due to the large size of the public sector in Kuwait, public spending dominates private spending, particularly in capital formation and investment. The fact that the private sector has limited role in economic activities induces it to increase its profitability by targeting a share in the heavy government spending schemes, mainly through the public sector procurement program. If the process of obtaining a governmental contract is not based on transparent efficient criteria, then the behaviour of the firm can be categorized as rent-seeking. For example, if a specific local firm obtains a lucrative governmental contract, and subsequently it sub-contracts it to another firm, then this firm has maximized its interest and increased its profit without adding to the without adding to the society's level of wealth.

7. CONCLUSIONS AND RECOMMENDATIONS

To summarize, Kuwait's public policies toward increased government spending and employment of nationals in the public sector, have negatively affected the business environment of the private sector. Enlarging the public sector work force has created unnecessary layers for unproductive labor. This would eventually result in the creation of many rules and procedures that have no economic value. The excessive rules and regulations would create hurdles and obstacles to the private sector and unconstructively affect its efficiency and profitability. Hence, the growth of the public sector in Kuwait has and will continue to undermine the performance of the private sector. This will deepen the structural imbalances leading to the apparent long-run deterioration of the economy.

This paper has reviewed and analyzed the theoretical relation between public and private sectors shares in the economy and economic growth. The analysis revealed a positive direct relationship between high GDP growth rate and the increased role of the private sector in the economy. The reviews of international experience in PSD have also shown that many transitional and developing economies have adopted a combination of privatization, FDI, SMEs, and overall improvement in business environment measures, in order to increase the role of the private sector and achieve high economic growth. The experience of transitional economies can be considered as an evidence of a rapid effective private sector growth.

Based on the analysis of large public sector in Kuwait, theoretical affirmation of the negative impact of large public sector, and the recent transitional economies experiences in constructive economic transformation, the paper proposes the following recommendations for Kuwait in order to progress the economy in the right direction: it is very significant and crucial that Kuwait should be implementing, as rapidly as it reasonably can, the regulatory and business environment improvements, which will enable an environment that is conducive to promote effective large scale private sector engagement in economic activities. Such improvements will create better conditions for all new businesses starting up in the country, as well as for the existing ones; and it will also facilitate higher volumes of investment, both by existing firms, government agencies and publicly owned firms. In order to energize the role of the private sector in economic activities, the government of Kuwait should acelerate the implementation of newly established privatization program. Privatization is an important economic/ political tool to rectify economic imbalances of a large public sector, and to speed economic growth through a vibrant private sector. Kuwait should also be taking action to adopt and implement the policies and regulatory changes to facilitate and promote FDI. Both privatization and FDI tend to be accompanied by significant benefits for the domestic economy in terms of management expertise, access to markets and market networks; innovation and new technology, knowledge of modern business methods, skills development and training programmes.

FUNDING

This Project was Partially Funded by Kuwait Foundation for the Advancement of Sciences under Project Code: 2010-1103-02.

REFERENCES

1. Central Statistical Bureau (CSB) (2011) Annual Statistical Abstract, State of Kuwait.
2. Hall, R.E. and Papell, D.H. (2005) Macroeconomics: Economic Growth, Fluctuations and Policy. 6th Edition, W. W. Norton & Company, New York.
3. World Bank (2002) Private Sector Development Strategy—Direction for the World Bank. World Bank, Washington DC.
4. Dabbah, M. (2010) Competition Law and Policy in Developing Countries: A Critical Assessment of the Challenges to Establishing an Effective Competition Law Regime. World Competition: Law and Economics Review, No. 457.
5. Bennett, J., Estrin, S. and Urga, G. (2007) Privatization Methods and Economic Growth in Transition Economies. Economics of Transition, 15, 661- 683.
6. Mavrov, H. (2007) The Size of Government Expenditure and the Rate of Economic Growth in Bulgaria. Economic Alternatives, 1, 52-63.
7. Ram, R. (1989) Government Size and Economic Growth: A New Framework and Some Evidence from Cross-Section and

Time-Series Data. The American Economic Review, 79, 218-284.

8. Barro, R. (1991) Economic Growth in a Cross-Section of Countries. Quarterly Journal of Economics, 106, 407-443.

9. Bairam, E. (1990) Government Size and Economic Growth: The African Experience 1960-85. Applied Economics, 22, 1427-1435.

10. Grossman, P.J. (1990) Government and Growth: Cross-Sectional Evidence. Public Choice, 65, 217-227.

11. Husnain, I. (2011) Is the Size of Government Optimal in Pakistan? Journal of Economics and Economic Education Research, 12, No. 2.

12. Scully, G. (1994) What Is the Optimal Size of Government in the US? National Centre for Policy Analysis. Policy Report, No. 188. http://www.ncpa.org/studies/s159/s159.html

13. Barro, R.J. (1990) Government Spending in a Simple Model of Endogenous Growth. Journal of Political Economy, 98, 103-126.

14. M. (2002) Community Interests and Insolvency Objective in Transition Economies? Europa-Universitaet Viadrina, Institut fur Transformationsstudien—FIT—Frankfurt an der Oder (Germany). http://www.opengrey.eu/partner/fiz

15. IMF (2000) Transition Economies: An IMF Perspective on Progress and Prospects. International Monetary Fund. http://www.imf.org/external/np/exr/ib/2000/110300.htm

16. The European Bank for Reconstruction and Development (EBRD) (1991-2010) Transition Report. The European Bank for Reconstruction and Development, London.

17. Brixiova, Z. and Kiyotaki, N. (1997) Private Sector Development in Transition Economies. Carnegie-Rochester Conference Series on Public Policies No. 46, 241-279.

18. Financial Division (2008) Public Budget Report. http://www.dof.gov.ae

19. Kanamori, T. and Zhao, Z. (2004) Private Sector Development in the People's Republic of China. Asian Development Bank Institute, Tokyo.

20. Callick, C. (2007) The China Model. www.american.com/archive/2007/november-december-magazine-contents/the-china-modelZheng, H. and Yang, Y. (2009) Chinese Private Sector Development in the Past 30 Years: Retrospect and Prospect. International House University of Nottingham, China Policy Institute.

21. Chandrashekahr, C.P. (2005) How Large Is China's Private Sector. India's National Magazine, 22, 8-21.Scully, G. (1989) The Size of the State, Economic Growth and the Efficient Utilization of National Resources. Public Choice, 63, 149-164. http://dx.doi.org/10.1007/BF00153397

22. Tullock, G. (2005) The Rent-Seeking Society: The Selected Works of Gordon Tullock, Vol. 5. Liberty Fund, Indianapolis.

9

CHAPTER

Is Tourism Development a Sustainable Economic Growth Strategy in the Long Run? Evidence from GCC Countries

Abdulkarim K. Alhowaish

Department of Urban and Regional Planning, University of Dammam, P.O. Box 2397, Dammam 31451, Saudi Arabia

ABSTRACT

The main objective of this study is to investigate the causal relationship between tourism development and economic growth in Gulf Cooperation Council (GCC) countries in a multivariate model, using panel data for the period 1995–2012. The study adopts a panel Granger causality analysis approach to assess the contribution of tourism to economic growth in GCC countries as a whole, and in each individual country. In the case of GCC countries as a whole, the results show a one-way Granger causality, from economic growth to tourism growth. Furthermore, Kuwait, Saudi Arabia, Qatar, and the United Arab Emirates follow the path of economy-driven tourism growth, as hypothesized. The reverse hypothesis (i.e., tourism-led growth hypothesis) holds true for Bahrain, while there is no causal relationship between tourism and economic growth in the case of Oman.

Keywords: tourism development; economic growth; panel causality; GCC countries

1. INTRODUCTION

The tourism industry has emerged as a key driver for a sustainable socio-economic development worldwide. The sector has become an increasingly important source of revenue and employment for many developing countries. According to the World Tourism Organization [1], due to the growing number of destinations opening up to and investing in tourism development, modern tourism has become a key driver for socio-economic progress. Tourism allows the creation of new jobs and enterprises, supporting infrastructure development, the protection of heritage and cultural values, and exporting earned revenues. The latest economic impact report provided by the World Travel and Tourism Council [2] indicated that the tourism industry generated US$ 7.5 trillion (9.8% of the world's GDP) and about 277 million jobs (1 in 11 jobs) globally, in 2014. The report also predicts that the industry is expected to generate more than US$ 11.3 trillion (10.5% of the world's GDP) and 357 million jobs for the world economy by 2025.

Given its increasing importance in the global economy, over the last few years, tourism has gained much attention among Gulf Cooperation Council (GCC) policymakers. GCC states, mostly rich oil countries, view the tourism industry not only as a source of revenue, but also, more importantly, as a way to diversify their economy and solve their unemployment problems [3].

The objective of this study is to investigate the relationship between tourism development and economic growth in GCC countries. It examines the causal relationship between tourism development and economic growth in GCC countries with a multivariate panel causality model, using panel data for the period 1995–2012. The remainder of the paper is organized as follows: Section 2 briefly presents the background of tourism development in GCC countries, Section 3 provides a brief literature review, Section 4 describes the estimation methodology and data sources, Section 5 presents the empirical results and Section 6 provides a summary, a brief conclusion, and some policy recommendations.

2. TOURISM DEVELOPMENT IN GCC COUNTRIES: AN OVERVIEW

Most GCC countries (Bahrain, Kuwait, Qatar, Oman, Saudi Arabia, and the United Arab Emirates) can be classified as newcomers to the global tourism agenda, especially in terms of attracting modern tourism, such as leisure, meetings, incentives, conventions and exhibitions, sport and adventure tourist activities. Over the last decade, massive projects in tourism infrastructure development have been undertaken in many GCC countries. All GCC countries have begun to establish national tourism development strategies and have tremendously expanded tourism through the adoption of positioning (re-positioning) strategies for tourist destinations and niche tourism initiatives [3,4]. Sport, leisure, event, hospitality infrastructures, and large-scale urban development have become a priority in such large-scale tourism initiatives. Ferrari Land, Formula One, Atlantis Dubai, Sharjah Biennale, the Asian Games, and the forthcoming Football World Cup are examples of these GCC tourism mega-projects. Today, more than 12 sites in GCC countries are listed on the UNESCO list of world cultural heritage [5]. Among them, the oasis of Al Ain in the Abu Dhabi emirate, Historic Jeddah (the Gate to Makkah) and At-Turaif District (ad-Dir'iyah) in Saudi Arabia, Qal'at Al-Bahrain, Bahla Fort, and Land of Frankincense in Oman, and Al Zubarah Archaeological site in Qatar.

In recent years, GCC countries have collectively played host to millions of tourists, with increasing number of visitors in most destinations. The number of international tourists increased from about 8.6 million in 1995 to almost 32 million in 2012 [6]. According to the economic impact reports on several GCC states provided by the World Travel and Tourism Council [2], travel and tourism directly supported 1,092,500 jobs in 2014 and around 1,597,000 jobs in 2015. However, the total contribution of travel and tourism to overall employment in GCC countries, including jobs indirectly supported by the industry, was about 1,957,500 jobs in 2014 and about 2,864,000 jobs in 2015. Indeed, tourism development provides great opportunities for GCC countries to diversify away from single resource economies. It also offers ways to help solve their socio-economic problems, such as unemployment [3].

The most recent tourism policy initiative in GCC countries was the development of intra-GCC tourism action plans [7]. The initiative was launched during the GCC tourism officials meeting in Doha on May 13, 2015. The focus of the meeting was on exploring mechanisms to enhance intra-GCC tourism, while building on the success of the Cruise Arabia Alliance, a regional collaboration that strengthens the Gulf's position as a cruise destination. The meeting also encouraged GCC officials to accelerate a joint GCC action to ensure that all member states benefit from mega events taking place in the region over the next decade, such as the Dubai Expo 2020 and the FIFA World Cup 2022.

3. LITERATURE REVIEW

Many governments around the world have engaged in tourism development to promote long-run sustainable economic growth and development. In the literature, long-term influence of tourism on economic growth is known as the tourism-led growth hypothesis. Advocates of this hypothesis argue that the economic growth of a country not only is a function of labor, capital, export, and other factors in that country, but it can also be affected by the number of tourists entering that country. Tourism can act as a growth engine; it contributes to GDP growth, job creation, and foreign exchange generation. Researchers [8,9,10,11,12,13,14,15] suggested many reasons for tourism to be a positive long-run factor in the economic growth of a country. These reasons are as follows:

- Tourism produces foreign exchange earnings that are essential to import both consumer goods and capital and intermediate goods;
- Tourism facilitates the use of resources that are in line with the factor endowment of a country;
- Tourism creates job opportunities in tourist destinations;
- Tourism promotes improvements in a country's infrastructures, benefitting not only tourists, but also residents;
- Tourism is considered a conduit for transferring new technological and managerial skills into an economy; and
- Tourism has the potential to create positive linkages with other sectors of the economy (e.g., agriculture, manufacturing, and other service industries).

On the other hand, economic growth also has a positive impact on tourism development. Economic growth can favor the tourism industry through the development of facilities and infrastructures, such as transportation development, information and communication technology development, electronic money, hotels, restaurants, and other entertainment services and facilities. The relationship between tourism development and economic growth has been a popular topic in the recent tourism-led growth literature. However, despite using research methodologies based on time series and/or panel data analytical techniques, empirical studies have shown mixed or even inconsistent results in terms of supporting the tourism-led economic growth hypothesis. Examples of studies that analyze the relationship between tourism and economic growth employing the Granger causality test with time series data analysis include Balaguer and Cantavella-Jorda [9], Durbarry [10], Gunduz and Hatemi-J [11], Brida, Carrera, and Risso [12], Chen and Chiou-Wei [13], Belloumi [16], Akinboade and Braimoh [17], Tang and Abosedra [18], and Tang and Tan [19].

These studies provide evidence in support of the tourism-led growth hypothesis. Furthermore, studies such as Dritsakis [14], Kim, Chen, and Jang [20], and Lee and Chien [21] support the validity of the feedback hypothesis, while Oh [22], Ozturk and Acaravci [23], Tang and Jang [24], and Payne and Mervar [25] present evidence of no relationship between the two variables. However, other empirical studies investigate the relationship between tourism development and economic growth using cross-section or panel data. Among these studies, Leitão [26], Tavares and Leitão [27], Leitão and Shahbaz [28], Sequeira and Campos [29], Lee and Chang [30], Po and Huang [31], Proenca and Soukiazis [15], Falk [32], Holzner [33], Ekanayake and Long [34], Lee and Brahmasrene [35], Aslan [36], Chou [37], Surugiu, Leitão and Surugiu [38], and Tugcu [39] obtain mixed results for the relationship between tourism and economic growth. Moreover, the results are sensitive to the specific group of countries under examination. For example, Balaguer and Cantavella [9] examined the tourism led-growth hypothesis for the first time. They used the Johansen-Juseliusco integration analysis in order to investigate the relationship between the tourism industry and long-run economic development in Spain, between 1975 and 1997. They reviewed the tourism led-growth hypothesis and concluded that during the study period, economic growth in Spain was strongly influenced by income from tourism. They also advocated that growth in the tourism industry had a positive long-run impact on economic development through a multiplier effect.

Eugenio-Martin, Morales and Scarpa [40] investigated the relationship between tourism and economic growth in 21 Latin American countries using GMM dynamic panel data analysis, over the period 1985–1998. Their results show that tourism has a positive and significant impact on the economic growth of Latin American countries. They also applied the Generalized Least Squares panel data model to explain foreign tourist arrivals, confirming the positive relationship between tourism and economic growth. The study suggested that developing infrastructure, education, and safety levels would increase tourism in Latin American countries, in general, and low income countries, in particular.

Lee and Chang [30] apply the heterogeneous panel co-integration technique to investigate the causal relationship between tourism and economic growth for two samples: OECD and non-OECD countries. They found evidence of panel co-integration between tourism development and GDP in both samples. Tourism development is shown to have a larger impact on GDP in non-OECD countries. In the long run, there is evidence of a unidirectional causal relationship from tourism development to economic growth in the case of OECD countries, and a bidirectional relationship in the sample of non-OECD countries.

Brida, Carrera and Risso [12] used the Johansen-Juselius econometrics method, the Granger causality test, and the impulse response analysis of shocks to investigate the long-run effect of tourism on economic growth in Mexico. The Johansen-Juselius test showed the presence of a co-integrated relationship among real GDP, tourism spending, and real exchange rate. The Granger causality test showed that causality goes unidirectional from tourism spending and RER to real GDP. They also found that a shock on tourism spending has a short-run, as well as a long-run positive effect on economic growth.

Chang, Khamkaev and McAleer [41] use a larger panel dataset that includes 159 countries, over the period 1989–2008. The panel threshold model shows a positive relationship between economic growth and tourism. However, the instrumental variable estimation indicates that tourism has a higher impact on economic growth in countries with a lower level of trade openness and investment.

Considering that GCC countries are new global destinations, where tourism-oriented development projects are on the rise, investigating if the tourism development strategy is a relevant growth factor for GCC economies would be of particular interest. To the best of the author's knowledge, the causal relationship between tourism and economic growth in GCC states has never been studied in a panel context, without exception.

4. DATA, METHODOLOGY AND RESULTS

4.1. Data

This empirical study uses annual data on six GCC countries (i.e., Bahrain, Kuwait, Oman, Qatar, Saudi Arabia, and the United Arab Emirates) over the period 1995–2012. The variables used in this study are real international tourism revenue (receipts) and real gross domestic product. International tourism revenue is expressed in billions of U.S. dollars. Real gross domestic product is measured in constant 2005 U.S. dollars. The source of the data is the World Economic Outlook Database [6]. Real international tourism revenue (LTR) is used to measure tourism development and real gross domestic product (LGDP) is used as an economic growth indicator. Both variables are expressed in natural logarithms. Summary statistics are provided in Table 1 and Table 2.

Table 1. Summary statistics of real GDP (constant 2005 U.S. dollars-unit: billion).

Country	Mean	Max.	Min.	Std. Dev.	Skew.	Kurt.	J–B
Bahrain	15.20	30.40	5.850	8.710	0.46	1.70	1.90
Kuwait	76.50	183.00	25.90	51.70	0.70	2.14	2.01
Oman	33.70	78.10	13.80	21.00	0.86	2.36	2.52
Qatar	58.50	192.00	8.140	59.30	1.07	2.87	3.44
Saudi Arabia	321.00	711.00	142.00	186.00	0.83	2.42	2.31
United Arab Emirates	179.00	384.00	65.700	105.00	0.59	1.94	1.90

Note: The sample period is from 1995–2012.

Table 2. Summary statistics of real international tourism revenue (unit: billion).

Country	Mean	Max.	Min.	Std. Dev.	Skew.	Kurt.	J–B
Bahrain	1.30	2.16	0.58	0.56	−0.02	1.42	1.88
Kuwait	0.46	0.78	0.29	0.14	0.68	2.44	1.64
Oman	0.72	1.78	0.19	0.48	0.86	2.76	2.25
Qatar	1.45	7.22	0.12	2.13	1.58	4.14	8.45
Saudi Arabia	5.13	9.32	3.42	2.04	0.66	2.00	2.08
United Arab Emirates	3.62	8.58	0.63	3.21	0.56	1.58	2.47

Note: The sample period is from 1995–2012.

The real GDP summary statistics in Table 1 indicate that Saudi Arabia and Bahrain had the highest and lowest average GDP: $321.0 and $15.2 billion dollars, respectively. The Jarque–Bera (J–B) normality test results indicate that the distribution of the real gross domestic products for these countries is approximately normal. Table 2 summarizes the descriptive statistics for international tourism revenue. Saudi Arabia and Kuwait received the highest and lowest mean tourism revenue, respectively. The Jarque–Bera (J–B) normality test results indicate that real international tourism revenues in these countries approximate a normal distribution.

4.2. Unit Root

One important step to investigate the causality between variables is to determine whether the series are integrated. To test for integration, the panel unit root tests developed by Levin, Lin, and Chu [42] and Im, Pesaran, and Shin [43] were used in this study. Both Levin, Lin, and Chu (LLC) and Im, Pesaran, and Shin (IPS) unit root tests consider the following panel ADF (Augmented Dickey–Fuller) specification:

$$\Delta y_{i,t} = \rho_i y_{i,t-1} + \sum_{j=1}^{\rho_i} \delta_{i,j} \Delta y_{i,t-j} + \varepsilon_{i,t} \qquad (1)$$

According to the LLC [42], the persistence parameters (ρi) are assumed to be identical across sections (i.e., ρi=ρ for all i), whereas the lag order (ρi) may freely vary. The LLC tests the null hypothesis (H0: ρi=0 for all i) against the alternative hypothesis (H1: ρi<0 for all i). Rejection of the null hypothesis indicates a possible panel integration procedure. The IPS [43] test differs from the LLC [42] test by assuming (ρi) to be heterogeneous across sections. The IPS tests the null hypothesis (H0: ρi=0 for all i) against the alternative hypothesis (H1: ρi<0 for all i). Rejection of the null hypothesis suggests that the series are integrated. The LLC and IPS tests were performed on the data; both in levels and first differences, and the results are reported in Table 3. It is evident that not all variables are stationary in level, but they become stationary in their first-difference.

Table 3. Panel unit root test results.

Dependent		H_0: All panels contain unit root			
		LLC		IPS	
	Variables	Constant	Constant + Trend	Constant	Constant + Trend
GCC Countries	GDP	0.606 (0.727)	−2.037 (0.021)	3.175 (0.999)	−4.326 (0.332)
	TR	0.021 (0.508)	−1.089 (0.138)	3.026 (0.998)	−0.050 (0.480)
	ΔGDP	−4.152 (0.000)	−3.520 (0.000)	−2.856 (0.002)	−1.193 (0.116)
	ΔTR	−5.730 (0.000)	−4.579 (0.000)	−5.599 (0.000)	−4.069 (0.000)

Note: Δ is the first-difference operator and *p*-values are in parentheses. The LCC test was performed using a Newey–West bandwidth selection with Bartlett Kernel. The Schwarz Bayesian Criterion was used to determine the optimal lag length.

4.3. Cross-Sectional Dependence

Another crucial step in panel causality analysis is to take into account possible cross-section dependences across countries. It is well documented that a high degree of globalization, international trade, and financial integration make a country more sensitive to external economic shocks. Thus, ignoring cross-section dependency leads to substantial bias and size distortions [44,45]. To test for cross-sectional dependency, the Pesaran's CD test statistic was used in this study [44]. The procedure for computing the CD test statistic is as follows:

$$CD = \sqrt{\frac{2T}{N(N-1)}\left(\sum_{i=1}^{N-1}\sum_{j=i+1}^{N}\hat{P}ij\right)} \quad (2)$$

where (T) is the time interval, (N) is the number of cross-section units, and (P^ij) is the pair-wise correlation between cross-sections. According to the test results given in Table 4, the null hypothesis is rejected for GCC countries at the 1% level of significance, meaning that a shock in one of these countries is transmitted to other GCC countries.

Table 4. Cross-section dependency test results.

Test	Statistic
CD_{BP}	248.19 (0.000)
CD_{LM}	41.479 (0.000)
CD_{LMadj}	41.302 (0.000)
CD	15.746 (0.000)

Note: *p*-values in parentheses.

4.4. Panel Causality Analysis

The existence of both cross-section dependency and heterogeneity across the six GCC countries under analysis requires a panel causality method to account for these dynamics. The panel Granger causality test developed by Dumitrescu and Hurlin [46] was employed in this study. Dumitrescu and Hurlin [46] proposed a panel causality test based on the individual Wald statistic of Granger non-causality, averaged across the cross-section units. The testing procedure considers both the heterogeneity of causal relationships and the heterogeneity in the regression model used for testing the Granger causality. The liner panel regression model is as follows:

$$y_{i,t} = \alpha_i + \sum_{j=1}^{J} \delta_i^j y_{i,t-j} + \sum_{j=1}^{J} \beta_i^j x_{i,t-j} + \varepsilon_{i,t} \qquad (3)$$

where (y) is real GDP, (x) refers to international tourism spending, and (J) is the lag length. Dumitrescu and Hurlin [46] state that "a homogenous specification of the relation between the variables (x) and (y) does not allow to interpret causality relations if any individual from the sample has an economic behavior different from that of the others." Thus, they propose an average Wald statistic that tests the null hypothesis of no causal relationship for any of the cross-section units (H0: βi=0, (i=1,...,N)), against the alternative hypothesis that a causal relationship exists for at least one subgroup of the panel (H1: $\beta i=0$, $(i=1,..N1)$; ($\beta i \neq 0$, $(i=N1+1,N1+2,...,N)$). Rejection of the null hypothesis with (N1=0) indicates that (x) Granger causes (y) for all (*i*), whereas rejection of the null hypothesis with (N1>0) provides evidence that both the regression model and the causal relations vary from one individual country or sample to another. Under these circumstances, the average of the individual Wald statistics generated by Dumitrescu and Hurlin [46] assumes the following form:

$$W_{N,T}^{Hnc} = \frac{1}{N}\sum_{i=1}^{N} W_{i,T} \tag{4}$$

where (Wi,T) is the individual Wald statistic for the *ì-th* cross-section unit. The results from the panel Granger causality analysis are reported in Table 5. In the case of GCC countries as a whole, the results show a one-way Granger causality running from economic growth to tourism development, statistically significant at the 1% level. For country specific hypotheses, the results show that Kuwait, Saudi Arabia, Qatar, and the United Arab Emirates follow the path of economic-growth-driven tourism; this hypothesis is significant at the 1% and 5% significance level, respectively. The feedback hypothesis is supported for Bahrain, implying that tourism receipts positively affect economic growth (the result is significant at the 1% level), and economic growth stimulates tourism growth (significant at the 10% level). Clearly, tourism growth is of great importance to the Bahraini economy. The empirical results show that there is no causal relationship between tourism revenue and economic growth in the case of Oman, in line with the results of previous studies.

With the exception of Oman, Table 5 exhibits some mixed results about the country specific hypotheses. These results are either theoretically or empirically consistent with the existing literature. As Chen and Chiou-Wei [13] state, the causal relationship between tourism and economic growth is not stable, and there might not be a unique relationship type among GCC countries. In this sense, Eugenio-Martin, Morales, and Scarpa [40], Chang, Khamkaev, and

McAleer [41], Leitão [26], Tavares and Leitão [27], Chou [37], and Tugcu [39] in their empirical investigation argued that, depending on different dynamics, such as economic and political structures, trade openness, initial tourism conditions, investment rate, sectorial linkages, and historical background of the countries, this relationship may vary. Therefore, different studies could show different results in these countries in the context of tourism-led growth, even for the same sample.

Table 5. Panel causality test results.

Cross-Section Units	Null Hypotheses			
	H_0: TR Does not Cause Growth		H_0: Growth Does not Cause TR	
	Wald	Decision	Wald	Decision
GCC Countries	3.410	Accept	9.625*	Reject
Bahrain	15.483*	Reject	4.884***	Reject
Kuwait	1.747	Accept	9.832*	Reject
Oman	2.769	Accept	2.498	Accept
Qatar	2.894	Accept	11.861*	Reject
Saudi Arabia	1.567	Accept	11.628*	Reject
United Arab Emirates	0.655	Accept	8.525**	Reject

Note: *, **, and *** indicate rejection of the null hypothesis at the 1, 5, and 10 percent levels of significance, respectively.

The empirical results indicate that, for four GCC countries (Kuwait, Saudi Arabia, Qatar, and the United Arab Emirates), the economy-driven tourism growth hypothesis holds true. These results also support the tourism-led growth hypothesis in the case of the Bahraini economy, while no relation between these variables in found for Oman. There are several possible explanations for such mixed results for GCC countries. One of the explanations for the direction of causality, from economic growth to tourism development, in most GCC countries may lie in the history of their tourism industry structure. It is worth noticing that nations (such as GCC oil-rich countries) with no long history of tourism development initiatives rely on their endowments to maintain tourist inflows, and that economic growth is the only way to invest in tourism and sustain tourist inflows in such countries [26,38,39]. In absence of economic growth, the tourism industry shrinks.

Another explanation may lie in the economic structure and the contribution of the tourism industry to the GDP of these countries. If this industry contributes only a small portion of the national GDP, their relationship is more likely to support an economy-driven tourism growth [14,19,25]. The direct contribution of the tourism industry to the GDP of these countries is very small, ranging from 1.5% for Kuwait to about 4.1% for UAE in 2015 [2]. Thus, GCC policymakers need to focus more on economy-oriented policies to promote tourism development as a potential source of economic growth. A third explanation may rely on the link between the tourism sector and the rest of the economy. Inter-sectorial linkages between tourism and the rest of the economy in GCC countries are either weak, or not strong enough. As Tugcu [39] points out, if linkages between the tourism industry and the rest of the economy are strong enough, economic growth may become an instrument to improve the efficiency of the tourism sector.

With respect to the Bahraini economy, one possible explanation for the impact of tourism on economic growth may lie in the tourism attraction policy adopted by Bahraini policymakers. Since the 1980s, Bahrain has become the regional hub for international banking and financial services and international leisure facilities [41,47]. It is well documented that countries with an established tourism attraction are likely to benefit from tourist inflows in the long run, which, in turn, fosters economic growth [25,38,39]. In the case of Oman, tourism development and economic growth do not seem to be sensitive to each other. One can attribute this to a relatively small contribution of tourism revenues to the overall economic output. Thus, tourism development has little or no impact on economic growth in this country. Therefore, the Omani policymakers need to develop travel and tourism policies that are not dependent on economic activities.

5. CONCLUSIONS

The main objective of this study is to investigate the causal relationship between tourism development and economic growth in Gulf Cooperation Council (GCC) countries in a multivariate model, using panel data for the period 1995–2012. The study adopts a panel Granger causality analysis approach to assess the contribution of tourism to economic growth in GCC countries as a whole, and in each individual country. In the case of GCC countries as a whole, the results show a one-way Granger causality, from economic growth to tourism growth. Furthermore, Kuwait, Saudi Arabia, Qatar, and the United Arab Emirates follow the path of economy-driven tourism growth, as hypothesized. The reverse hypothesis (i.e., tourism-led growth hypothesis) holds true for Bahrain, while there seem to be no causal relationship between tourism and economic growth in the case of Oman.

Given the fact that GCC countries have similar climate and natural resources, attracting international tourists may require some degree of specialization to offer unique services and activities. GCC policymakers intended to establish an intra-GCC tourism-oriented approach with the goal of enhancing GCC countries as a tourist destination. For the intra-GCC tourism policy to succeed, policymakers should formulate their tourism policy based on country-specific comparative advantages, rather than competitive advantages. In terms of recommendations for their economic policy, we argue that GCC countries should continue to promote the tourism sector and, at the same time, strengthen the link of the tourism industry with the rest of the GCC economy. To this end, a new GCC tourism framework should be designed, based on the notion of sustainable tourism in the region, and it should be managed following the three principles of sustainability. The economic, social, and cultural benefits of sustainable tourism need to be the focus of the sustainable development of the sector. Worldwide, the path towards sustainability in the tourism and hospitality industry has been a long process and remains an unfinished business, while in GCC countries this path has just begun. Therefore, GCC governments should play a major role in boosting and maintaining the path of sustainable tourism and hospitality industry within their regional destinations.

CONFLICTS OF INTEREST

The authors declare no conflict of interest.

REFERENCES

1. The World Tourism Organization. *Tourism Highlights*, 2010 ed.; WTO: Geneva, Switzerland, 2010.
2. The World Travel and Tourism Council–WTTC. *Yearbook of Tourism Statistics*; WTTC Database: Madrid, Spain, 2015.
3. Al-Hamarneh, A.; Stephenson, N. *International Tourism Development in the GCC: Opportunities and Challenges*; Gulf Research Center: Cambridge, UK, 2013.
4. Alhemoud, A.M. Tourism Marketing Plan for Kuwait and other GCC Countries. *J. Int. Bus. Entrep. Dev.* **2003**, *1*, 52–57.
5. Atalla, G.; Shediac, R.; Nasr, A. Reinventing Tourism in the GCC. Available online: http://www.strategyand.pwc.com (accessed on 24 June 2016).
6. International Monetary Fund. *World Economic Outlook Database, IMF Data and Statistics*; International Monetary Fund: Washington, DC, USA, 2015.
7. Marhaba, D. GCC Tourism Officials Meet in Doha to Boost Tourism Within GCC. Available online: http://marhaba.qa/gcc-tourism-officials-meet-in-doha-to-boost-tourism-within-gcc/ (accessed on 24 June 2016).
8. Modeste, N.C. The impact of growth in the tourism sector on economic development: The experience of selected Caribbean countries. In Proceedings of the XXVI Annual Conference of the Regional Programme of Monetary Studies, Genova, Italy, 23–26 November 1994.
9. Balaguer, J.; Cantavella-Jorda, M. Tourism as a long-run economic growth factor: The Spanish case. *Appl. Econ.* **2002**, *34*, 877–884.
10. Durbarry, R. Tourism and economic growth: The case of Mauritius. *Tour. Econ.* **2004**, *10*, 389–401.

11. Gunduz, L.; Hatemi, A. Is the tourism-led growth hypothesis valid for Turkey? *Appl. Econ.* **2005**, *12*, 499–504.

12. Brida, J.; Carrera, E.; Risso, A. Tourism's Impact on long-run Mexican economic growth. *Econ. Bull.* **2008**, *3*, 1–8.

13. Chen, C.; Chiou, W. Tourism Expansion, Tourism Uncertainty and Economic Growth: New Evidence from Taiwan and Korea. *Tour. Manag.* **2009**, *30*, 39–44.

14. Dritsakis, N. Tourism as a long-run economic growth factor: An empirical investigation for Greece using causality analysis. *Tour. Econ.* **2004**, *10*, 305–316.

15. Proenca, S.; Soukiazis, E. Tourism as an economic growth factor: A case study for Southern European Countries. *Tour. Econ.* **2008**, *14*, 791–806.

16. Belloumi, M. The relationship between tourism receipts, real effective exchange rate and economic growth in Tunisia. *Int. J. Tour. Res.* **2010**, *12*, 550–560.

17. Akinboade, O.A.; Braimoh, L.A. International tourism and economic development in South Africa: A Granger causality test. *Int. J. Tour. Res.* **2010**, *12*, 149–163.

18. Tang, C.F.; Abosedra, A. Small sample evidence on the tourism-led growth hypothesis in Lebanon. *Curr. Issues Tour.***2012**.

19. Tang, C.F.; Tan, E.C. How stable is the tourism-led growth hypothesis in Malaysia? Evidence from disaggregated Tourism Markets. *Tour. Manag.* **2013**, *37*, 52–47.

20. Kim, H.J.; Chen, M.H.; Jang, S. Tourism expansion and economic development: The case of Taiwan. *Tour. Manag.***2006**, *27*, 925–933.

21. Lee, C.C.; Chien, M.S. Structural breaks, tourism development, and economic growth: Evidence from Taiwan. *Math. Comput. Simul.* **2008**, *77*, 358–368.

22. Oh, C.O. The contribution of tourism development to economic growth in the Korean economy. *Tour. Manag.* **2005**, *26*, 39–44.

23. Ozturk, I.; Acaravci, A. On the causality between tourism growth and economic growth: Empirical evidence from Turkey. *Transylv. Rev. Adm. Sci.* **2009**, *25*, 73–81.

24. Tang, C.H.; Jang, S.S. The tourism-economy causality in the United States: A sub-industry level examination. *Tour. Manag.* **2009**, *30*, 553–558.

25. Payne, J.E.; Mervar, A. The tourism-growth nexus in Croatia. *Tour. Econ.* **2010**, *19*, 1089–1094.

26. Leitão, N.C. Portuguese Tourism Demand: A Dynamic Panel Data Analysis. *Int. J. Econ. Financ. Issues* **2015**, *5*, 673–677.

27. Tavares, J.M.; Leitão, N.C. The Determinants of International Tourism Demands for Brazil. *Tour. Econ.* **2016**.

28. Leitão, N.C.; Shahbaz, M. Economic Growth, Tourism Arrivals and Climate Change. Bulletin of Energy Economics (BEE). *Econ. Soc. Dev. Organ. (TESDO)* **2016**, *4*, 35–43.

29. Sequeira, T.; Campos, C. International tourism and economic growth. *Nat. Resour. Manag.* **2005**, *14*, 1–25.

30. Lee, C.C.; Chang, C.P. Tourism development and economic growth: A closer look at panels. *Tour. Manag.* **2008**, *29*, 180–192.

31. Po, W.C.; Huang, B.N. Tourism development and economic growth—A nonlinear approach. *Phys. A* **2008**, *387*, 5535–5542.

32. Falk, M. A dynamic panel data analysis of snow depth and winter tourism. *Tour. Manag.* **2010**, *31*, 912–924.

33. Holzner, M. Tourism and economic growth: The beach disease? *Tour. Manag.* **2011**, *32*, 922–933.

34. Ekanayake, E.M.; Long, A.E. Tourism Development and Economic Growth in Developing Countries. *Int. J. Bus. Financ. Res.* **2012**, *6*, 51–63.

35. Lee, J.W.; Brahmasrene, T. Investigating the influence of tourism on economic growth and carbon emissions: Evidence from panel analysis of the European Union. *Tour. Manag.* **2013**, *38*, 69–76.

36. Aslan, A. Tourism development and economic growth in the Mediterranean countries: Evidence from panel Granger causality tests. *Curr. Issues Tour.* **2013**.

37. Chou, C.M. Does Tourism Development Promote Economic Growth in Transition Countries? A Panel Data Analysis. *Econ. Model.* **2013**, *33*, 226–232.

38. Surugiu, C.; Leitão, N.C.; Surugiu, M.R. A Panel Data Modelling of International Tourism Demand: Evidences for Romania. *Econ. Res. Ekon. Istraž.* **2011**, *24*, 134–145.

39. Tugcu, C.T. Tourism and Economic Growth Nexus Revisited: A Panel Causality Analysis for the case of the Mediterranean Region. *Tour. Manag.* **2014**, *42*, 207–212.

40. Eugenio-Martín, J.L.; Morales, N.M.; Scarpa, R. Tourism and Economic Growth in Latin American Countries: A Panel Data Approach. Available online: http://home.wlu.edu/~caseyj/spring07devseminar/latinAmtourand%20dev.pdf (accessed on 24 June 2016).

41. Chang, C.; Khamkaev, T.; McAleer, M. IV Estimation of a Panel Threshold Model of Tourism Specialization and Economic Development. *Soc. Sci. Res. Newt.* **2010**.

42. Levin, A.; Lin, C.F.; Chu, C.S. Unit root tests in panel data: Asymptotic and finite-sample properties. *J. Econ.* **2002**, *108*, 1–24.

43. Im, K.S.; Pesaran, M.H.; Shin, Y. Testing for unit roots in heterogeneous panel. *J. Econ.* **2003**, *115*, 53–74.

44. Pesaran, M.H. *General Diagnostic Tests for cross Section Dependence in Panels*; Cambridge Working Papers in Economics No. 0435; Faculty of Economics, University of Cambridge: Cambridge, UK; June; 2004.

45. Bai, J.; Kao, C. On the estimation and inference of a panel cointegration model with cross-sectional dependence. In *Panel Data Econometrics: Theoretical Contributions and Empirical Applications*; Baltagi, B.H., Ed.; Elsevier: Amsterdam, The Netherlands, 2006; pp. 3–30.

46. Dumitrescu, E.I.; Hurlin, C. Testing for Granger non-causality in heterogeneous panels. *Econ. Model.* **2012**, *29*, 1450–1460.

47. Mansfield, Y.; Winckler, O. The Role of the Tourism Industry in Transforming a Rentier to a Long-Term Viable Economy: The Case of Bahrain. *Curr. Issues Tour.* **2008**, *11*, 237–267.

10
CHAPTER

Made in Oman: Promoting Manufacturing and Export in the Sultanate of Oman

Tyler Philip Eldridge McWilliam

SIT Study Abroad,

ABSTRACT

Oman's manufacturing sector has shown promising growth during the past decades. This paper analyzes the role of the manufacturing and export sector in economic growth and development. Then, after analyzing government policy toward manufacturing in Oman, this paper uses research gathered from companies in Rusayl to determine the biggest problems currently facing manufacturing in Oman and the effectiveness of government policy toward the sector. Problems found included excessive bureaucracy, Omanization, and transport costs. These findings were then presented to the appropriate public institutions, with their reactions documented. Recommendations for change include streamlining government services, expediting the construction of the Gulf Railway, and implementing an innovative credit-based solution to Omanization.

INTRODUCTION

During the past four decades, one of the most salient policies of the Omani government has been the diversification of the national economy away from oil revenue. Each of Oman's eight five-year-plans, issued under Royal Decrees 1/76, 1/81, 1/86, 1/91, 1/96, 1/2001, 1/2006, and 1/2011, has addressed the issue in some form. In Oman's Vision 2020 development goals, issued in 1996 under Royal Decree 1/96, there is an entire chapter dedicated to economic diversification, with other chapters addressing issues ancillary to it. The importance of diversification for Oman increases with each passing year. As the oil reserves, which have supported Oman's economy for the past 40 years, dwindle, Oman is forced to find alternate sectors on which its economy can rely. Sectors such as tourism and agriculture have shown significant growth and should not be ignored, but relative to the size of the national economy they cannot seriously be expected to support the country. According to statistics published by the Ministry of the National Economy in August 2010, the two sectors combined contributed less than 3% of the national GDP (MONE 4). However, one sector which has shown promising growth is manufacturing. Manufacturing, a sector which is second in size only to petroleum- based activities, accounts for slightly over 12% of the national economy – however, with time and prudent governmental policy the manufacturing sector has the potential to grow substantially, especially as more companies begin to export to foreign markets. However, it has been observed that the manufacturing sector development has been met with a lack of enthusiasm by public institutions. For example, on its website the Ministry of the National Economy has no public data available for this sector, despite having significant data in others. This paper aims to identify current governmental policies toward manufacturing and identify faults within or ways in which they can be improved.

The paper is structured such that Section 1 provides a basic overview of the role of manufacturing in economic development, including case studies, Section 2 gives an overview of development in Oman since 10970, Section 3 covers the research and conclusions drawn from field research undertaken for this paper, and Section 4 concludes with recommendations for policy change.

METHODOLOGY

Research data for this document was gathered through the following methods:

- Direct interviews with representatives from companies located in the Rusayl Industrial Estate (RIE). Interviews were conducted during a two week period in April 2011.

- Direct interviews with representatives from the Minister of Commerce and Industry (MOCI), the Chamber of Commerce (OCCI), and the Public Establishment for Industrial Estates (PEIE). Interviews were conducted during a three week period in April-May 2011.

- Questionnaires distributed to companies in RIE. Questionnaires were distributed without regard to company size or product. Of the 21 companies approached, responses were received from only 15. Data was gathered during a two week period in April 2011.

As a result of insupressible concerns over anonymity for both themselves and their company from the representatives interviewed, very few of the interviews conducted in Rusayl were recorded - written notes were taken and significant statements (appearing in quotations) were noted verbatim. A similar problem was observed with government officials over their desire not to be recorded 'officially' – the same process was used for them as well.

Section 1: The Role of Industry in Development

Previous Findings on Manufacturing and Export Development

Because of the importance of manufacturing as well as its potential to fundamentally change and economy, there have been incredible amounts of research pertaining to the subject. While industrialization, as a concept, has existed since the 19th century, this paper is mainly focused on more recent findings - specifically regarding manufacturing and its role in global integration. During the past century there have been several successful cases of manufacturing development, two of which, Thailand and Ireland, will be explored later. However, there have also been many cases of failed developmental programs - which also will be explored later in the paper. Manufacturing development is therefore an inherently risk-heavy undertaking which, if handled improperly, can have long-lasting repercussions.

One strategy for development is free market 'shock therapy', referring to rapid removal of trade barriers. This form of market liberalization, a concept championed by Adam Smith, is a policy which, until recently, was long-championed by institutions such as the International Monetary Fund (IMF). It reasons that humans, being inherently rational, actin their best interest, and thus any established trade barrier which stops someone's actions only serves to hinder humans from achieving total efficiency. For example, some economists argue that government intervention can lead to distortion in resource allocation (AlRawas 16). While the concept is appealing, economists like Bruce Greenwald have shown that this only holds true under very specific market conditions, conditions which have yet to occur in any market (Greenwald 2).

Moreover, market liberalization before adequate infrastructure is in place can have dire consequences, as was seen during the liberalization of Russia (Stiglitz 133). So government intervention is argued as just as it can correct market failures and facilitate a proper business environment.

Another strategy for manufacturing development is import substitution industrialization (ISI). This model posits that if imports of foreign manufactured products are barred, the market will respond by manufacturing those products itself, thus achieving industrialization. This model, used in Latin America extensively during the 1950s and 60s, has been observed to show initial industrial growth, but, usually because of the small size of the domestic population, the growth eventually subsides (Primo Braga 4). Latin American governments attempted to stimulate more growth through increased spending, however this only served to build foreign debt, thus leading to the Balance of Payment crisis in the 1980s (Primo Braga 5). Today, ISI has largely been disregarded as a sustainable development model, recommended in use in only very limited circumstances with newly developing countries.

A more recent model of development, one which has largely replaced ISI as the preferred, is the export-intensive development (EOD) model, used intensively in East Asia during the 1980s and 90s. This model, rather than employing isolationist ISI policies, encourages rapid, but controlled, global economic integration, with an economy focusing on exports. This is developed through encouraging local industries, building the skills of the labor-force, and especially through attracting foreign direct investment (FDI). FDI is critical as it brings capital into a country.

Foreign firms, mostly multi-national corporations, invest in regional production facilities, hiring local labor and thus increasing capital flows.

Although industrial development strategies must be used on a case-by-case basis, economists today tend to favor gradual market liberalization coupled with an export-intensive structure, with government services ensuring fair business practices (Stiglitz Ch. 2).

Vaulting the Resource Curse

A well-known and much-studied phenomenon regarding countries endowed with natural resources is the resource curse. The resource curse refers to the seemingly inverse relationship between the presence of natural resources and economic prosperity. In countries like Nigeria, the number of people living in poverty actually increased during the exploitation of natural resources (Stiglitz 134). The resource curse also wreaks havoc on development. There is a tendency for the presence of natural resources in a nation's economy to detract resources away from other sectors, manufacturing in particular. When one sector proves to be more lucrative than the others, capital and human resources flock to it. As a result, when the lucrative sector is inevitably exhausted, the economy finds itself with little development in other sectors.

Another element of the resource curse is the 'Dutch Disease', so called because of its associations with the discovery of a major natural gas reserve in the Netherlands in 1959. The Dutch Disease is the increase in valuation of a nation's currency, which in effect raises the cost of goods produced in the economy. This effectively stymies the economy's ability to export its products abroad, as its high-production costs can no longer compete in foreign markets (Stiglitz 148). A solution to this problem, presented in detail in (Stiglitz 149), is the creation of a stabilization fund – a mechanism designed to lower the impact of the Dutch Disease through investment, which usually takes the form of buying foreign debt. This preserves the value of the oil revenue while at the same time keeping the currency stable, thus largely averting the Dutch Disease.

Thailand: The Surprise Asian Tiger

A country which has shown great successes in fostering its fledgling manufacturing sector is Thailand. In the decades leading up to the 1980s, Thailand's economy focused on the export of primary goods and ISI development policies (Hussey 2). While growth was observed, this was mainly a result of the realization of its agricultural sector and the United States' involvement in Vietnam, which increased Thailand's foreign aid substantially. The 1979 oil crisis, falling prices for Thai goods, and the exhaustion of agricultural expansion opportunities all combined to make Thailand's economy one of the slowest growing in Asia during the early 1980s. In response to this decline, government officials and local entrepreneurs considered developing the manufacturing sector. Thailand began implanting policies designed to aggressively attract foreign investment, and it worked. Industrial investment rose from 2,867 baht in 1986 to 24,562 baht in 1989, most of which was focused on companies which exported 80-100% of their products (Hussey 5). Thailand's success in manufacturing development has been attributed to good timing, availability of cheap, trainable labor, sufficient port, air, road, and utility infrastructure, tax incentives, and streamlined, non-bureaucratic government procedures. Also, Thailand had political and racial stability. Finally, unlike its neighbors, such as Malaysia, Thailand did not mandate Thai employment (Hussey 6). The Thai manufacturing sector grew so effectively that, despite only employing 15% of the workforce, it contributed to 50% of the country's GDP.

Critics of Thailand's industrialization policies point out its neglect of impoverished rural farmers, which constitute 49% of the population, its environmental impact, and the 1997 financial crisis. It has been said that Thailand is not an industrialized country, but rather Bangkok is an industrialized city (Hussey 19). Outside of Bangkok there is little sign of Thailand's advancements. Secondly, the rapid, unrestrained industrial process has also taken a toll on Bangkok's environment. Bangkok's water networks once led the city to be called the 'Venice of the East'. However the water today, much to the distress of the Thai tourism industry, has been replaced by a black sludge (Hussey 23).

Finally, given Thailand's rapid growth in the years leading up to 1997, it would seem as though the financial crisis was caused by the development policies. However, as explained by (Stiglitz 95), this crisis came as a result of an 'attack' by currency speculators holding inactive assets in Thailand's currency, the Baht. Investors responded to Thailand's short term debt, thinking that the currency would devalue, by selling their assets, thus causing the currency, and with it the country, to crash.

Ireland: The Celtic Tiger

Another country which surprised the world through its emergence as a world manufacturing hub is Ireland. Ireland, a country which was previously wrought with political turmoil and, to a lesser extent, ethnic stereotyping from abroad, was able to foster a highly advanced manufacturing sectoring during the 1990s. Whereas Thailand capitalized on its availability of cheap, trainable labor, Ireland adopted policies directed towards advancing the skillset of its labor force and aggressively attracting foreign investment through specifically targeted **promotion and incentives.**

Ireland's model has been dubbed the 'flexible development state' (FDS) (O'Higgins 1), as it created a strong bond between society and state. In its Programme for National Recovery (PNR), started in 1987, the government focused on matching the needs of society, such as companies and employees, with the needs of the government. By altering policy and adjusting to societal needs, the government followed a very personal, flexible development path.

Ireland also benefited from the results of previous initiatives. Free secondary education was provided by the government in 1967 (O'Higgins 3), as a result, by the 1990s over 80% of the labor force had completed secondary education, and more than 40% had third-level education experience. This large supply of skilled labor effectively lowered Irish skilled-labor costs relative to other European countries. Additionally, its labor force was comprised on English speakers, which, especially for high tech, internet oriented companies, made Ireland all the better as a location.

The biggest factor in Ireland's development was FDI (O'Higgins 4). Ireland's Industrial Development Agency (IDA) played a key role in this. The IDA established offices in key cities across the USA, marketing Ireland and establishing personal links with multi-national corporations (MNCs). It was given autonomy and funding to negotiate deals with firms and expedite services to meet demand. This specifically targeted marketing strategy came at a cost, but it worked. With its cheap supply of skilled, English speaking labor, and intensive government campaigns to market Ireland abroad, high tech companies from abroad flocked to the country. High tech MNCs, especially those in the Americas, saw Ireland as a gateway to Europe's 300 million-strong consumer market, opening regional branches across the country.

Zambia: Lessons from a Failed State

While there have been stunning examples of manufacturing development leading to massive economic overhauls, it should be noted that some countries have not been as fortunate, such as Zambia. At its independence in 1964, 90% of Zambia's export earnings came from raw copper sales. The government, devoted to industrializing the country, nationalized nearly all industries, owning 80% of the economy by 1969 (Osei-Hwedie 2). Using revenue from copper sales, the government implemented policies with the set goals of diversification away from copper, Zambianisation, infrastructure development, and employment creation. However these policies were wrought with flaws. The ISI policies instituted were unsustainable and growth quickly dropped, leading to the government injecting a constant stream of capital to keep the policies in place. As most copper revenue was devoted to this by the time the government invested in infrastructure there was little left to save. Without this savings fund Zambia's economy was vulnerable to fluctuations in world copper prices. The ISI subsidized companies proved to be monopolistic, inefficient, and uncompetitive. Additionally, state intervention led to heavy bureaucratization and with it corruption and uncertainty, thus discouraging any meaningful private investment.

At the recommendation of the World Bank and the IMF, Zambia began to liberalize its economy in 1983 (Osei-Hwedie 7). However this served only to worsen Zambia already troubled economy. Foreign aid, which increased after Zambia's announcement of liberalization, was mostly diverted to debt reduction rather than development. Additionally, attempts to privatize manufacturing failed miserably, corruption ran rampant, and with Zimbabwean and South African products entering Zambian markets, the country's manufacturing sector was effectively killed. While it once held middle income-status, Zambia now stands as one of the poorest countries in the world (Osei-Hwedie 10).

Section 2: Industrialization in Oman

Industrial Growth in Oman

Oman's manufacturing sector has made a great deal of progress since 1970. Figure 1, below, shows Oman's value added growth in the sector since 1961.

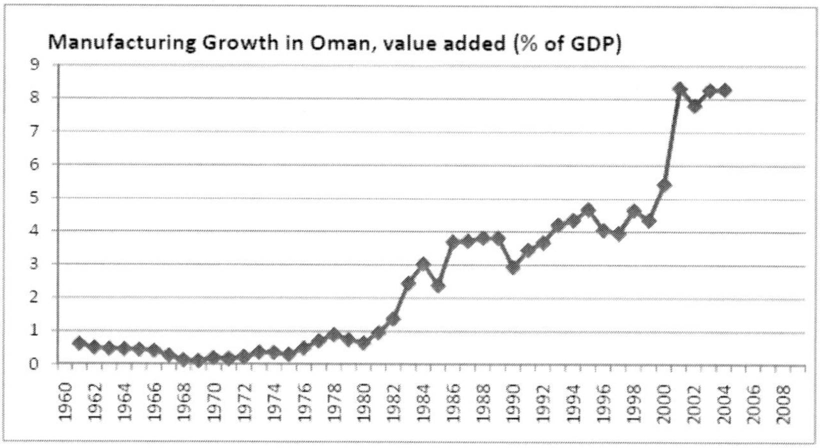

Source: World Bank (2011)

Figure 1

Before 1970, Oman's economy was largely agricultural, showing very slow development. The recent discovery of oil showed a promising future, but was not being used to its full potential. Upon the ascension of HM Sultan Qaboos, sweeping changes were made to the way oil revenue was being invested. Universal primary education was made a priority, the Oman stabilization fund was created, and infrastructure systems were rapidly constructed. The initial industrial strategy was ISI-based. To attract industry, the Rusayl industrial Estate (RIE) was established in 1983, providing infrastructure needs like electricity, water, and gas. This proved successful, with the manufacturing sector showing significant growth in the following years. By the 1990s, the development strategy shifted from ISI to diversification away from oil. To help increase multiplier effects on other sectors, the government emphasized the creation of linkages between companies. Instead of just export-led development, the government wanted to see companies use local materials.

In 1996, HM Sultan Qaboos issued the Vision 2020 development plan. This plan laid the groundwork to achieve a lofty vision of heavily diversified Oman, with a skilled labor force, global economic integration, and a promising future. By 2020, Oman would get only 19% of its GDP from oil and gas, be globally integrated, and boast an educated labor force. This put a great deal of pressure on government institutions. Industrial states were improved and expanded, infrastructure further developed, and more initiatives were taken to promote Oman abroad.

In November 2000, Oman joined the World Trade Organization (WTO). This has generally been the reason attributed to the increased growth between 2000 and 2002. This gave Oman greater access to international markets to which manufacturers could export. Later, in 2006, Oman entered into a free trade agreement with the US, opening the US consumer market to Omani goods.

Oman's Current Development Initiatives

While Dubai has already earned the dubious distinction of the 'Gulf Tiger', Oman still has the potential to emerge as a key economic player. Oman is politically stable, infrastructurally sound, and maintains an excellent geoeconomic location.

As identified in (Abdulrazzaq 5), there are five significant challenges currently facing all GCC countries. These are economic diversification, human resource development, private sector development, export promotion, and infrastructure development. Not incidentally, each of these obstacles has implications on the manufacturing sector. Oman, in its development plans, has taken notice of this and has put in place initiatives to help overcome these challenges.

Economic Diversification: A very broad term, economic diversification refers to the development of any economic sector that can move the Omani economy away from oil dependency. The Vision 2020 goals laid out programs to help Oman diversify its economy. As was mentioned earlier, Oman hopes to see 81% of GDP come from non-oil and gas revenue. In order to achieve these goals it focuses diversification into sectors like tourism, agriculture, and manufacturing (Vision 2020). In promoting manufacturing growth, the Vision 2020 goals most notably promise export-led development, increased focus on SMEs, the transfer of technology, and increasing R&D (Vision 2020 4-4).

An institution that was created to help encourage diversification was the Oman Development Bank (ODB). Established in 1997, with a reorganizing in 2006, the ODB is designed to provide loans to entrepreneurs looking to start a business in a sector other than the petroleum industry. Unlike private banks, which, acting in their best interests, avoid granting loans to risk-heavy undertakings, a public development bank, which has no vested interest in making a profit, is more likely to give loans to more risk-laden entrepreneurial ventures and thus help development.

Human Resource Development: Potentially the biggest and most pivotal challenge facing the Omani manufacturing sector is human resource development. Since 1970, there have been three noticeable stages of human development and education in Oman (Issan 1). Stage one was quantitative, focusing on increasing the number of Omanis attending schools. Stage two, started during the 1980s, focused on the quality of education in Oman. Oman is currently in Stage three, which began in 1995 with the declaration of the Vision 2020 development goals.

This stage focuses on preparing Omanis to join the labor force through skill-building and post- secondary education (Issan 1). The most recent five year plan, issued this past January, created programs providing local internships, support for specialized programs abroad, and physical support for national training projects (Oman Observer).

The Ministry of Manpower has implemented several programs dedicated to building the skills of the Omani workforce. Through its Occupational Standards and Testing Center (OSTC), the Ministry of Manpower works with job-seekers to help improve the quality and efficiency of their training. The key to effective training is clear and continuous cooperation between training institutions and the private sector. For the private sector this means providing training institutions with instructions and requirements for the skills they need, and for institutions this means making the private enterprises aware of the importance of properly trained staff.

Through effective communication with the private sector, both the skillset of the national workforce can and its net effectiveness can grow (Jax). In addition to providing training services to Omanis the OSTC also, through its SANAD-programme, provides both funding and counseling

services to help skilled, job-seeking Omanis with self-employment projects (Jax).

Private Sector Development: Historically, the public sector has been the Sultanate's primary economic actor. Unfortunately, as is frequently the case with public enterprise, it has been marked by inefficiency and low productivity. By transitioning economic power into the hands of the private sector, as the argument goes, it will allow for competition to force an economy to run at full efficiency. Encouraging foreign direct investment (FDI) is crucial to building the private sector. One of the most significant measures taken by the Omani government towards this goal was the creation of the Omani Center for Investment Promotion and Export Development (OCIPED) in 1996 under Royal Decree No. 59/96. OCIPED encourages foreign investment by marketing Oman to potential investors abroad. This is through exhibitions and road shows, marketing campaigns, data collection, and finding investment partners (ociped.com).

A piece of FDI-attracting policy championed by the Omani government is the US-Omani free trade agreement (OFTA). While this agreement has been criticized as being one-sided on the part of the United States (Stiglitz 97), both Omani and American representatives have held it in very high regard (PEIE). By giving American businessmen national status, which allows them to start and own businesses just like Omani citizens, the Omani government hopes to see US investors flock to the country.

In addition to these explicit measures, there are several soft elements which help encourage FDI into the Omani economy. Many of Oman's more resource-endowed neighbors, such as Saudi Arabia, Iran, and Qatar, have used the stability of their wealth to promote controversial political goals. Fortunately, Oman has not had such luxury and has remained politically neutral during Sultan Qaboos' tenure. This has helped to make Oman a more attractive place for foreign investors, as Oman is seen as more stable and thus less risky (Wilson 1).

Export Promotion: One of the key elements of global integration is the export of Omani products. Oman is an excellent location geographically. At the base of the Arabian Peninsula it is better able to accept materials imported from abroad at cheaper costs than its neighbors. As a result it has the potential to serve as the supplier for the rest of region.

As OCIPED's name would suggest, in addition to promoting FDI it also works towards export development. OCIPED's primary methods of assistance are promotion through exhibitions and helping companies locate potential market opportunities (OCIPED).

The Omani government also hopes that the OFTA will help promote Omani exports. By eliminating trade barriers with the United States, the largest consumer market in the world, the sale of Omani goods to America is expected to increase substantially in the near future.

Finally, to help combat the effects of the Dutch Disease, Oman established the State General Reserve Fund (SGRF) in 1980. While owned by the Omani government and administered by the Ministry of Finance, the SGRF is a sovereign institution. Its assets are currently valued at over $8 billion USD (Investopedia).

Infrastructure Development: One of the most valuable elements of industrialization is FDI. If a government can entice a firm to start a company there, the company, acting independently, will inevitably bring revenue into the country. One of the best ways governments can spur development is by creating a system in which a company can work effectively. Infrastructural development is critical in this goal. Generally speaking, Oman's infrastructural development has made massive improvements since 1970, however to be globally competitive, it will need to be improved further.

Oman currently has three port facilities – one each in Salalah, Muscat, and Sohar. Currently, the Omani government is working on the construction of a major port and dry dock at Duqm (Oman Observer). The Duqm port, at an expected cost of OR 1.7 billion, is expected to be completed in 2012. The port is designed to be the catalyst for the development of Duqm as a city of industry.

One of the most significant projects Oman has planned for the future is its contribution to the Gulf Railway. Oman, in a joint effort between six Gulf States, will help construct a 2,000 kilometer railway network (Prabhu). The rail will run from Kuwait to Southern Oman, and potentially further into Yemen. The rail network, which will include freight service, is expected to drastically cut the cost of transportation within GCC states. At staggering total cost estimates of up to $25 billion USD, the Gulf Railway is a serious investment, and there is still the inherent risk that it won't spur the economic growth needed to justify its construction.

Section 3: The Implications of Oman's Industrial Development Policies: Have They Worked?

Response from Companies

The primary purpose of this paper is to determine the effect that governmental policies have had on Oman's manufacturing and export sector. Although the sector has shown significant growth during the past decade, this cannot be off-handedly attributed to Oman's economic policies. This paper aims to determine the causality of this growth, and then, working from research gathered from companies in the Rusayl Industrial Estate (RIE) as well as public institutions like the Ministry of Commerce (MONI), formulate policy changes which would serve to improve Oman's manufacturing and export industry. The first element of this study was gathering research data from Omani manufacturing companies in the form of surveys and interviews.

Problems Facing Manufacturing Companies in Oman

The surveys distributed to the companies focused on two categories. The first half covered general problems the company faced. The latter half centered specifically on the company's relations with public institutions. The survey results concerning general problems faced by the company are given in Figure 2. (Data is given in percentages)

Statement	Strongly Disagree	Disagree	Neutral	Agree	Strongly Agree
Our products can't compete in American and European Markets	35.71	42.86	0	21.43	0
There is a lack of skilled management in Oman	28.57	42.86	7.14	21.43	0
Omanization policies have made it difficult to find labor	7.14	28.57	21.43	42.86	0
The US-Omani Free Trade Agreement has helped our sales abroad	0	23.01	46.15	15.38	7.69
Rusayl has enough infrastructure for our business to grow	0	14.29	21.43	57.14	7.14
Omani customs duties hinder our operations	14.29	42.86	21.43	21.43	0
The government does not effectively market Oman internationally	0	53.85	30.77	15.38	0
It is more expensive to produce in Oman compared to elsewhere	0	53.85	15.38	30.77	0
Government services have improved during the past five years	0	0	15.38	76.92	7.69
There aren't enough opportunities to market our product abroad	7.69	38.46	7.69	38.46	7.69
Our company owes much of its success to government assistance	0	38.46	7.69	53.85	0
The US-Omani Free Trade Agreement has harmed our business	7.69	53.85	38.46	0	0
Not enough Omanis are studying what is needed for our business	0	23.08	15.38	53.85	7.69
Shipping costs are prohibitively expensive	0	7.69	23.08	61.54	7.69
Imported foreign machinery is affordable	0	28.57	7.14	64.29	0
The government is doing all it can to help us	0	15.38	30.77	46.15	7.69
There are better ways the government can help us	0	7.69	0	84.62	7.69

Source: McWilliam, Tyler (Fieldwork, April 2011)

Figure 2 – Survey Statements

To what extent do you agree with these statements? (Mark the best response; leave blank if not applicable)

Before the analysis of the dataset, it is important to note that these data cannot be read like election results. A majority reporting no problems does not mean that problems do not exist; it means that there is a minority with problems. Under the increasingly liberalized system of global trade networks, in which competition is intense, small problems or areas of even minor inefficiency can have hugely impactful results.

However with that, generally speaking, the survey respondents gave very positive responses to the above statements. None of the respondents disagreed that the government services have improved over the past five years, and only fifteen percent thought the government was not doing everything it could. However, with that a shocking 92% of companies agreed that there are better ways the government can help them, indicating that there is indeed inefficiency in government services.

While company owners did not think that any government services were useless, they did give various suggestions to improve them. From the surveys, suggestions included streamlining government services to a single 'one-stop-shop', allowing for more expats to be hired, training Omanis, improving online service, more proactive 'problem-solving' services working within a specific time frame, implementing Omanization more gradually, and one company simply requested 'better service'.

One company manager talked about his problems with government bureaucracy, saying that "to solve a problem, you need to drive to one place, wait in line, drive to another place, wait in line, wait many weeks, and then maybe after that maybe your problem is fixed," (Personal Interview 2011). He complained that government services do not work within a specified time frame, so when companies need a problem fixed by a certain date, they cannot rely on the government for assistance.

Interestingly enough, few of the companies reported having been positively affected by the OFTA. Only slightly over 20% responded that it has helped sales abroad, with a majority reporting either neutrally or in disagreement. In an interview, the manager of one company even said "We used to export to the US and Canada, but we stopped six months ago because of rising costs" (Personal Interview 2011). The OFTA also seemed to do little in terms of promoting American investment into manufacturing. In an interview with a representative from PEIE, an American-owned company was cited as being an example of the success of the OFTA. However, in an interview with the manager of that company, it was discovered that it had in fact been recently bought buy an Indian investment firm, with "rising costs" being cited as the reason for the sale (Personal Interview 2011). It is important to note that implementing the OFTA came was not free for the Omani government. During negotiations the US insisted that if an FTA were to be made then conditions in the Sultanate needed to be on par with America. As a result the FTA contains passages addressing issues like labor rights, intellectual property guidelines, telecommunications, and business ethics (Tepitino 41). This means that in exchange for access to American markets and investors, Oman now has to pay to enforce copyrights, meet labor needs, and provide infrastructure. If the OFTA fails to live up to its expectations these costs would have been in vain.

While most companies faced no problems with the infrastructure in Rusayl, a shortage of natural gas has wreaked havoc for gas-burning companies planning to expand. The manager of a steel-rolling mill in Rusayl explained how this shortage of natural gas had "caused [the company's] plans for a new factory, a $12 milion USD project, to be stopped," (Personal Interview 2011). An interview with an employee from another company revealed that they were facing problems with the lack of physical space. He lamented that in order to make room for their latest factory expansion, "[The company] had to break many mountains," (Personal Interview 2011). These faults in infrastructure availability hinder growth, and, if the problem persists, can potentially discourage FDI and local entrepreneurship.

Whereas one of Oman's goals is creating 'upstream' enterprises, or enterprises that are vertically linked, only 35% of the responding companies used Omani raw materials, with the remaining 65% relying on foreign imports. When questioned about this, companies primarily cited the lack of domestic resource availability as the reason for import.

In 2003, under the direction of the Dubai-based Gulf Research Center, a survey including similar questions was distributed to 31 companies in the Sohar Industrial Estate (SIE), from which 14 responses were received. The following Figure 3 shows the results of select questions from the Sohar study matched with their appropriate counterpart from this study. (Data from 2003 is on the left, represented by darker shades)

Figure 3 – Improvements Since 2003

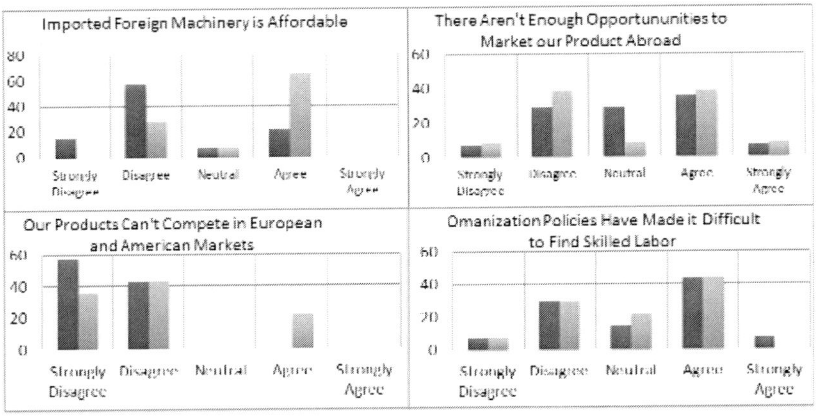

Source: McWilliam, Tyler (Field Work, April 2011); Bakheet, Adil-Hassan (Fieldwork, June-August 2003)

This comparison works on the assumption that problems facing companies in Sohar can be applied to companies operating in the Rusayl Industrial Estate. Under this assumption, one can observe a clear change in the question "Imported foreign machinery is affordable" Whereas in 2003 nearly 60% of companies cited this as a problem, the results were nearly reversed come 2011, with just over 60% agreeing that machinery costs are manageable. Both the 2003 and 2011 survey results showed a clear split on whether or not there were enough opportunities to market abroad. If anything, there was a drop from 'neutral' to 'disagree' during the past decade. This indicates that government services towards helping promotion abroad have largely stagnated since 2003. Omanization was and still is a problem for many companies. Results from 2003 are nearly identical to 2011, showing that there still is not a sufficient supply of skilled and willing Omani laborers.

It was also observed that there was a correlation between responses and the relative size of the business. For example, larger businesses tended to have little difficulty meeting Omanization requirements, less trouble meeting costs, and more favorable opinions of government policies. A selection of responses where these differences were particularly noticeable is shown below in Figure 4. (Size was determined by the respondents own judgment)

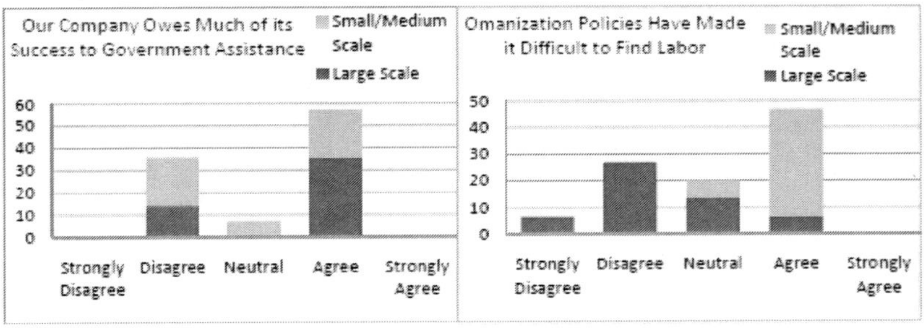

Source: McWilliam, Tyler (Fieldwork, April 2011)

Figure 4 – Responses by Company Size

It is apparent that there exists a duality between new, smaller companies and the more established, larger ones. This duality is the most noticeable in the response to Omanization. Omanization policies negatively affected SMEs far more often than they did large scale enterprises. Additionally, a higher proportion of large scale companies owed their success to government policies. However, despite this difference, in interview, companies of all sizes cited the hard work of their employees as their primary force for success. One manager of a large enterprise who described himself as "100% capitalist" said that government plays only a minor role in how he runs his business, saying that "the only times I talk to them is when I need their permission for something," (Personal Interview 2011)

The second part of the distributed surveys focused on the relationship between companies and public institutions. This was divided into two parts, the amount of communication and the amount of help received. The raw data is shown below in Figure 5.

How much do you communicate with the following institutions? (1 Not at all; 2 A little; 3 Some; 4 A lot; 5 A great deal)

Institution	1	2	3	4	5
OCIPED	3	3	3	2	0
The Chamber of Commerce and Industry (OCCI)	1	5	3	4	0
The Ministry of Commerce and Industry (MOCI)	1	1	5	5	0
The Public Establishment for Industrial Estates (PEIE)	1	1	4	5	1
The Ministry of Manpower	1	1	5	2	4

How much do the following institutions help your business?

Institution	1	2	3	4	5
OCIPED	2	4	3	2	0
The Chamber of Commerce and Industry (OCCI)	1	4	4	4	0
The Ministry of Commerce and Industry (MOCI)	1	3	4	4	0
The Public Establishment for Industrial Estates (PEIE)	0	5	4	2	2
The Ministry of Manpower	0	6	2	2	3

Source: McWilliam, Tyler (Fieldwork, April 2011)

Figure 5 - Relationship with Public Institutions

One of the most troubling results from these two datasets is the amount of help provided by OCIPED. Most companies reported OCIPED as helping either a little bit or not at all. While some reported OCIPED's services as helping 'a lot', this number is not as high as it should be. Half of OCIPED's purpose is the promotion of exports, so it would be expected that their assistance would be higher than reported.

Companies, when asked to describe how these institutions help them, mainly cited 'approvals', 'market statistics', and 'infrastructure'. While these help companies start and plan their business, they do not, with the exception of 'market statistics', help companies once they have begun operating.

From the research, it would appear that, once established, companies have generally been responsible for their own growth. Institutions like the Oman Development Bank and industrial zones like Rusayl have helped encourage companies to start, but after that government services tend to wane in their efficiency.

Response from Public Institutions

The above research data and conclusions were presented to appropriate public institutions. Their responses varied from concurrence with the data to its outright rejection.

One public official working in the Ministry of Commerce remarked how several of the results found matched his expectations. In relation to the problems facing SMEs, he said "SMEs are very important, they account for ninety percent of businesses in Oman, but only produce three or four percent of GDP; they must be developed more," (Personal Interview 2011). He recognized the faults of Omanization, saying that Omanis have a tendency to leave jobs shortly after being hired, making them not as dependable as expat workers.

Despite the faults, he expressed confidence in manufacturing growth. He explained that "[Oman] has the potential to have a good manufacturing sector because of oil revenue," and that, with current growth trends, the manufacturing sector will far surpass the 15% of GDP goal set forth by the Vision 2020 goals.

In response to the natural gas shortage, a representative at PEIE explained that "it is not under [PEIE's] authority". He said that natural gas is under the jurisdiction of the Ministry of Oil and Gas, expecting them to fix it sometime during 2012.

Although no date was given, he said PEIE also plans to have increases in online service and the eventual creation of a 'one-stop shop' which could better assist companies.

One official, speaking on behalf of the Chamber of Commerce and Industry, remarked that the sample size of the survey was too small to determine true national interest. He determined that "the only way to truly discover the companies' interests is through a comprehensive survey administered by Omani businesses," (Personal Interview May 2011) He argued that companies were too self-interested, using their membership in the chamber only to promote their own companies goals. In relation to international exhibitions, he said that "it is in the national interest is to promote Oman, however the companies want only to secure contracts," He cited conflicts of interest and how the policies proposed by companies focus on very specific issues. With respect to the official, this is a very jaded view. Companies, in a free-market system, do not advertise nations, they advertise products. It is to be assumed that companies, and their representatives, will work primarily towards bettering their own situation. The OCCI is facing a form of the principle-agent problem. While those in charge of the OCCI want to see it work towards their interests, those composing it want to see it work towards theirs. Companies will produce recommendations which help companies. The OCCI is a semi-governmental institution, serving only an advisory role in policy making. Recommendations from its members channel upwards to the chief of the committee. However, it is under his discretion whether or not these recommendations actually proceed from the Chamber to the Ministries. If they are judged to be not in line with national interest, they are discarded. This creates a great deal of inefficiency.

Section 4: Recommendations for Policy Change

As explained earlier, the purpose of this document is to find ways that the government can better help to provide for its fledgling manufacturing and export sector. Recommendations were formulated using the input from companies in Rusayl as well as officials from the Ministry of Commerce and Industry, the Chamber of Commerce and Industry, OCIPED, and the Oman Development Bank. Based on this research, this document presents five recommendations for policy change that will better help facilitate manufacturing and export development in the Sultanate.

Government Streamlining

Private enterprise dependency on government support is a bad thing. The Omani private sector would seem to agree, as it has become apparent through conversations with business owners (some Omani, some expat) that they don't want to rely on the government for support. Several factory managers, purely free-market capitalist in their outlook, simply wanted the government to provide a business environment in which they can freely operate.

Many factory managers expressed frustration with the complexity of government services. By streamlining services to a single window, or better yet, a single website, factory owners would be able to focus more on running their business. The 'one-stop shop' promised by PEIE helps to meet this, but it should be expanded to cover the services provided by all government institutions. As was seen with the natural gas shortage in Rusayl, there is still the potential for problems to simply be handed off to other ministries. Streamlined service would allow for a single administration to handle any problems companies would face.

To help attract FDI, OCIPED should be restructured after Ireland's IDA. It should be given more autonomy and the funding to open offices in key cities around the world, such as Silicon Valley, Seoul, and Tokyo. This would help to establish personal contacts between potential foreign investors and also in finding potential contracts for Omani businesses. Government services should help to improve the availability of information. As one of the causes of market failure is imperfect information, services should help to provide companies with contract opportunities, material prices, and potential investors. These facilities should also be made readily available online.

Omanization

One of the biggest problems facing companies in Rusayl, especially SMEs, is Omanization. Omanization policies, while they cost the government little to enact, are not free. The costs of Omanization flow directly to companies. When companies need skilled labor, and the supply is not available in Oman, they must look abroad for expat labor. However, when Omanization policies prevent them from hiring more foreign labor, costs are incurred. Some companies simply accept running inefficiently with unsuitably skilled employees, while other companies may hire an Omani in a 'window seat' position, one which has little real responsibility or productivity, simply so they can open up space to hire more skilled expats.

SMEs have proven to be critical in industrial development, as was seen in the case of Thailand, wherein fifty percent of companies employed less than twenty workers (Hussey 8). It is important that the government therefore ensure that they are not being overlooked when drafting policy.

It would appear as if the Omani government is faced with two options: either continue Omanization policies at the expense (and potential loss) of fledgling SMEs – thus leading to continued unrest from disgruntled Omani business owners, or, cancel Omanization and face continued unrest from unemployed Omanis, disgruntled by the governments apparent apathy toward their plight. This would seem to be a Morton's Fork of sorts, a decision wherein each choice leads to the same, unpleasant outcome. However, a solution to this dilemma has been presented by (Al-Rawas 2009).

As was mentioned earlier, there is a duality between SMEs and large-scale companies. While the SMEs struggle to meet Omanization requirements and keep costs down, large-scale companies far surpass their requirements. An ingenious solution for this problem which capitalizes on this duality was developed by Basil Ahmed Al-Rawas. Al-Rawas, inspired by the credit-based cap-and-trade system developed to lower carbon emissions, suggests that Omanization can be improved through the creation of labor credits. Al-Rawas explains the following:

"Firms achieving more than 35 percent Omanization can gain extra credits points. For instance, firm A could receive 5 points if it achieves 40 percent Omanization. It could then sell these credits to firm B that has a 30 percent Omanization ratio and cannot achieve the target ratio of 35 percent. The price of the permits, (5 percent of Omanization), that would be paid by firm B to firm A would not exceed the marginal

cost of firm B of achieving the extra 5 percent Omanization. The payment would go

directly to the MMP which will transfer the credit to firm A in the form of free training programs for their extra Omani workers," (Al-Rawas 43)

Expats from South-Asia generally live away from their families, sending money to them home in the form of remittances. Al-Rawas explained in an interview that, "If [South-Asian expats] fear that they will be replaced, they will be more hesitant to bring relatives to Oman, and instead will keep sending money out of Oman," (Personal Interview 2011). This credit-based system of Omanization would give expats more job security, and thus they would bring their families to Oman, which would help to keep the money from flowing from the country.

A perceived flaw in this program is buying the credits from the Ministry of Manpower and funding sales with training programs. If the companies themselves were able to sell their credits, there would be more of an incentive to meet Omanization requirements. Credits would be seen as a valuable commodity with a tangible value. The revenue from credit sales could then be spent under the company's own discretion, which might even include the training programs.

As was seen in the case of Thailand, which was able to outcompete its neighbor Malaysia because of its lack of mandatory Thai employment, labor force nationalization policies can wreak havoc on attracting FDI and development. This solution would help to lower the costs Oman has undoubtedly incurred through Omanization.

Building the Skills of the Omani Labor Force

The Omani government is well aware of the need to create a skilled local labor force, and it has established policies to help facilitate it. While it is hard to judge the effectiveness of current initiatives, as it will not truly be known until students enter the labor force, there are changes that can be made to these policies that would better help the manufacturing industry.

Specialized vocational and technical education programs should be more readily available and subject to government subsidy. While formal education and the creation of experts would be ideal and should still be developed, these are long processes and will not produce results until several years from now. Technical schools are able to help Omanis join the labor force in far less time.

On-the-job training programs, which are used by many of the manufacturers in Oman, should be subsidized by the government. By eliminating the cost of training, companies would be more likely to consider hiring unskilled Omanis over skilled expats. Additionally the savings on training could be used on to help the company in other ways, such as R&D.

Infrastructural Development

It was observed that shipping costs proved prohibitively problematic for nearly all companies surveyed. Currently, Oman's plans for the Gulf Railway have it run south from the UAE border and eventually terminate in the southern port city of Duqm. This paper cannot stress enough the importance of this rail network and applauds the initiative of the Omani government. The speedy completion of this network should be a top priority for government authorities.

Additionally, the possibility of extending the terminus further west to the Yemeni border has been considered. However, this is not yet official. This document strongly recommends taking this course of action. Although Yemen is currently facing devastating problems in economic development as well as political unrest, the fact remains that Yemen's situation will eventually improve.

Yemen has the potential to become a key export market for Oman. With a population of nearly thirty million, rivaling that of Saudi Arabia, Yemen's burgeoning consumer market will demand great amounts of imported goods. This of course could take many decades, but if Omani companies are able to establish their products early in the Yemeni markets, it could prove to be a very valuable investment when the time eventually comes.

Increased Government Openness

This recommendation comes not from the companies interviewed, but rather from the researcher's personal opinion. Most factory owners interviewed showed a distinct apprehensiveness when learning of the purpose of this research. This was even more visible when managers were pushed to give their own personal opinions on government effectiveness. It is feared that this apprehensiveness may have even affected the survey results.

It is no secret that public criticism of the Omani government is highly discouraged and in some cases even illegal. Companies are extremely hesitant to criticize government policies, even when they have suggestions, which in some cases may even be better than the current policies. A representative of the Chamber of Commerce and Industry argued that "government represented by OCCI and OCIPED opened the door to commercial openness," (Personal Interview May 2011). The OCCI, which is made up of private sector representatives, helps, but many businesses, specifically SMEs, cannot afford to represent themselves, and there is still hesitation to publicly oppose policies. This is not about political philosophy, but rather economic efficiency. Can a government which does not encourage constructive criticism be as effective as one that is open to suggestions? The rentier-state model, of which Oman is an example, suggests that citizens give up personal liberty in exchange for government benefits.

This is generally done to help ensure that the current government remains in place. However, in Oman there is a genuine respect for the government. It has, historically, acted in the best interests of its people and improved life in the Sultanate greatly over the past 40 years. It has earned the trust of its people. However, it is in the opinion of this researcher that through the government's closed-door tendency it has missed the opportunity to hear the true problems faced by SMEs and thus has failed to reach its fully efficient potential.

Conclusion

Despite the critical approach taken by this paper, it is important to note that many of the survey responses were indeed supportive of most government policy, indicating that much of Omani policy has indeed worked. However, the recommendations given in this paper, if followed, will enhance the growth of Oman's manufacturing and export sector. Of course, it is entirely possible that the Omani government has considered taking the actions recommended above, yet has chosen not to enact them. This could be because the Omani government simply does not want to see Oman become a major manufacturer. This would explain its heavy emphasis on national image and tourism, which, in this researcher's opinion, is disproportionate to the emphasis placed on manufacturing. The creation of an export-intensive economy would drastically change Oman's image, and image held highly by the Omani government.

Oman has worked to create its international image as one of a historically rich people, with a country decorated with forts, castles, dhows and mountains. To create an economy based on industry and manufacturing would serve to potentially disrupt or possibly even destroy this image. This research understands that the government may simply not wish to see its country change in such a way. But as oil revenues decrease and eventually cease, the time Oman has to commit to a sustainable path to development slims. What is the cost of protecting this image when faced with such a closing window of opportunity? This is a decision that must soon be made by the Omani government.

So there it is.

Works Cited

O'Higgins, Eleanor. "Government and the Creation of the Celtic Tiger: Can Management Maintain the Momentum?." Academy of the Management Executive. 16.3 (2002): 104-120.

Ciccone, Antonio. "Input Chains and Industrialization." Review of Economic Studies. 69.3 (2002): 565-587.

Hussey, Antonia. "Rapid Industrialization in Thailand 1986-91." Geographical Review. 83.1 (1993): 14-28.

Bakheet, Adil Hassan. Problems Facing the Industrial Establishment in Sohar. Dubai, UAE: Gulf Research Center, 2005. eBook.

Wilson, Rodney. The Changing Composition and Direction of GCC Trade. Abu Dhabi, UAE: The Emirates Center for Strategic Studies and Research, 1998.

Abdulrazzaq, Ali, Kamal Naser, and Peter Sadler. The Role of Industrial and Development Finance Institutions in the GCC States: ensions and Policies. Abu Dhabi, UAE: The Emirates Center for Strategic Studies and Research, 2002.

Sultanate of Oman. Monthly Statistical Bulletin. Muscat: MONE, 2010.

Sultanate of Oman. Export Development and Facilitation. Muscat: OCIPED, 2009. Web. 1 May 2011.

Xia, Ying, and Jochen Ropke. "Creating Entrepreneurial Energy and the Dutch Disease: How to Create Innovation and Entrepreneurship in a Resource-Rich Country." International Workshop for Higher Education and Entrepreneurship. University of Tehran: Marburg, Germany, University of Marburg. 2006.

Primo Braga, Carlos. "Import Substitution Industrialization in Latin America: Experience and Lessons for the Future ." Seminar in Honor of Werner Baer. Washington DC, USA, The World Bank. 2006.

Yasser. Personal Interview by Tyler McWilliam. 21 Apr 2011. Public Establishment for Industrial Estates. 1 May 2011.

Greenwald, Bruce, and Joseph Stiglitz. "Externalities in Economies with Imperfect Information and Incomplete Markets." Quarterly Journal of Economics. 101.2 (1986): 229-64. Print.

Stiglitz, Joseph. Making Globalization Work. W. W. Norton & Company, 2006.

Osei-Hwedie, Bertha. "Development Policy and Economic Change in Zambia: A Re-Assessment."DPMN Bulletin. 10.2 (2003):

Al-Rawas, Basil. " Small and Medium Enterprises(SMEs) in Oman: Problems and Prospects for Development ." University of Applied Sciences, Berlin. (2009):

World Bank Online Database. Washington DC, USA: World Bank Group, 2011. Web. 5 May 2011.

<http://data.worldbank.org/?display=graph>.

Tipitino, Demic. "Can Bilateral Free Trade A greements Be a Catalyst for Widespread Economic Change." Muscat, Oman: SIT Oman , 2010. Print.

Issan, Salha. "Post Basic Education Reforms in Oman: A Case

Study." Literacy Information and Computer Educat ion Journal. 1.1 (2010): Print.

Prabhu, Conrad. "Rail Project Network Gains Pace."Oman Observer 01 Feb 2011: n. pag. Web. 8 May 2011.

" State General Reserve Fund." Investopedia .com. Investopedia LUC, 2011.

Web. <http://www.investopedia.com/terms/s/state-general- reserve-fund.asp>

" Duqm Port to Boost Development." Oman Observer23 Apr 2011: n. pag. Web. 8 May 2011. <http://main.omanobserver.om/node/48491>.

Field Interviews, Rusayl. Made in Oman Personal Interviews by Tyler McWilliam. Apr 2011. SIT Oman.

Ministry of Commerce and Industry. Made in Oman Personal Interview by Tyler McWilliam. Apr 2011. SIT Oman.

Public Establishment for Industrial Estates. Made in Oman Personal Interview by Tyler McWilliam. Apr 2011. SIT

Oman.

Oman Chamber of Commerce and Industry. Made i n Oman Personal Interviews by Tyler McWilli am. Apr 2011. SIT Oman.

Jax, Antonius. "Efficient Human Resource Development for the Private Sector in the Sultanate of Oman." Lecture Series 2011. World Learning Center. Muscat, 10 April 2011.

"Full text of the National Economy Minister 's address outlining the 8th Five-Year Plan and State's General Budget for 2011." Oma n Observer 03 Jan 2011: n. pag. Web. 9 May 2011.

Sultanate of Oman. Vision 2020. , 1995Print..

11
CHAPTER

The Role of Entrepreneurship in Economic Development in Saudi Arabia

Yusuf N[1*] and Albanawi Ni[2]

[1]Department of Economics and Administration, Jamia Street, King Abdul-Aziz University, Jeddah-21551, Saudi Arabia

[2]King Abdul-Aziz University, Jeddah, Saudi Arabia

ABSTRACT

One of the key objectives of modern economics is to determine factors that influence the economic development. This paper, therefore, seeks to discuss entrepreneurship as one of the factors that influence the economy of a nation, either directly or indirectly. It is a fact that entrepreneurship plays a significant part in shaping the landscape of a country's economy. Economists and policy makers recognize this fact. In fact, entrepreneurship is the engine of economic growth and it has come to be perceived as a catalytic agent for expansion and promotion of productive activities in every sphere of economic life all over the world. This research will focus on finding out how entrepreneurship influences the economy of Saudi Arabia. The paper will begin with a brief introduction of the topic before proceeding to present a comprehensive review of literature relevant to the topic. It will then proceed to present an overview of relevant variables used in determining the role played by entrepreneurship in the economy of Saudi Arabia. There will then follow a discussion on the disadvantages of entrepreneurship to the economy. The paper will end with a conclusion summarizing all the keys points discussed, research limitations, and recommendations for further research.

Keywords: Consumption factors; **ECONOMIC DEVELOPMENT**; Entrepreneurship; **GROSS DOMESTIC PRODUCT**; Saudi Arabia

INTRODUCTION

Entrepreneurship is generally described as the ability of an individual or a group of individuals to create or discover an opportunity and utilize it to the benefit of the society, which, in turn, will bring success to the innovators and their organization. The relationship between entrepreneurship and economic growth of a country has increasingly gained a lot of interest from economists and policy makers over the years. However, while some view it as a direct relationship, others see it as an indirect kind of relationship. According to Sarkar [1], this interest has been fueled by the desire to understand how entrepreneurship influences the economy of a country. Both the economists and policy makers recognize the effect of entrepreneurship on the economy of a country. In fact, entrepreneurship has been considered as the engine of economic growth and it has come to be perceived as a catalytic agent for expansion and promotion of productive activities in every sphere of economic life all over the world. According to Sarkar [1], entrepreneurship spreads through every aspect of economic growth, it does not only drive economic development by introducing new combinations, but it also introduces incremental improvements that exert large cumulative impact over time.

In addition, entrepreneurship continually mixes up newly introduced and already existing productive resources among competing uses hence enhancing the efficiency of allocation [1]. It also creates the overall prices within which business decisions are made and influences the rules of the game through which production and exchange are carried out [1]. In developing countries, the process of economic growth is largely dependent on the entrepreneurial activities of the population. The well-planned and well-coordinated activities of entrepreneurs in a nation can bring about a high economic growth rate. In Saudi Arabia, entrepreneurship is one of the key factors that contribute to the balanced and rapid growth of the country's economy [2]. In addition, entrepreneurship largely contributes to proper utilization of resources, establishment of a developed self-sufficient society, and creation of employment opportunities in Saudi Arabia [3]. This paper discusses how the entrepreneurial spirits of the people living in Saudi Arabia contribute to the rapid development of the country's economy.

LITERATURE REVIEW

Kayed and Hassan [4] argue that in the face of numerous challenges that confront the course economic development in Saudi Arabia must pursue, or at least consider, a viable diversification strategy in order to deal with such challenges. Some of the diversification strategies that have enabled Saudi Arabia to confront challenges that hinder its economic growth are the promotion of entrepreneurial spirit among its citizens and creation of policies that promote entrepreneurship. In the past, entrepreneurship was rarely practiced in Saudi Arabia due to unfavorable environment and lack of entrepreneurial skills among the citizens. However, following the introduction of entrepreneurial training programs and implementation of favorable policies by the government, the image of Saudi Arabia has changed drastically in respect of entrepreneurship [5]. Now the economic growth rate of the country has increased significantly owing to a large number of entrepreneurs that have emerged, especially in the field of technology. The effort of the Saudi government towards entrepreneurial **MOTIVATION** and development has yielded a positive impact on the country's economy. Kayed and Hassan [4] believe that because of the environment that is favorable for entrepreneurship, Saudi Arabia currently has a huge number of new breed of entrepreneurs that is gradually shaping the country's economic landscape. According to Sarkar [1], these devoted male and female entrepreneurs are 'pushing the envelope' in their individual communities and defying old conjectures regarding risk aversion and value creation in the Arab world [1].

Faria et al. [6] argue that entrepreneurship is the engine of economic growth in Saudi Arabia, and it has come to be perceived as a catalytic agent for expansion and promotion of productive activities in all spheres of economic life in every part of the country. According to Hamod [3], entrepreneurship is one of the key factors that have contributed to the balanced and rapid growth of the country's **ECONOMY**. Hamod [3] believes that entrepreneurship in Saudi Arabia has spread through every aspect of economic growth, thus it does not only drive economic development by introducing new combinations, but it also introduces incremental improvements that exert large cumulative impact on the economy over time. In addition, entrepreneurship has largely contributed to proper utilization of resources, establishment of a developed self-sufficient society, and creation of employment opportunities in Saudi Arabia. Kayed et al. [4], assert that entrepreneurs play a major role in the economic growth in Saudi Arabia. With the help of their strong initiative, skill, drive, and spirit of innovation, entrepreneurs have brought significant changes in the process of economic growth. "Entrepreneurs are highly motivated individuals who are always action oriented and prepared to take all risks to attain their economic goals" [7].

Daniel Smith, in his article titled "The Role of **ENTREPRENEURSHIP** in Economic Growth" argues that even though a number of classical factors of economic development influence entrepreneurship in Saudi Arabia, it remains as one of the key factors that influence economic development of a nation [8]. He argues, "If there is a single factor that influence entrepreneurship not included among the classical factors of economic development and entrepreneurship does have an impact on economic development, then entrepreneurship ought to be considered as an additional separate factor of economic development" [8].

DISCUSSION

In a bid to appreciate the role played by entrepreneurship in shaping the economy of a state, the ensuing discussion tries to pursue the practicability aspect of it. In order to understand fully the role of entrepreneurship in economic development, it is prudent to consider it in light of dependent and independent variables. One way in which entrepreneurship contributes to the economy of a country is, rather obviously, through the creation of job opportunities. In many cases, the economic wellbeing of a country is measured by the rates of employment. In Saudi Arabia, the situation is not different. Throughout the years, entrepreneurship has played a key role in shaping the country's economy, a factor which has led it to be rated among the fastest growing economies in the world.

The employment plan of 2014, Saudi Arabia has seen an increase in the level of employment. According to the country's ministry of labor, although there has been a slight increase in the number of those who are unemployed, there rate at which people have been recruited for jobs has increased compared to previous years [9]. Such growth has been majorly attributed to entrepreneurial activities in the country, and in particular, the small and medium size enterprises, which are said to create about thirty five thousand job opportunities annually. The sentiments are shared by the Central Department of Statistics and Information, which, in 2013, produced a report to the effect that the unemployment rate stood at 5.5%. That was a decrease in the unemployment rates, compared to the 6.3% in 2006. Going by the **STATISTICS** provided at the national level, therefore, there is no doubt as to the role played by entrepreneurship in job creation in Saudi Arabia. The growth witnessed in the private sector has seen many individuals, especially young adults, finding means of earning a living, as illustrated in the **FIGURE 1**.

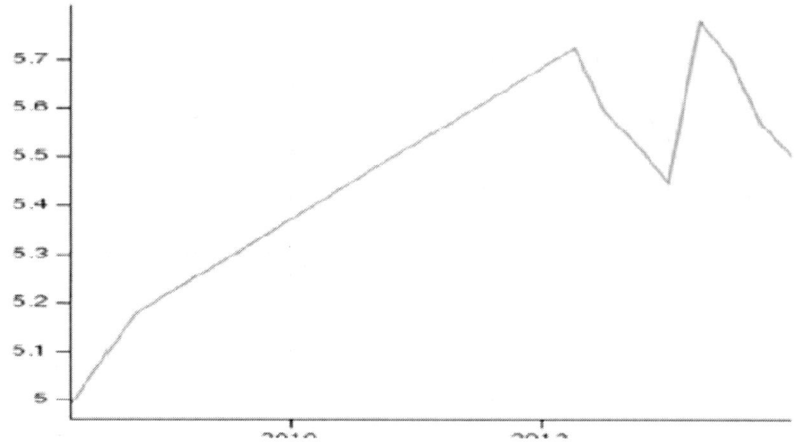

FIGURE 1: Unemployment rate in Saudi Arabia [16].

As it can be seen on the graph, the unemployment rate in Saudi Arabia has been on the fall since 2013. Another way in which entrepreneurship has contributed to the development of the economy of Saudi Arabia is through resource and wealth distribution. In previous years, it was only the capital city and a few urban areas, which used to reap the benefits of entrepreneurship. The reason behind this was the fact that most of the large and well-established companies avoided conducting **BUSINESS** in rural areas, for the fear that they would incur losses. Consequently, there resulted economic imbalance in the country, since resources and wealth were concentrated in the capital city and a few urban centers.

However, this is no longer the case. The ministry of labor, upon realizing this, started various programs to support young entrepreneurs who were willing to start business in rural areas. A good example is the entrepreneur development program, which seeks to identify young talents and mentor them on matters to do with entrepreneurship and economics. As a result, there has been a re-distribution of wealth and resources across the country, hence creating some sort of economic balance, though this is still a work-in-progress.

Entrepreneurship has also played a major role in Saudi Arabia's **GROSS DOMESTIC PRODUCT** (GDP) growth rate [10]. As economics dictate, the growth of a country is measured by its GDP in one year. Simply put, GDP is the aggregate value of the final goods and services produced in a country within a period of one year. GDP, therefore, reflects the economic status of a country, since it shows how rich or poor a country is at a specific time. In the last few years, there has been consistent GDP growth rate in Saudi Arabia, leaving no doubt that the country's productivity is constantly on the rise, as shown in the **FIGURE 2**.

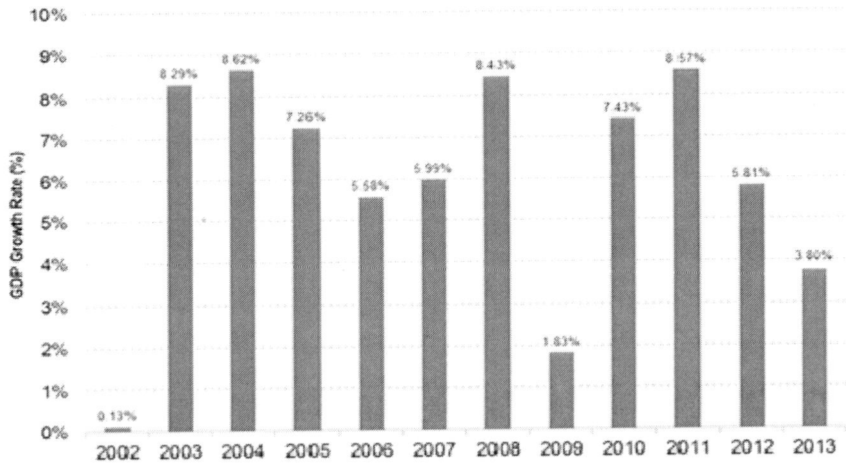

Source: World Bank, 2015

FIGURE 2: Saudi Arabia annual GDP growth rate.

Judging from the **FIGURE 2**, although there have been variations in the growth rate; Saudi Arabia's GDP has always been increasing on an annual basis. The presence of a positive growth works to prove that the value of goods and services produced in one particular year, is always higher than the previous year.

Judging from the **FIGURE 2**, although there have been variations in the growth rate; Saudi Arabia's GDP has always been increasing on an annual basis. The presence of a positive growth works to prove that the value of goods and services produced in one particular year, is always higher than the previous year. Increased productivity in the country is largely attributed to increased entrepreneurial activities compared to the previous years. For instance, many young adults have taken up the challenge through innovation, a factor that has intensified competition in the various industries within the economy.

It is highly undisputable that in deed entrepreneurship has greatly contributed to the production of goods and services in Saudi Arabia. In essence, it is through entrepreneurial activities that the major factors of production are brought together in order to produce goods and services. The entrepreneur development programs across the country have acted as a catalyst in unleashing the potential in young adults, something that was not so prevalent about a decade ago.

Increased exports is another result of entrepreneurship in Saudi Arabia. As it is widely known, the country is the second largest producer of oil after Russia, something that has worked to boost its economy [11]. Moreover, it is the largest producer and exporter of **PETROLEUM PRODUCTS** in the world. For instance, the **FIGURE 3**, below shows the external destinations of Saudi Arabian oil in the year 2013.

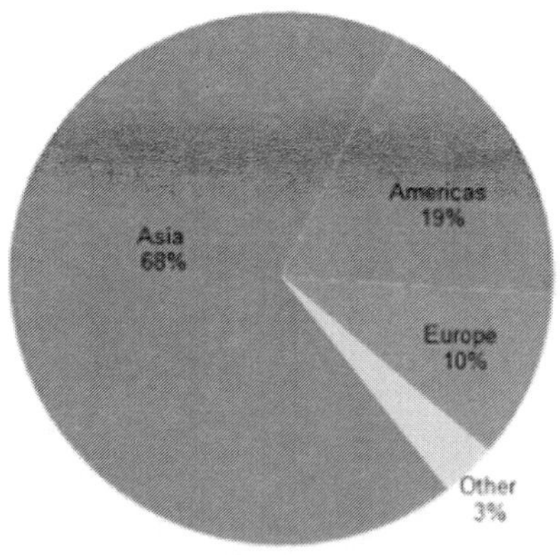

Source: Global Trade Information Services [15]

FIGURE 3: The external destinations of Saudi Arabian oil in the year 2013.

The pie chart above clearly shows that majority of Saudi Arabia's export market lies within the Asian continent, with China being the major market. Africa is included among the 3%, reason being most African countries import oil from either the Far East, or West African countries. Just as crucial as the exportation of a major product is to any country, oil production and exportation is the backbone of Saudi Arabia's economy. The country exports seven million barrels of oil a day. Bearing in mind that one barrel of oil goes at about $125, the contribution it has to the economic growth and stability of the country cannot be underestimated. The **FIGURE 4**, below serves as prove of the increased oil production in 2015.

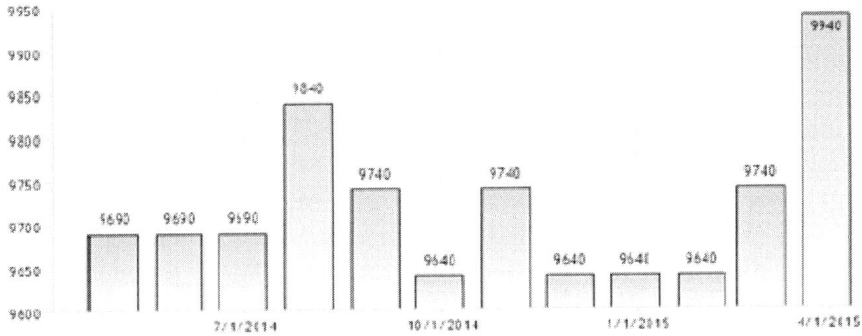

Source: Trading Economics [17].

FIGURE 4: Saudi Arabia crude oil production.

A keen observation from the figure above indicates that during the month of April 2015, the barrels of oil produces in the country are the highest in the last one year. The increase is highly attributed to the increased investments in the oil production industry, which has seen many entrepreneurs take risks to invest their capital towards oil production [12].

Largely also, entrepreneurship has promoted creativity and innovation in Saudi Arabia [13]. One major advantage of entrepreneurship, not only in Saudi Arabia, is that it promotes creativity and innovation in the country. In fact, the desire to produce goods and services different from the ones already existing in the market is always the driving force behind entrepreneurship. Identification of a market niche is followed by creativity and innovation, since the product, which an entrepreneur is anticipating to introduce in the market has to be of a unique nature.

The economic wellbeing of Saudi Arabia largely depends on the value of its products in the international market. The value of a country's products in the **INTERNATIONAL MARKET** depends on their quality as compared to products of the same nature from other countries. Saudi Arabia's economy has been growing consistently, thanks to the competitiveness of its products at the international market. Increase in entrepreneurial activities in the country is what has yielded such results, hence stabilizing the economy of the country. This is because the increase in innovation has led to improved technologies, which are used in the production of large quantities of quality goods and services. Innovation is closely related to the creation of new markets, which is another role played by entrepreneurs in the economic development of Saudi Arabia. As earlier discussed, the desire of entrepreneurs is to succeed in the market. However, due to the congestion in the Saudi Arabian market, many entrepreneurs opt to penetrate external markets, hence clearing the way for products that are locally manufactured. The rate of new markets creation in this context is a dependent variable that relies on entrepreneurship, in that the more players there are in the economy, the more new external markets will be created.

Another key role played by entrepreneurship in shaping the economy of Saudi Arabia is the improvement of living standards. As earlier discussed, entrepreneurship facilitates the creation of jobs in the country, a factor which creates income to individuals. Because of the increased income, individuals gain more purchasing power, and hence are able to purchase the goods and services available to them through the market. This is based on the economic assumption (Keynesian theory) that expenditure increases with income. In such a case, expenditure is a dependent variable that depends on income as the independent variable, as shown in the **FIGURE 5**.

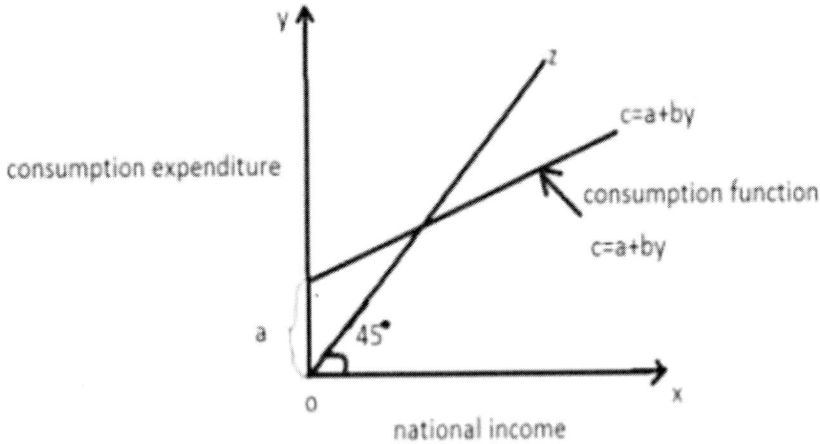

FIGURE 5: The consumption factor.

In the figure above, the X-axis represents the national income, what can also be considered earnings of individuals, while the Y-axis represents expenditure. Curve "z" suggests that the relationship between income and expenditure is directly proportional in that, an increase in income leads to an increase in expenditure. However, it should be noted that in this case, the x-axis represents the independent variable and the y-axis represents the dependent variable. The result is that the economy of the country is boosted by a large extent.

Finally, another important aspect about entrepreneurship is that it is a source of government revenue. This is achieved in a number of ways, for example, the taxes levied on the locally produced goods and services, as they enter the market. Saudi Arabia's economic growth is attributed to the increased annual revenues collected by the government. This is due to the increased scales of production, due to an increment in the entrepreneurial activities in the kingdom. Another way of earning government revenue is through the excise duty taxed at the port when entrepreneurs are importing raw materials, machinery and other products from the external market into the country. The benefits of all these are usually reflected in the country's economy.

SHORTCOMINGS OF ENTREPRENEURSHIP ON ECONOMIC DEVELOPMENT

As much as entrepreneurship plays a significant role in the economic development of Saudi Arabia, there are also ways in which it undermines the growth of the economy. One of the ways in which it impacts undesirably on the economy, is the inflation. Simply defined in economic terms, inflation refers to an instance in the economy of a country, where there is too much circulation of its currency in the economy. An entrepreneurial culture in a state creates a situation whereby people are willing to invest in the production of local goods and services. For instance, the most commonly produced goods in Saudi Arabia are petroleum related. Since petroleum is the most readily available resource, almost all the entrepreneurs produce goods of the same nature. In order to be able to sell their products in the competitive markets, some will be willing to sell less than the true value, hence leading to inflation in the country.

The other shortcomings of entrepreneurial activities in Saudi Arabia is environmental degradation. As entrepreneurs invest in production, they end up over-exploiting the natural resources to depletion. Such resources include the mineral resource (copper and gold), oil and water. This has seen the government come up with various policies in order to control the level of natural resource exploitation, to safeguard the future generation. The danger of over-exploitation of natural resource is that it places the future of the country's economy in jeopardy, since there might be no more natural resources in future from which to produce. Therefore, if not well regulated, entrepreneurship may cause the economy more destruction than that which is fathomable.

CONCLUSION

Up to this point, it is worth appreciating the key role played by entrepreneurship in the development of the economy. In some instances is direct while in others it can be indirect [14]. The bottom line is that it is such a crucial factor that cannot be ignored. The government of Saudi Arabia, therefore, should endeavor to promote an entrepreneurial culture in the country. There are so many young talents willing to take up the challenge. However, lack of capital and the relevant knowledge and skills acts as deterrents. This paper has majorly focused on the role played by entrepreneurship in the economic growth of Saudi Arabia. This, however, is not exhaustive. On the other hand, the disadvantages of entrepreneurship to the economy should not be ignored either. This is because they pose a great danger to the future of the economy.

There is a great need for the country to promote entrepreneurship through formulation of supportive policies. However, this calls for the policy makers to understand first what factors influence entrepreneurship [5]. The curriculum in the higher institutions of learning should also be structured in a way to incorporate entrepreneurship. Majority of the institution's curriculum have nothing to do with this, and this poses a danger to the future of the entrepreneurship culture in the country. Incorporating entrepreneurial values and principles in school curriculum will work to impart the necessary knowledge and skills among students with regard to self-employment. Such a system has been tested and has been proved to yield results in countries such as China and Japan [15].

However, it is still not certain as to what extent should such be incorporated in the learning curriculum. This is one of the important questions should be answered by future research. This research has focused on this relationship, aiming to explore how entrepreneurship influences the economy of a nation. In particular, this paper has sought to discuss how the entrepreneurial spirits of the people living in Saudi Arabia contribute to the rapid development of the country's economy [16,17]. All the literature reviewed in this study showed that there is direct relationship between entrepreneurship and economic development of a country. This is confirmed by the results from the regression equation, which depicted that entrepreneurship significantly influences the economic growth of a nation.

There is recommended a more expansive and exhaustive future research on this. All the same, the findings of this study are equally important for economists and policy makers in Saudi Arabia as they show that the nation should focus on promoting entrepreneurship as one of enhancing the economic development. The connection between entrepreneurship and economic development of a country has continuously received a lot of from policy makers and scholars across the world. Yet, existing literature presents remarkably diverse views about this relationship.

REFERENCES

1. Sarkar S (2014) International Journal of Finance and Policy Analysis. London: Universal Publishers.

2. Kelley D, Bosma N, Amoros J (2010) Global Entrepreneurship Monitor (GEM). Global Report: Babson.

3. Hamod D (2010) Cultivating the entrepreneurial ecosystem in Saudi Arabia. US-Arab Tradeline, XVII spring pp1-3.

4. Kayed R, Hassan K (2013) Islamic Entrepreneurship: Durham Modern Middle East and Islamic World Series. New York: Routledge.

5. Thurik R, Carree M, Stel A, Audretsch D (2008) Does self-employment reduce Unemployment? Journal of Business Venturing 23: 687-698.

6. Faria J, Cuestas J, Mourelle E (2010) Entrepreneurship and unemployment: a nonlinear bidirectional causality? Economic Modelling 27: 1282-1291.

7. Tiwari A (2007) Entrepreneurship development in India. Mumbai: Sarup& Sons Publishers.

8. Smith D (2010) The Role of Entrepreneurship in Economic Growth. Undergraduate Economic review: 6: 1-19.

9. Muhammad F (Nd) Entrepreneurship in the Kingdom of Saudi Arabia. Retrieved from Young Saudi Entrepreneurs.

10. Salem MI (2014) Building an Entrepreneural Economy: Evidence From Developing Countries. International Business and Economic Research Journal 13.

11. Summers D (2012) How Saudi Arabia Will Influence The Oil Market to Benefit Their Economy.

12. Alhajji A (2015) Saudi Arabia Oil Prices and Shale Energy.

13. Alsodais, S. (2013, 9). Science, Technology and Innovation in Saudi Arabia. WIPO.

14. Bathelt H (2001) Competence and economic Recovery: Divergent Growths Paths in Bostons High Technology Economy. Entrepreneurship and Regional Development 13: 287-317.

15. GTI (2013) Exports Today.

16. Quandl (2015) Saudi Arabia Unemployment Summary.

17. Trading Economics (2016) Saudi Arabia GDP Annual Growth Rate.

12

CHAPTER

Sustainable Energy Development in Saudi Arabia

Mounir Belloumi [1,2,†,*] **and Atef Saad Alshehry** [2,†]

[1] *Laboratoire du Management d'Innovation et du Developpement Durable, University of Sousse, Sousse 4023, Tunisia*

[2] *College of Administrative Sciences, Najran University, Najran 1988, Saudi Arabia*

ABSTRACT

The main objective of this research is to study the role of energy consumption in economic growth in Saudi Arabia over the period of 1971–2012 using the autoregressive distributed lag (ARDL) cointegration procedure, and based on neoclassical growth, endogenous growth, and ecological-economics viewpoints. Our empirical results show the existence of a cointegrating relationship between the different variables investigated. In addition, all the inputs (conventional and non-conventional) Granger cause economic growth in both the short and long runs. Our findings confirm the energy-led growth hypothesis in the case of Saudi Arabia. Hence, energy conservation policies may deteriorate economic growth in Saudi Arabia if they are not followed by measures that improve energy efficiency, energy saving technologies and encourage the investment and use of renewable energy sources such as solar and wind energies that can participate in the attenuation of climate changes.

Keywords: ARDL bounds testing; energy-led growth hypothesis; Saudi Arabia

1. INTRODUCTION

Even though neoclassical theory states that energy is neutral to economic growth, historically, energy shocks have affected global economic growth. This observation shows the key role of energy consumption in economic growth [1,2]. According to the ecological and biophysical models, energy is the main factor of production [3,4] . The production of goods is straightly related to the use and the availability of energy, which is considered as the primary factor of production. The main aim of this study is to examine the role of energy consumption in economic growth for an oil producing and exporting country (OPEC), such as Saudi Arabia, using the autoregressive distributed lag (ARDL) Bounds testing to cointegration over the period 1971–2012. In order to control for potential omitted-variable biases and take into account the neoclassical, endogenous growth and ecological economics view points, we consider a model where real GDP is explained by employment, capital, and human capital in addition to energy consumption (for more details, see [4,5,6]). Generally, it is known that the level of energy consumption is very high in the majority of OPEC members, and mainly in Saudi Arabia, due to the low levels of national fuel prices and energy efficiency. Energy is over subsidized in Saudi Arabia. Nowadays, the country is under pressure to increase fuel prices and reduce fuel subsidization. If we find that energy consumption boosts economic growth in Saudi Arabia, a policy aiming to reduce energy consumption might lead to undesirable results concerning economic growth. We should suggest some other measures such as energy efficiency, investment in renewable energies such as solar and wind energies and capital formation that could lead to economic growth and increase employment, where the demand for labor is increasing.

The causal relationship between energy consumption and economic growth has been well studied since the seminal paper of [7]. However, until now the empirical findings are divergent sometimes, even for the same country. Different empirical research has used a variety of econometric techniques and variables over various periods for different countries or groups of countries at aggregated and disaggregated levels. In this context, by using a meta-analysis of 51 works on energy-growth nexus, Menegaki (2014) [8] found that the long run impact of energy consumption on economic growth is dependent of the variables investigated, the data span, and the cointegration technique used.

The role of energy in economic growth has interested researchers since the first oil crisis of 1973. It continues to interest researchers for many reasons. Firstly, the high volatility of fossil fuel prices has largely affected global economic activities and even food security. Secondly, since the industrial revolution, energy has been used in all economic activities. It has become the main engine of the global economy. Thirdly, the use of energy (mainly fossil fuels) is not without negative effects on the global environment and its consequences on climate change has adversely affected human activities.

As reviewed and reported by previous research, there is a large literature on the causal relationship between energy use and economic growth. In this study, we survey mainly the studies including employment and capital as inputs in the energy-growth nexus. The first work on this subject is that of Kraft and Kraft (1978) [7] who studied the relationship between gross national product (GNP) and energy for the United States over the period 1947–1974. By using the Sims causality test, they showed that energy consumption does not cause GNP but the reverse holds. Comparatively to the work of Kraft and Kraft (1978) [7], Akarca and Long (1980) [9] changed only the period of study but they did not find the same result. Their finding showed the absence of causality between the gross national product and energy use for the U.S. over the period 1950–1970. Eight years after the first work of Kraft and Kraft (1979) [7], Erol and Yu (1987) [10] studied the causal relationship between energy consumption and GNP for another six developed countries (Canada, France, Germany, Italy, Japan and the United Kingdom). The authors used both tests of causality of Sims and Granger. The neutral hypothesis of energy was verified for both countries of France and the United Kingdom, whereas the energy-led growth hypothesis held only for

Canada. The feedback hypothesis was verified for Japan while the conservation hypothesis was found for Germany and Italy.

The above studies considered only the tests of causality between two macroeconomic series. Later many researchers showed that these types of models suffer from the problem of omission of some other variables, which could affect the results. In order to resolve this problem, when studying the relationship between energy consumption and economic growth, many studies have included other variables such as employment, capital, carbon dioxide emissions, *etc.* For example, when investigating the causal relationship between energy consumption and GNP in United States, Yu and Hwang (1984) [11] included employment as a control variable. Their findings showed the absence of causality in both directions between energy consumption and GNP. The results confirmed the neutral hypothesis.

However, all these previous studies did not check for the non-stationarity of the macroeconomic time series. Hence, since the work of Yu and Hwang (1984) [11], many studies have used the cointegration approaches of Engle and Granger (1987) [12], and Johansen and Juselius (1990) [13] to resolve this problem. As an example of work using the Engle–Granger cointegration technique, Cheng and Lai (1997) [14] studied the relationship between real GDP, energy consumption and employment in the case of Taiwan. They found unidirectional causality running from real GDP to energy consumption. This means that conservative hypothesis holds.

Contrarily to the previous technique, the Johansen–Juselius cointegration approach has been widely used (e.g., [15,16,17,18,19]). For example, Chang *et al.* (2001) [15] studied the dynamic causal relationships between economic output, energy consumption and employment for Taiwan for the period covering January 1982 to November 1997. Their results supported the energy-led growth hypothesis. Ghali and El-Sakka (2004) [16] used a neo-classical production function where economic output is explained by capital, labor and energy use for Canada. They found bidirectional causality between economic growth and energy use. Yuan *et al.* (2008) [18] studied the causal relationships between energy consumption, labor, capital and economic output for China using a neo-classical aggregate production function. They used energy consumption at both aggregated and disaggregate levels (electricity consumption, oil consumption and coal consumption). The authors found that the series are cointgrated at both aggregated and disaggregated levels. The results of short run causality are mixed. Stern and Enflo (2013) [19] studied the relationship between energy, capital, labor and economic growth for Sweden over the three periods of 1900–2000, 1950–2000 and the whole period of 1850–2000. Using a VECM, they found that energy Granger causes economic growth for the whole period of 1850–2000, whereas economic growth causes energy for the two other periods.

However, the Johansen's cointegration approach has been criticized by many researchers when using small samples, because the usual unit root and cointegration tests are not powerful in this case. In order to control for the problems associated with small samples, some researchers have made appeal to other methods such as the ARDL bounds testing approach (e.g., [20,21]) and panel unit root and cointegration tests (e.g., [22]).

Sari *et al.* (2008) [20] studied the relationships between disaggregate energy consumption (coal, natural gas, fossil fuels, conventional hydroelectric power, solar energy, wind energy, wood, and waste), employment and industrial output in the United States using monthly data covering the period of January 2001 to June 2005. They found unidirectional causality running from industrial production to disaggregate energy consumption; except for the case of coal consumption, the reverse holds. Shahbaz *et al.* (2011) [21] included employment as an additional variable to electricity consumption and economic growth when studying the causal relationships between the three variables for Portugal over the period of 1971–2009. Their results showed that there is bidirectional causality between the three variables in the long run. The feedback hypothesis was validated. Lee *et al.* (2008) [22] analyzed the relationships between energy consumption, capital stock and economic output for a set of 22 OECD countries over the period 1960–2001. They found that the three series are cointegrated and there is a bi-directional causality between economic growth and energy consumption. By studying the energy-growth nexus in 17 Arab countries using the ARDL approach over the period 1980–2011, Shahateet (2014) [23] found that neutrality hypothesis is verified in 16 out of 17 Arab countries including Saudi Arabia.

By taking into account the non-normality assumption, Yildirim and Aslan (2012) [24] studied the causal relationships between energy use, employment, gross fixed capital formation, and economic growth for 17 highly developed OECD countries using the Toda–Yamamoto test framework and the leveraged bootstrapped simulation technique. Their findings indicate the neutrality in the case of Australia, Canada, and Ireland. In the same line, Yalta and Cakar (2012) [25] used a maximum entropy bootstrap to investigate the relationship between energy consumption and economic growth over the period 1971–2007 in the case of China. Overall, their results support the neutrality hypothesis. Salamaliki and Venetis (2013) [4] argued that no previous studies took into account the indirect causality. To do so, they studied the causal relationships between energy consumption, real GDP and capital stock in the group of seven advanced countries by employing two recent methods of Dufour–Pelletier–Renault (2006) [26] and Hill (2007) [27] in order to detect direct and indirect causal effects. They found that in general, real GDP causes energy consumption for this group of countries. Ayres and Voudouris (2014) [28] studied the nonlinear relationships between economic growth with energy use, labor and capital stock in Japan, United Kingdom and United States. They argued that since the industrial revolution, capital stock and energy have played an important role in economic growth.

For the case of Saudi Arabia, empirical studies on energy consumption-economic growth nexus are very restricted. To our knowledge, there are only two studies (Alqudair [29,30]) that focused on Saudi Arabia as a single-country, whereas many other studies ([31,32,33,34,35,36,37,38]) focused on Saudi Arabia in the context of a multi-country study. The results of these studies are mixed and sometimes contradictory. The results of [30,31,32,37] are conforming to the conservative hypothesis that implies economic growth Granger causes energy consumption in the long run. Squalli (2007) [33], Narayan and Smyth (2009) [34], Sadorsky (2011) [35] and Mohammadi and Parvaresh (2014) [38] validated the feedback hypothesis that states bidirectional causality between energy consumption and economic growth in the long run. Contrarily, Hossein *et al.* (2012) [29] and Alkhathlan *et al.* (2012) [36] found an absence of causality between energy consumption and economic growth in the long run. Their findings are conforming to the neutrality hypothesis.

Our study complements the work of Alkhathlan *et al.* (2012) [29], which is the only one of these studies that used the production function approach. The study of Alqudair [30] is limited to a two-variable specification that investigated the energy use-economic growth nexus. Alkhathlan *et al.* (2012) [29] studied the relationship between economic growth, carbon dioxide emissions, employment and energy consumption in Saudi Arabia over the period 1980–2008 using both approaches of ARDL Bounds testing and Johansen multivariate cointegration. The authors used a production function framework where they explained economic output by energy consumption, employment and CO_2 emissions. Compared to this previous study, we do not integrate CO_2 emissions; we add real fixed capital formation and human capital as explanatory variables of economic growth and extending the period from 1971 to 2012.

The remainder of our paper is organized as follows. In Section 2, we present the material and methods used to investigate the relationship between real GDP, energy consumption, real fixed capital formation, employment and human capital in the case of Saudi Arabia. We present the data and the different procedures of ARDL cointegration Bounds testing framework. Section 3 presents the empirical results. In Section 4, we discuss our different findings. Finally, Section 5 concludes by some policy implications and recommendations.

2. MATERIAL AND METHODS

2.1. Data Descriptions

This study is based on annual time series data on real GDP, energy consumption, real fixed capital formation, employment and human capital over the period 1971–2012. Except employment, all the four other time series are sourced from [39]. Time series data on employment are taken from [40].

The variable real GDP is expressed in million 2005 US$. We note its natural logarithm by Y. Energy consumption refers to the use of primary energy before transformation to other end-use fuels. It is expressed in kiloton of oil equivalent and its natural logarithm is noted by X_1. Since a time series on the capital stock is not directly available for Saudi Arabia, it is proxied by the real value of gross fixed capital formation (GFCF). This proxy for capital stock has been used in many previous studies ([41,42]). It is expressed in million 2005 US$ and its natural logarithm is noted by X_2. Employment is measured by the number of people employed in the different economic activities in Saudi Arabia. It is expressed in thousands of persons and we note its natural logarithm by X_3. Human capital is proxied by the ratio of gross tertiary school enrollment. According to the World Bank, it is defined as the ratio of total enrollment, regardless of age, to the population of the age group that officially corresponds to this level of education. We note the natural logarithm of this variable by X_4. Descriptive statistics of all variables at their levels and growth rates are presented in Table 1.

Table 1. Descriptive statistics.

Statistics	Variable Levels					Growth Rates (%)	
	Real GDP	Energy Consumption	Real Gross Fixed Capital Formation	Employment	Human Capital	Real GDP	Energy Consumption
Mean	239,836.9	80,256.39	392.200	4813.400	16.123	4.69	8.01
Median	223,325.0	74,413.64	299.901	4883.000	11.292	4.96	6.68
Maximum	497,620.1	197,000.0	1118.271	8935.555	50.936	24.28	40.81
Minimum	72,547.85	6250.783	25.773	1539.199	1.635	−11.76	−16.30
Standard Deviation	97,242.47	56,313.61	290.294	2261.481	12.045	7.11	11.35
Observations	42	42	42	42	42	41	41

Figure 1 gives a plot of the annual growth rates of real GDP and energy consumption over the period 1971–2012.

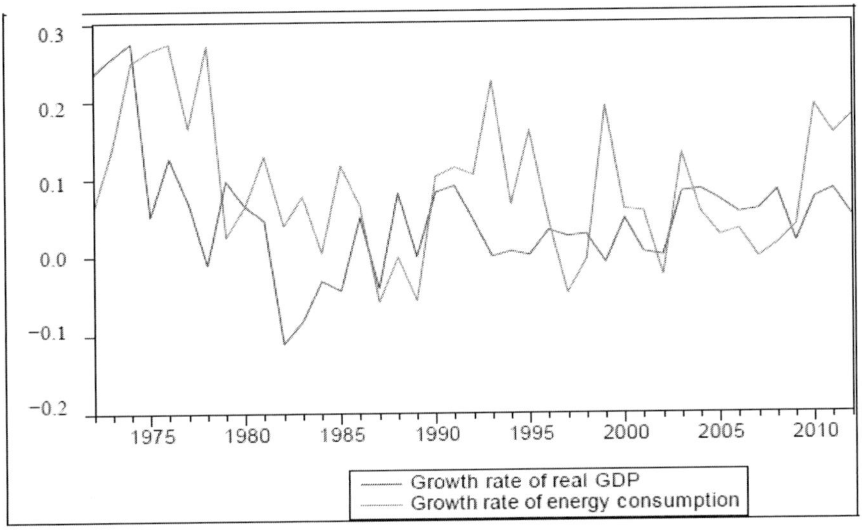

Figure 1. Annual growth rates of energy consumption and real GDP.

2.2. ARDL Bounds Testing

Our study is based on Autoregressive-Distributed Lag (ARDL) models and bounds testing for cointegration approach. Pesaran and Shin (1999) [43] and Pesaran *et al.* (2001) [44] initially developed the ARDL cointegration framework. The ARDL models have been used extensively over the last fifteen years to test for the existence of long-run relationships between macroeconomic variables. They are playing a very important role in the modeling of non-stationary series since they have three advantages in comparison with Johansen cointegration framework ([45]). The first one is that the ARDL framework does not require all the variables under study be integrated of the same order and it can be applied when the underlying variables are integrated of order one (I(1)), order zero (I(0)) or fractionally integrated. The second advantage is that the ARDL Bounding test is relatively more efficient in the case of small and finite sample data sizes. The last and third advantage is that by applying the ARDL technique, we obtain unbiased estimates for the long-run model ([46]).

The single equation ARDL model is presented by Giles (2013) [45] as follows:

$$y_t = \beta_0 + \beta_1 y_{t-1} + \ldots + \beta_p y_{t-p} + \sum_{j=0}^{q_1} \alpha_j x_{1t-j} + \sum_{j=0}^{q_2} \alpha_j x_{2t-j} + \ldots + \sum_{j=0}^{q_k} \alpha_j x_{kt-j} + \varepsilon_t \quad (1)$$

where ε_t is the random error term that is assumed to be serially independent. It is not necessary that the model contains the current values of the explanatory variables and each explanatory variable can have its own maximum lag length ([45]). The ARDL model is essentially used to implement the bounds test in order to check for the existence of the long-run relationships between the various time series investigated.

When implementing the ARDL method, we have to follow four steps. The first step is to verify that all the variables are I(0) and/or I(1) (none of the variables are I(2)). We use the unit root tests such as the Augmented Dickey–Fuller (ADF) ([47]), Phillips and Perron (PP) ([48]) and DF-GLS ([49]) tests to check that none of the variables investigated are I(2). We use also the DF-GLS test because it is well known that it is more efficient in the presence of small sample size.

The second step is to define an unrestricted error-correction model (UECM), which is given by transforming Equation (1). Suppose there are five variables that we are interested in modeling: a dependent variable, y, and four other explanatory variables, x_1, x_2, x_3 and x_4. We recall that a conventional ECM for cointegrated variables has the following form:

$$\Delta y_t = \beta_0 + \sum_{i=1}^{p} \beta_i \Delta y_{t-i} + \sum_{j=0}^{q_1} \gamma_j \Delta x_{1t-j} + \sum_{j=0}^{q_2} \delta_j \Delta x_{2t-j} + \sum_{j=0}^{q_3} \mu_j \Delta x_{3t-j} + \sum_{j=0}^{q_4} \lambda_j \Delta x_{4t-j} + \eta\, ECT_{t-1} + \varepsilon_t \quad (2)$$

where ECT is the error-correction term that represents the OLS residuals derived from the long-run relationship model given by:

$$y_t = \alpha_0 + \alpha_1 x_{1t} + \alpha_2 x_{2t} + \alpha_3 x_{3t} + \alpha_4 x_{4t} + vt \quad (3)$$

The error correction term is given by the following equation:

$$ECT_{t-1} = y_{t-1} - a_0 - a_1 x_{1t-1} - a_2 x_{2t-1} - a_3 x_{3t-1} - a_4 x_{4t-1} \quad (4)$$

where a_0, a_1, a_2, a_3 and a_4 are the OLS estimates of α_0, α_1, α_2, α_3 and α_4.

In doing so, we estimate the following model:

$$\Delta y_t = \beta_0 + \sum_{i=1}^{p} \beta_i \Delta y_{t-i} + \sum_{j=0}^{q_1} \gamma_j \Delta x_{1t-j} + \sum_{j=0}^{q_2} \delta_j \Delta x_{2t-j} + \sum_{j=0}^{q_3} \mu_j \Delta x_{3t-j} + \sum_{j=0}^{q_4} \lambda_j \Delta x_{4t-j} + \theta_0 y_{t-1} + \theta_1 x_{1t-1} + \theta_2 x_{2t-1} + \theta_3 x_{3t-1} + \theta_4 x_{4t-1} + \varepsilon_t \quad (5)$$

This model is similar to the usual or regular error correction model but we have now replaced the error-correction term, ECT_{t-1} with the terms y_{t-1}, x_{1t-1}, x_{2t-1}, x_{3t-1} and x_{4t-1}. We call this model an UECM because we are not restricting their coefficients.

This step needs the determination of appropriate lag structure of the UECM, the verification of autocorrelation of the error terms of this model, and making sure that the model is dynamically stable. Firstly, we choose the maximum lags, p, q_1, q_2, q_3 and q_4 by using the information criteria such as Akaike information criterion (AIC), Schwartz criterion (SC) or Bayesian information criterion (BIC), and Hannan–Quinn information criterion (HQ), *etc.* We also pay attention to the statistical significance of the coefficients in the model. Once we have our preferred specification, we check that there is no remaining autocorrelation using the LM test. If we find serial dependence of errors, we should need to lengthen the maximum lags, even if the terms are not significant. "We set a maximum lag length and then look at all possible combinations of lags within this constraint. The model with the smallest information criteria is chosen. That will involve many possible combinations. We suggest taking account of significance to reduce this set of possibilities. Start with lots of lags, and test down, not the opposite. We can omit 'intervening' lags if this is suggested by lack of significance" [45]. Normality and heteroskedasticity of the errors can also be tested. As the model has an autoregressive structure, so we have to check that the model is dynamically stable.

The third step is to implement a bounds test in order to detect if there is a cointegrating relationship between the different investigated variables by estimating the model (5) and testing the hypothesis, H_0: $\theta_0 = \theta_1 = \theta_2 = \theta_3 = \theta_4 = 0$; against the alternative that H_0 is not true. As in conventional cointegration testing, the acceptance of the null hypothesis implies the absence of a cointegrating relationship between the time series. A rejection of H_0 implies that we have a long-run relationship. To decide on this, we perform an F-test.

Critical values for the F-test are supplied by Pesaran *et al.* (2001) [44] and complemented by Narayan (2005) [50] for smaller and finite samples. For different sample sizes, different levels of probability and different numbers of variables, there are lower and upper critical values. The lower critical value is determined by considering that all of the series are stationary on levels, whereas the upper critical value is determined by supposing that all the time series are integrated of order one. We obtain that the variables are cointegrated when the value of the F-statistic exceeds the upper critical value, whereas we reject the cointegrating relationship when the value of the F-statistic is inferior to the upper critical value. Otherwise, the test is not conclusive. Narayan (2005) [50] gives critical values for less than 80 observations.

In the fourth step, if the variables are found to be cointegrated, we estimate a long-run "levels model" given in Equation (3), as well as a separate restricted error correction model (RECM) given by Equation (2) to determine the short-run effects and the speed of adjustment If we have established that there is a long-run relationship between the various variables, we will keep all the variables in the long-run model, even some variables are individually not significant.

2.3. Granger Causality Tests

As noted by Granger (1988) [51], if the variables are cointegrated, we should test for short and long run causality between the dependent variable of economic growth and the explanatory variables of energy consumption, real gross fixed capital formation, employment and human capital using the restricted error correction model given in Equation (2). The long run causality is determined by testing the significance of the coefficient of the error correction term. We say that there is a long relationship between economic growth and the different explanatory variables if this coefficient of ECT_{t-1} is negative and statistically significant at a level of 5%. The short run causality between the dependent variable of economic growth and each of the explanatory variables of energy consumption, real gross fixed capital formation, employment and human capital is determined by testing, respectively, the following hypotheses:

Ho: $\gamma_1 = \gamma_2 = \ldots = \gamma_{q1} = 0$; implying that x_1 does not Granger-cause Y in the short run;

Ho: $\delta_1 = \delta_2 = \ldots = \delta_{q2} = 0$; implying that x_2 does not Granger-cause Y in the short run;

Ho: $\mu_1 = \mu_2 = \ldots = \mu_{q3} = 0$; implying that x_3 does not Granger-cause Y in the short run;

Ho: $\lambda_1 = \lambda_2 = \ldots = \lambda_{q4} = 0$; implying that x_4 does not Granger-cause Y in the short run.

We can also test for strong long run causality between economic growth and the explanatory variables of energy consumption, real gross fixed capital formation, employment and human capital by testing, respectively, the following hypotheses:

Ho: $\eta = \gamma_1 = \gamma_2 = \ldots = \gamma_{q1} = 0$; implying that x_1 does not strong Granger-cause Y;

Ho: $\eta = \delta_1 = \delta_2 = \ldots = \delta_{q_2} = 0$: implying that x_2 does not strong Granger-cause Y;

Ho: $\eta = \mu_1 = \mu_2 = \ldots = \mu_{q_3} = 0$: implying that x_3 does not strong Granger-cause Y;

Ho: $\eta = \mu_1 = \mu_2 = \ldots = \mu_{q_3} = 0$: implying that x_4 does not strong Granger-cause Y.

All these tests are determined by the F-statistic of Wald test on coefficient restrictions in restricted ECM given in Equation (2).

3. EMPIRICAL RESULTS

Contrarily to previous studies using the ARDL bounds test to cointegration in the context of VECM, our study is based on a single equation VAR model. As the ARDL bounds test is based on the assumption that the variables are I(0) or I(1), so, before applying this test, we determine the order of integration of all variables using the unit root tests. For all the variables, we use their natural logarithms. The objective is to ensure that none of the variables is integrated of order two because of spurious results and we cannot interpret the values of F-statistics provided by [44] or [50] when we have I(2) variables.

In order to check that none of the variables is integrated of order two, we apply the ADF, PP and DF-GLS tests. The results of the three tests applied to the levels and first differences of the variables are shown in Table 2. According to the three tests of ADF, PP and DF-GLS, we find that real GDP is not stationary at its level, whereas its first difference is found to be stationary. In addition, the three-unit root tests show that energy consumption is integrated of order one. The level of real gross fixed capital formation is found to be not stationary due to ADF and DF-GLS tests whereas it is shown to be stationary due to PP test at a 10% level. According to the three tests, the first difference of real gross fixed capital formation is stationary. The variable employment is found to be integrated of order one according to ADF and DF-GLS tests, while it is shown to be integrated of order zero due to PP test. Finally, human capital is found to be integrated of order zero according to ADF test, while it is shown to be integrated of order one due to PP and DF-GLS tests. Apparently, there are sometimes conflicts between the outcomes of tests; however, we can conclude that neither of variables is integrated of order two.

Table 2. Results of unit root tests.

Variables	ADF	PP	DF-GLS
Y	2.467 (0)	−2.067 (0)	1.021 (0)
x_1	−2.167 (0)	−1.910 (2)	−0.423 (1)
x_2	−2.148 (1)	2.819 (4) ***	−0.561 (1)
x_3	−2.538 (1)	−3.545 (4) **	−0.201 (1)
x_4	−3.730 (1) **	−2.756 (0)	−1.592 (0)
ΔY	−3.337 (0) *	−3.337 (0) *	−1.648 (1) ***
Δx_1	−4.485 (0) *	−4.497 (1) *	−2.896 (0) *
Δx_2	−2.495 (0) **	−2.448 (1) **	−1.832 (0) ***
Δx_3	−3.219 (0) ***	−3.188 (2)	−3.205 (0) **
Δx_4	−3.894 (0) *	−3.937 (2) *	−3.936 (0) *

Note: *, ** and *** denote the significance at the 1%, 5% and 10% levels, respectively; SC determines the optimal lag orders for ADF and DF-GLS tests, while the bandwidth for PP test is determined by the Newey-West using Bartlett kernel' The values between parentheses are the maximum lag length.

The results shown by the different unit root tests suggest the use of bounds test for cointegration framework. In doing so, we estimate a 1-equation VAR model (called also unrestricted ECM) given by Equation (5). This needs to implement the information criteria for selecting the lag-lengths. This is somewhat difficult for the lags of exogenousregressors.

Looking at the different values of Akaike information criterion (AIC), Schwarz criterion (SC) and Hannan–Quinn information criterion (HQ), we see that SC suggests a maximum lag of one. The results of lag order selection criteria are shown in Table 3.

Table 3. Results of lag order selection criteria for unrestricted ECM.

Lag Order	AIC	SC	HQ
1	−3.051	−2.418 *	−2.822
2	−3.026	−2.173	−2.720
3	−3.441 *	−2.364	−3.058 *

Note: * indicates minimum value.

After that, we check for the significance of exogenous variables. As the span of the period is small and finite (41 years), we estimate the model given in Equation (5) by OLS by taking three years as the maximum lag length order for the exogenous regressors. After that, we choose only the regressors, which are significant. The selected ARDL model is of order (1, 1, 3, 0, 0).

The results of diagnostic tests applied to ARDL (1, 1, 3, 0, 0) are shown in Table 4.When we check for the serial independence of the errors of this model using the Breush-Godfrey Lagrange multiplier (LM) test, we find that they are serially independent at the 5% level up to order twelve.

Table 4. Results of diagnostic tests applied to ARDL (1, 1, 3, 0, 0).

Breush-Godfrey LM Test			Normality Test		ARCH Test	
Lag	LM stat	*p*-value	χ^2 *stat*	*p*-value	χ^2 *stat*	*p*-value
1	2.994	0.083	0.812	0.666	0.061 (1)	0.803
2	1.529	0.216				
3	3.127	0.077				
4	3.566	0.058				
5	0.041	0.839				
6	0.001	0.970				
7	1.509	0.219				
8	0.384	0.535				
9	0.0001	0.990				
10	0.829	0.362				
11	0.933	0.333				
12	0.121	0.727				

Value between parentheses is the order of diagnostic test.

The p-values corresponding to the Jarque–Bera normality test indicate that we accept at a 5% level the normality of the error disturbances. The result of the autoregressive conditional heteroskedasticity (ARCH) test shows that the errors of the ARDL model are not heteroskedastic as its p-value is equal to 0.803. Finally, before proceeding to the bounds testing, we verify for the inverse roots of the autoregressive characteristic of our unrestricted ECM. As shown by Figure 2, all these roots are inside the unit circle, which implies that the ARDL model is dynamically stable.

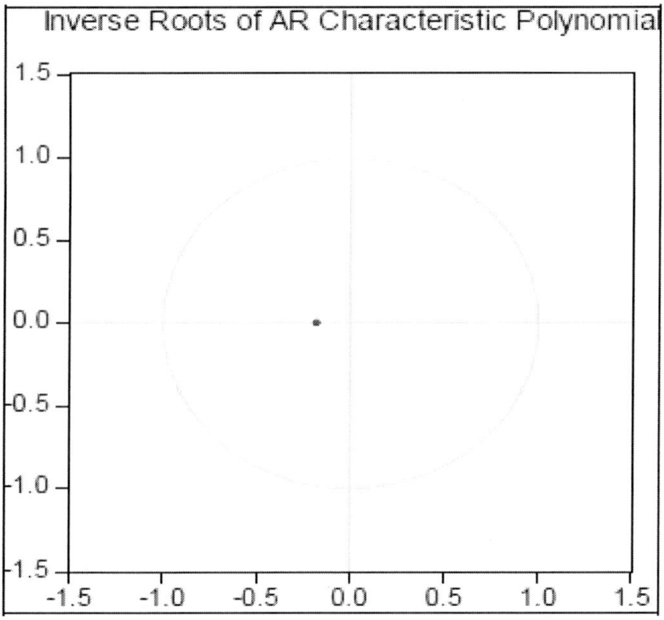

Figure 2. The inverse roots of the associated characteristic ARDL model.

Since the ARDL model passes all diagnostic tests without problem, we apply the bounds testing by checking for the null hypothesis, H_0: $\theta_0 = \theta_1 = \theta_2 = \theta_3 = \theta_4 = 0$. Results of the test are shown in Table 5. The value of F-statistic is equal to 5.355. Therefore, when we go to the bounds test tables of critical values, we use the number of regressors (k = 4). We have not constrained the intercept of our model, and there is no linear trend term included in the ARDL model. As the number of observations is small (T = 42), critical values are collected from [50] for T = 40. The lower and upper bounds at the 10%, 5%, and 1% significance levels are equal to [2.483, 3.647], [2.962, 4.268], and [4.045, 5.898], respectively.

Table 5. The results of ARDL bounds test.

	Bounds Testing for Cointegration	
F-statistic	Optimal lag length	F-statistic
$F_Y(Y/x_1, x_2, x_3, x_4)$	1, 1, 3, 0, 0	5.355 **
	Critical Values	
Significance level	Lower bounds $I(0)$	Upper bounds $I(1)$
1% level	4.045	5.898
5% level	2.962	4.268
10% level	2.483	3.647

Note: The asterisks *, ** and *** denote the significance at 1%, 5% and 10% levels, respectively.

As the value of the F-statistic exceeds the upper bound at the 5% significance level, we can conclude that there is a relationship between economic growth and the various explanatory variables (energy consumption, real gross fixed capital formation, employment and human capital) in the long run.

For testing the dynamic causal relationships between economic growth and the various explanatory variables, we estimate the long run equilibrium model given in Equation (3) by OLS, construct the residuals series, deduce the error correction terms given in Equation (4) and estimate by OLS the restricted ECM given in Equation (2). The results show that the coefficient of the error-correction term, ECT_{t-1}, is negative and significant at 1% level. If the result of the ARDL bounds test shows that there is cointegration between the variables, but the coefficient of the error correction term is positive or negative, but not significant, the model may be misspecified. In addition, if the coefficient of the error-correction term is smaller than −1, it makes no sense and it implies that there is an "over-correction" towards equilibrium ([45]). This is expected because there is cointegration between the various investigated variables. The coefficient of the error-correction term represents the speed of adjustment per period after a short-run shock to the equilibrium relationship. It is equal to −0.637. The magnitude of this coefficient implies that the speed of adjustment is rapid. Nearly 64% of any disequilibrium between economic growth and the inputs is corrected within one year. Thus, given the negative ECT sign, real GDP "moves" to close the disequilibrium gap within two years.

The restricted error correction model, which represents short run dynamics, passes also the diagnostic tests without problems. Results of diagnostic tests are shown in Table 6. Figure 3 shows that the model is dynamically stable because the only root is inside the unit circle and it lies on the X-axis. Accordingly, the short-run dynamics associated with the model are not complicated.

Table 6. Results of diagnostic tests applied to residuals of ECM.

	LM test		Normality test		ARCH test	
Lag	χ^2 *stat*	*p*-value	χ^2 *stat*	*p*-value	χ^2 *stat*	*p*-value
1	1.964	0.161	1.686	0.430	0.693 (1)	0.405
2	5.48×10^{-5}	0.994				
3	2.044	0.152				
4	2.507	0.113				
5	1.177	0.277				
6	0.013	0.906				
7	2.416	0.120				
8	0.901	0.342				
9	0.225	0.634				
10	0.679	0.409				
11	0.701	0.402				
12	0.264	0.606				

Values between parentheses are the order of diagnostic tests.

As shown in Table 6, the results of LM test applied to residuals of ECM imply that the error disturbances are serially independent up to order twelve.

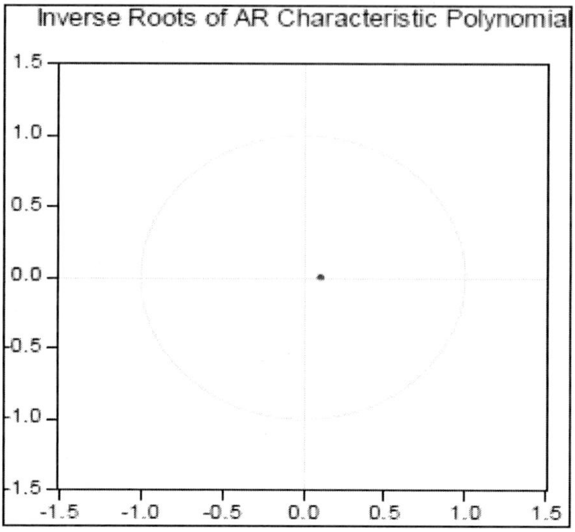

Figure 3. The inverse roots of the associated characteristic RECM.

As we find that the variables are cointegrated when the economic output is the dependent variable, we should employ the Granger causality test in the ECM to determine which exogenous variables can cause economic growth for Saudi Arabia. Long-run causality is determined by the t-significance of the one period lagged error-correction term ECT_{t-1}, whereas short run causality is determined by the joint significance F tests of the lagged explanatory variables. The results of different types of short and long run Granger causality are shown in Table 7. In the short run, the conventional inputs (capital and employment) Granger cause economic growth at 1% level, whereas energy consumption and human capital Granger cause economic growth at a level of 5%. For the long-run causality, the estimated coefficient of ECT_{t-1} is negative and significant at a level of 1%, implying that there is unidirectional causality running from energy consumption, capital, employment and human capital to economic output in the long run. When checking for the strong long run causality, we find that all inputs Granger cause economic growth at even 1% level.

Table 7. The results of Granger causality tests.

Depend. Variable: Δy	$\sum \Delta x_{1j}$	$\sum \Delta x_{2j}$	$\sum \Delta x_{3j}$	$\sum \Delta x_{4j}$	Long-run causality
	F statistics [p-values]				ECT_{t-1} [t-statistic]
Short-run causality	5.98 ** [0.05]	17.21 *** [0.00]	6.88 * [0.00]	4.50 ** [0.03]	−0.637 * [−4.44]
Strong Long-run causality	20.19 * [0.00]	35.50 * [0.00]	21.63 * [0.00]	19.96 * [0.00]	

Note: The asterisks ***, ** and * denote the significance at the 1%, 5% and 10% levels, respectively.

For robustness, as the unit root tests suggest that the five time series can be I(1), we can also use the multivariate cointegration approach of [52,53]. Before applying this test, we determine the lag length for the VAR model. Due to the criterion of AIC, the maximum lag length is equal to 1 whereas it is equal to 5 according to the criteria of SC.

For a lag length equal to 1, the results of trace and Max-Eigen tests are summarized for the five cases in Table 8. According to Max–Eigen test, there is only one cointegrating relationship between the five variables for all the five cases. However, the trace test gives that there are 3 cointegrating relationships for the first case (no intercept or trend in CE or test VAR), and only 1 cointegrating relationship for the four remaining cases. We can conclude that there is significant evidence in favor of only one cointegrating relationship between the five variables, as the second case (intercept but no trend in CE, no intercept in VAR) is more suitable for our study.

Table 8. Results of trace and Max–Eigen tests.

Data Trend	None	None	Linear	Linear	Quadratic
Rank or No. of CEs	No Intercept No Trend	Intercept No Trend	Intercept No Trend	Intercept Trend	Intercept Trend
	Number of Cointegrating relations by model at 5% level				
Trace test	3	1	1	1	1
Max-Eigen test	1	1	1	1	1

When estimating the vector error correction model (VECM), the coefficient of error correction term is negative and statistically significant in only the equation where the dependent variable is economic growth. This implies that the only long run relationship exists when economic growth is the dependent variable. The results given by the multivariate cointegration approach of [52,53] confirm those obtained using the ARDL bounds testing to cointegration framework.

4. DISCUSSION

According to our findings, we affirm that energy consumption strongly causes economic growth, and these results are contradictory to those obtained by previous studies for Saudi Arabia ([31,32,33,34,35,36,37,38]). Hence, our results support the energy-led growth hypothesis. The economic growth of Saudi Arabia may benefit from the extensive use of oil and the high subsidization of oil price. Firstly, energy plays an important role as an input in the production function. From that perspective, the results show a positive contribution of energy consumption to economic activity. In addition, Saudi Arabia is subsidizing fossil fuel products (oil and natural gas products) and electricity. This subsidization is mainly in favor of domestic consumption and domestic and foreign investors.

Saudi Arabia is one of the largest energy consumers in the world. As it is the world's first largest producer of oil and due to the low levels of energy prices, there is a vast wasteful use of energy. Saudi Arabia consumes more than one quarter of its energy production. Total energy primary production is equal to 3.29 times the total energy consumption in 2012 ([54]). The growth rate of total energy consumption is equal to 5.6% (2.2% in the world) per year over the period of 2000–2012 in Saudi Arabia. It is one of the countries, which have a high growth rate of energy consumption in the world after China (7.0%), and Kazakhstan (6.6%). In addition, comparatively to other countries, energy intensity of GDP is very high in Saudi Arabia. For example, for the Saudi Arabia energy intensity of GDP at constant purchasing power parities (expressed in koe/$2005) is equal to 0.310 in 2012, while it is equal to only 0.184 in the world ([54]).

As energy consumption leads to economic growth, energy conservation measures can restrain the economic development of the country. Hence, the energy conservation measures should be based on energy efficiency and addressed with caution. Such measures should include the use of various tariff rates, insulation materials in buildings, more training of energy-efficiency personnel, certification for energy managers and auditors, energy efficiency information and awareness, energy efficiency labels and standards for new equipment, energy audits, and enforcement of energy conservation laws ([55,56]).

According to [55], the use of renewable energy resources (wind and solar) adding to energy efficiency measures can lead to a reduction of 10% in energy consumption in Saudi Arabia. These measures can benefit Saudi Arabia about $6 billion per year as supplementary revenue from fuel exports ([55]). The share of renewable energies in primary consumption is less than 0.1% in Saudi Arabia while it is 12.9% in the world. For example, in Norway that is a natural gas and oil producing country, renewable energies represent about 43.1% of primary energy consumption in 2012.

Energy subsidy plays a major role in the overuse of energy in Saudi Arabia. In Saudi Arabia, energy subsidies were estimated at 10% of its GDP in 2011. These subsidies can create distortions in markets and incentives for wasteful ([57]).

5. CONCLUSIONS

This study tests the energy-led growth hypothesis by examining the relationship between real GDP and energy consumption, employment, real fixed capital formation and human capital using the ARDL bounds testing to cointegration approach for the case of Saudi Arabia. Our results show the presence of a long run relationship between the various variables. Robustness of the results of ARDL testing to cointegration is tested by employing the Johansen multivariate cointegration technique. The two approaches give approximately the same results. All the inputs (conventional and non-conventional) Granger cause economic growth in both the short and long runs. While our results show the importance of energy use to economic activity through the various channels of production, consumption and investment in Saudi Arabia, this must not neglect its environmental consequences and the investment in renewable energy sources. Our findings reaffirm the previous studies stating that energy is not neutral to economic growth.

We are motivated by testing the energy-led growth hypothesis due to the impact of the various conservation policies on economic growth. Energy policies are based, in part, on the energy-growth nexus. Knowing the relationship between economic growth and energy use can help policy makers taking the best decisions of energy management, which are important for environmental and climate changes.

As we find that energy consumption Granger causes economic growth, the adoption of energy conservation policies can limit Saudi economic growth. Hence, policy measures should be based on energy efficiency and the investment in renewable energy sources such as solar and wind where Saudi Arabia has also abundant resources.

Energy efficiency plays both roles. It saves money that can be used in the investment in renewable energies and it reduces greenhouse gases to meet the international commitments on climate change. The investment in renewable energies should help Saudi Arabia to be prepared in the long run to the low carbon economy that is based on clean technologies. Adding to that as suggested by the International Monetary Fund, energy subsidy reforms should be planned in Saudi Arabia.

As energy is overused in Saudi Arabia, future researches on this subject should be dedicated to energy efficiency and environmental efficiency. Reducing the conventional energy use in developed and developing countries is considered an important element in the world's ability to grow sustainably. Likewise, reducing energy consumption is considered a practical solution to many of today's common challenges including global energy shortages; mitigating against further changes in the climate; and health impacts of local air and water pollution. Understanding the factors that influence fluctuations in energy use are of first-order importance for academics and policymakers.

ACKNOWLEDGMENTS

The research leading to this paper was sponsored by Najran University, Kingdom of Saudi Arabia.

AUTHOR CONTRIBUTIONS

Atef Saad Alshehry collected the data, whereas Mounir Belloumi conceived and performed the

experiments using the analysis tools. Both authors analyzed the data and wrote the paper.

CONFLICTS OF INTEREST

The authors declare no conflict of interest.

REFERENCES

1. **Stern, D.I. Energy and economic growth in the USA: A multivariate approach. *Energy Econ.*** 1993, ***15*, 137–150.**

2. Stern, D.I. A multivariate cointegration analysis of the role of energy in the US macroeconomy. *Energy Econ.* **2000**, *22*, 267–283.
3. Cleveland, C.J.; Costanza, R.; Hall, C.A.S.; Kaufmann, R.K. Energy and the US economy: A biophysical perspective. *Science* **1984**, *225*, 890–897.
4. Salamaliki, P.K.; Venetis, I.A. Energy consumption and real GDP in G-7: Multi-horizon causality testing in the presence of capital stock. *Energy Econ.* **2013**, *39*, 108–121.
5. Stern, D.I. The role of energy in economic growth. *Ecol. Econ. Rev.* **2011**, *1219*, 26–51.
6. Pirlogea, C.; Cicea, C. Econometric perspective of the energy consumption and economic growth relation in European Union. *Renew. Sustain. Energy Rev.* **2012**, *16*, 5718–5726.
7. Kraft, J.; Kraft, A. On the relationship between energy and GNP. *J. Energy Dev.* **1978**, *3*, 401–403.

8. Menegaki, A.N. On energy consumption and GDP studies; A meta-analysis of the last two decades. *Renew. Sustain. Energy Rev.* **2014**, *29*, 31–36.
9. Akarca, A.T.; Long, T.V. Relationship between energy and GNP: A reexamination. *J. Energy Dev.* **1980**, *5*, 326–331.
10. Erol, U.; Yu, E.S.H. On the causal relationship between energy and income for industrialized countries. *J. Energy Dev.* **1987**, *13*, 113–122.
11. Yu, E.S.H.; Hwang, B. The relationship between energy and GNP: Further results. *Energy Econ.* **1984**, *6*, 186–190.
12. Engle, R.F.; Granger, C.W.J. Co-integration and error correction: Representation, estimation, and testing. *Econometrica* **1987**, *55*, 251–276.
13. Johansen, S.; Juselius, K. Maximum likelihood estimation and inference on cointegration with applications to the demand for money. *Oxf. Bull. Econ. Stat.* **1990**, *52*, 169–210.
14. Cheng, B.S.; Lai, T.W. An investigation of cointegration and causality between energy consumption and economic activity in Taiwan. *Energy Econ.* **1997**, *19*, 435–444.
15. Chang, T.; Fang, W.; Wen, L.F. Energy consumption, employment, output and temporal causality: Evidence from Taiwan based on cointegration and error-correction modelling techniques. *Appl. Econ.* **2001**, *33*, 1045–1056.
16. Ghali, K.H.; El-Sakka, M.I.T. Energy and output growth in Canada: A multivariate cointegration analysis. *Energy Econ.* **2004**, *26*, 225–238.
17. Soytas, U.; Sari, R. The relationship between energy and production: Evidence from Turkish manufacturing industry. *Energy Econ.* **2007**, *29*, 1151–1165.
18. Yuan, J.; Kang, J.; Zhao, C.; Hu, Z. Energy consumption and economic growth: Evidence from China at both aggregated and disaggregated levels. *Energy Econ.* **2008**, *30*, 3077–3094.
19. Stern, D.I.; Enflo, K. Causality between energy and output in the long-run. *Energy Econ.* **2013**, *39*, 135–146.
20. Sari, R.; Ewing, B.T.; Soytas, U. The relationship between disaggregate energy consumption and industrial production in the United States: An ARDL approach. *Energy Econ.* **2008**, *30*, 2302–2313.

21. Shahbaz, M.; Tang, C.F.; Shahbaz Shabbir, M. Electricity consumption and economic growth nexus in Portugal using cointegration and causality approaches. *Energy Policy* **2011**, *39*, 3529–3536.
22. Lee, C.C.; Chang, C.P.; Chen, P.F. Energy-income causality in OECD countries revisited: The key role of capital stock. *Energy Econ.* **2008**, *30*, 2359–2373.
23. Shahateet, M.I. Modeling Economic Growth and Energy Consumption in Arab Countries: Cointegration and Causality Analysis. *Int. J. Energy Econ. Policy* **2014**, *4*, 349–359.
24. Yildirim, E.; Aslan, A. Energy consumption and economic growth nexus for 17 highly developed OECD countries: Further evidence based on bootstrap-corrected causality tests. *Energy Policy* **2012**, *51*, 985–993.
25. Yalta, T.; Cakar, H. Energy consumption and economic growth in China: A reconciliation. *Energy Policy* **2012**, *41*, 666–675.
26. Dufour, J.-M.; Pelletier, D.; Renault, E. Short run and long run causality in time series: Inference. *J. Econometr.* **2006**, *132*, 337–362.
27. Hill, J.B. Efficient tests of long-run causation in trivariate VAR processes with a rolling window study of the money-income relationship. *J. Appl. Econometr.* **2007**, *22*, 747–765.
28. Ayres, R.; Voudouris, V. The economic growth enigma: Capital, labor and useful energy? *Energy Policy* **2014**, *64*, 16–28.
29. Alkhathlan, K.; Alam, M.; Javid, M. Carbon dioxide emissions, energy consumption and economic growth in Saudi Arabia: A multivariate cointegration analysis. *Br. J. Econ. Manag. Trade* **2012**, *2*, 327–339.
30. Alqudair, K. Causal Relationship between Energy Consumption and Economic Growth in the Kingdom of Saudi Arabia. *J. Energy Dev.* **2012**, *37*, 129–142.
31. Al-Iriani, M.A. Energy–GDP relationship revisited: An example from GCC countries using panel Causality. *Energy Policy* **2006**, *34*, 3342–3350.
32. Mehrara, M. Energy consumption and economic growth: The case of oil exporting countries. *Energy Policy* **2007**, *35*, 2939–2945.

33. Squalli, J. Electricity consumption and economic growth: Bounds and causality analyses for OPEC members. *Energy Econ.* **2007**, *29*, 1192–1205.
34. Narayan, P.K.; Smyth, R. Multivariate granger causality between electricity consumption, exports and GDP: Evidence from a panel of Middle Eastern countries. *Energy Policy* **2009**, *37*, 229–236.
35. Sadorsky, P. Trade and energy consumption in the Middle East. *Energy Econ.* **2011**, *33*, 739–749.
36. Hossein, A.; Yazdan, G.F.; Ehsan, A.G. The Relationship between Energy Consumption, Energy Prices and Economic Growth: Case Study (OPEC Countries). *OPEC Energy Rev.* **2012**, *36*, 272–286.
37. Damette, O.; Seghir, M. Energy as a driver of growth in oil exporting countries? *Energy Econ.* **2013**, *37*, 193–199.
38. Mohammadi, H.; Parvaresh, P. Energy consumption and output: Evidence from a panel of 14 oil-exporting countries. *Energy Econ.* **2014**, *41*, 41–46.
39. WDI. *World Development Indicators*; World Bank: Washington, DC, USA, 2013.
40. The Conference Board Total Economy Database™, January 2014. Available online: Http://www.conference-board.org/data/economydatabase/ (accessed on 13 May 2014).
41. Balasubramanyam, V.N.; Salisu, M.A.; Sapsford, D. Foreign direct investment and growth in EP and IS countries. *Econ. J.* **1996**, *106*, 92–105.
42. Belloumi, M. The relationship between trade, FDI and economic growth in Tunisia: An application of the autoregressive distributed lag model. Economic Systems **2014,** 38, 269–287.
43. Pesaran, M.; Shin, Y. An Autoregressive Distributed Lag Modeling Approach to Cointegration Analysis. In *Proceedings of the Econometrics and Economic Theory in the 20th Century: The Ragnar Frisch centennial Symposium*; Econometric Society Monographs Book 31; Strom, S., Ed.; Cambridge University Press: Cambridge, UK, 1999.

44. Pesaran, M.H.; Shin, Y.; Smith, R. Bounds testing approaches to the analysis of level relationships. *J. Appl. Econometr.* **2001**, *16*, 289–326.
45. Giles, D.E. ARDL models–Part II–Bounds Tests. Available online: http://davegiles.blogspost.com/ 2013/06/ardl-models-part-ii-bounds-tests.html (accessed on 13 April 2014).
46. Harris, R.; Sollis, R. *Applied Time Series Modelling and Forecasting*; Wiley: Chichester, UK, 2003.
47. Dickey, D.A.; Fuller, W.A. Distribution of the estimators for autoregressive time series with a unit root. *J. Am. Stat. Assoc.* **1979**, *74*, 427–431.
48. Phillips, P.C.B.; Perron, P. Testing for a unit root in time series regression. *Biometrika* **1988**, *75*, 335–346.
49. Elliot, G.; Rothenberg, T.J.; Stock, J.H. Efficient tests for an autoregressive unit root. *Econometrica* **1996**, *64*, 813–836.
50. Narayan, P.K. The saving and investment nexus for China: Evidence from cointegration tests. *Appl. Econ.* **2005**, *37*, 1979–1990.
51. Granger, C.W.J. Causality, cointegration and control. *J. Econ. Dyn. Control* **1988**, *12*, 551–559.
52. Johansen, S. Estimation and hypothesis testing of cointegrated vectors in Gaussian vector autoregressive models. *Econometrica* **1991**, *59*, 1551–1580.
53. Johansen, S. *Likelihood-Based Inference in Cointegrated Vector Autoregressive Models*; Oxford University Press: Oxford, UK, 1995.
54. BP Statistical Review of World Energy June 2013. Available online: http://www.bp.com/ statisticalreview (accessed on 12 May 2014).
55. Alyousef, Y.; Abu-ebid, M. Energy Efficiency Initiatives for Saudi Arabia on Supply and Demand Sides, Energy Efficiency—A Bridge to Low Carbon Economy; Morvaj, Z., Ed.; InTech: Rijeca,Croatia, 2012.
56. Alshehri, A.; Hussain, A.; Mobarak, Y. Energy-conversion measures in the industries of Saudi Arabia and development of methodology for certification of energy personnel in the Kingdom. *Energy Policy* **2014**, *64*, 203–208.

57. International Monetary Fund (IMF). Energy Subsidies in the Middle East and North Africa: Lessons for Reform. Available online: http://www.imf.org/external/np/fad/subsidies/pdf/menanote.pdf (accessed on 21 April 2014).

13

CHAPTER

Review of Women and Society in Saudi Arabia

Yahya Al Alhareth[1],, Yasra Al Alhareth[1], Ibtisam Al Dighrir[1]

[1]*General Administration of Education in Najran Region, Ministry of Education, Riyadh, Kingdom of Saudi Arabia*

ABSTRACT

Saudi society is a unique mix between religion and culture, which poses difficulties for the government over education for women. The position of women in this society is complicated and they have to face a lot of barriers to get an education as they live under male authority all the time. Thereby, this paper will review the literature on women and society in Saudi Arabia and its relation to their educational achievement, considering several different aspects including: Feminist theory, Islamic feminism in Saudi society, the status of women in Saudi society and the Holy Book of the Muslims (Qur'an) as well as their comparison in both.

Keywords: Feminist theory, Islamic feminism, Saudi society, women's situation

1 INTRODUCTION

Saudi Arabia is a socially and religiously conservative country [24]. Its has a high cultural homogeneity based on tribal and Islamic affiliations and therefore has a unique and complex culture. Hence it is difficult to differentiate between Islamic principles and Arabic customs [2]. Some customs, such as the belief that women should not drive cars or practise Law or Engineering are not from Islamic law but have become entrenched in the culture [16]. Women's function in wider society is limited and Saudi Arabia has one of the lowest participation of women in the workplace, particularly from graduates. Yet, this is needed for the country to achieve progress [ibid]. Therefore, the government faces great challenges if it is to achieve its goal of development and fundamental changes in the way society is conducted are needed.

2. FEMINIST THEORY

Feminism is a belief in social, economic as well as political equality of the two genders [17]. It recognises and criticises male supremacy while making efforts to change it. According to reference [17], this theory was born out of the movement that seeks to empower women all over the world. It focuses on gender inequality through women's social roles and experiences, social relations with males and also the promotion of women's rights [6]. Feminism seeks to demonstrate the role as well as the importance of women in society, to reveal that women in the past have been subordinates to their male counterparts, and to create gender equality. Feminists generally fight for gender equality *"and argue that women should have an equal share in society's opportunities"* as well as other resources that are scarce [17-21][17].

In principle, the philosophical understanding of the feminist theory explicates the world view of gender inequality [31]. In this regard, the theory explains the social roles of women in society including their feminist politics and experiences in diverse field discourses [9]. The principal relevance of the feminist theory is to define and analyse the critical possibilities affiliated to gender inequality [31]. Feminism asserts that the position of the woman in society is determined by institutional and social factors, in addition, there is ample evidence demonstrating that women have been continuously treated as inferior citizens [13]. As a mode of analysis, feminism is grounded in the link between the social institutions which influence the daily life of individuals and in a desire for social change. As a theory, feminism is both scientific and political. According to reference [13], feminist scholars are identified by their political interest in protesting against women's oppression and view their scholarly work as a contribution to comprehensive understanding of why and how liberation of women should be achieved.

It is important to note that feminism has no universally accepted or single definition. An analysis of feminism demonstrates that the theory is diverse in its definitions [17]. They include a description of the present situation or issue, an explanation of its roots, a review of the positive and negative aspects of the current issue, and proposals as well as strategies to produce social change in the pursuit of the declared goals and values [ibid].

In the recent past, the government has developed campaigns against gender segregation with the major stakeholders endeavouring to ensure change in the education processes within the Saudi political system and promoting equality by institutionalising more female learning institutions to enhance the number of Saudi women reaching higher education [23]. Importantly, the scrutiny on women's rights to bring about gender equality, particularly in education and leadership, defines the value-free direction within the political systems, not only in Saudi Arabia, but also in global political systems [26]. The processes involved in mitigating this sexual objectification and stereotyping directed against women in Saudi society with regard to education achievement include education equity by opening more institutions of higher learning for women, mainstreaming the school curricula for girls' institutions of learning and incorporating subjects and career fields that do not discriminate against the interaction between the males and females in this society [16]. Transitions from social and humanity fields to technology fields are including incorporation of ICT in the girls' curriculum which is the major effort. Essentially, this incorporation will foster the use of ICT to engender e-learning in such schools [25].

Feminist strategies concerning technology generally involve looking for non-threatening ways that can be used to enable women enhance their technical competence so they rely less on men. These efforts are however faced by a general problem which makes achievement of the intended goals a challenge. The main problem is that predicting the effects of new technologies is not always possible and by the time negative consequences become apparent, the technology's artifactual form as well as social interests that characterise it usually have become so embedded that they present a major barrier to change [31]. Feminists therefore argue that there is a need for strategies to be developed to mediate the process of designing new technologies as well as the use of these technologies. This study draws from this notion and assumes that the use of e-learning can help Saudi women to achieve their educational goals but their ability to access and use it freely should firstly be understood.

2.1. Islamic Feminism

Islamic feminism attempts to work within the values of Islam, not against them, by offering social benefits in a culturally satisfactory and sustainable way to families through enhanced opportunities for daughters, sisters, wives and mothers [7]. Applying feminism in a Muslim society can however be challenging. Reference [22]explains that feminism in Islamic societies is often viewed as a secular and Western ideology or 'an alien' assault to the Islamic religion and is often not supported. Reference [22] also notes that achieving equality in the family is a major challenge for Muslim feminists. Reference [1] explains that though some equality has been achieved in the public domain for many countries, gender inequality in families is still very common and sustained by state-backed laws which are based on Islamic beliefs. This might affect the achievement of the main goal of this study, which is to enhance women's ability to access and use e-learning freely. Gender inequality might hinder some families from allowing the womenfolk to take online courses because of the traditional belief that the place of the woman is at home and not 'out there' as explained by reference [29].

The ideology of feminism as an attempt to empower women globally following the acknowledgment and critique of male dominion as well as the efforts to bring change to this norm, is the foundation of Islamic feminism, which entails definition of the roles of an Islamic woman [18]. Principally, it is a movement that requires women's rights support with a focus on social justice and gender equality from an Islamic focal point [20]. In this regard, gender manipulation in terms of dressing, religious practices, politics and public life, which directly affects education achievement in the Muslim fraternity are considered for transition. Although the concern is mainly due to references to feminism within an Islamic construct, the utility of secular and non-Islamic feminism discourses incorporated is shown from a global feminist approach to ensure change in the Middle-Eastern world, Saudi Arabia included [15].

The political and social constructs embraced by Arabian countries such as Saudi Arabia are established within the dominion of male bigots and advocacy of women's leadership is not common place [ibid]. Under the current transition plans, restructuring of the education system, which is the pillar of knowledge, achievement and equity, is the main agenda in which females are provided with tailored education curricula, not only to suit women in their social and biological functional life, but also to develop them in diverse subject areas such as architecture, medicine, engineering and other technology-oriented fields [20].

The expansion of the knowledge base for Muslim women is geared by the feminist paradigm and mitigation of menial superiority complex in order to perpetuate naturalisation and recuperate gender equality as the core idea in the Islamic being [23]. A better understanding of the Islamic feminism paradigm is provided by the force of Muslim women who explain their educational needs beyond the passive common knowledge, but also by the engagement of religious practices such as Ijtihad (Rethinking Islam) without the salience rooted in the thinking and activism of their gender [18]. The manner brought by education limitations has so far surpassed considering the increased awareness of the importance of knowledge and skills garnered via education achievement, and the willingness to implement reforms within the education system delivery processes.

3. SAUDI SOCIETY

Saudi society is built around tribal and Islamic affiliations [24] and it is difficult to differentiate between Islamic laws and Arabic traditional norms [2]. Major cities are generally less conservative than the remote areas and smaller towns and cities, though Riyadh, the capital and centre of Wahabism in the middle of the country, is seen to be more conservative than the second city, the coastal port of Jeddah in the West, which is more cosmopolitan [8]. Saudi citizens embrace the cultural and religious attributes of society in totality while the norms for public behaviour are highly regarded as conservative.

3.1. The Status of Women in Saudi Society

The position of women in Saudi society, especially in the public domain, is complicated [15]. The concept of male guardianship has been, and still is, one of the strong norms for Islamic women in Saudi Arabia [16]. This phenomenon has impacted on women taking up higher education and in particular women seeking education from international countries. Every woman is entitled to a male guardian, regardless of her age, by law. Politically, women have not been allowed to participate in any form of elections [ibid]. Recently, the king is pledging to allow women candidates to run for seats in the consultative assembly in the local elections and they will be allowed to vote [4].

The power imbalance between men and women in Saudi Arabia is not specifically stated in the laws of the country, but rather, is embedded in the social and government structures and practices [12]. Women lack access to the justice system and thus rely on their male counterparts to represent them. Such imbalance also affects their education since it is difficult for women to voice any concerns that they may have about the existing education system. This practice implies that women's ability to be and do whatever they want is limited, which must be improved. Another important area that needs improvement is the overall freedom of women in Saudi Arabia since current limitations mean that they are unable to travel beyond their home, hence their access to education opportunities is limited. This is another requirement of women's capability which needs to be focused on and should not be ignored.

In addition, the extent to which women participate in decisions relating to their own marriage is restricted by the family and male counterparts [12]. This indicates that Saudi women suffer from the exclusion from participating and playing vital roles in their society and the deprivation from getting their rights. In this regard, reinforcing women's power is required to enhance their ability to be a valuable person in their society by doing things that are important to them and live as they want. As these practices develop from the nature of Saudi society with participation from government policies, according to reference [30, p. 15], they fall under *active* exclusion *"done by the government"* and *passive* exclusion *"result from a set of circumstances"*, the conservative and tribal society culture in this study. The women in Saudi Arabia lack equal access to employment and economic opportunities, on top of what the scope for women to manage their own wealth is limited by social and religious factors [12]. As a result, women are not in a position to take up education opportunities. Even methods such as e-learning, which as a new form of delivery could open up opportunities for women to engage with education more freely, require substantial investment from the leaner.

The Sharia laws, as well as the tribal culture, define the gender-based roles within Saudi society [20]. These cultural aspects, particularly the tribal cultural practices, have helped shaping the position of women in society and subjugating women to gender segregation in diverse aspects of society. From a broader perspective, approximately 80% of women in Saudi society, as depicted by a government poll in 2006, are opposed to the practices of women driving or working in the same environment as men [ibid]. This shows that the majority of women are against the reforms which might release them from their often perceived suppression [28]. However, there are other groups of women, who live in the main cities e.g. Riyadh, Jeddah and in the Eastern region, who have got a high education degree, probably obtained from abroad, and who are not happy with the current status of women in society. They are highly motivated to enhance their situation so they try from time to time to put pressure on the government to change and improve their status within the community by calling women all over the country to drive cars in spite of the government and society not allowing them to do so. This shows that some changes are happening within the Saudi women community which the government needs to be ready to face by taking some decisions in favour of women as King Abdullah did when allowing 30 women to take a place in the Shura Council (called Majlis Al-Shura) [5]. This exercise of capability should be improved as it would lead women to moving forward towards being treated as humans in their society.

Notably, women make up only 21% of the Saudi workforce [28]. With the adoption of the current changes to transform male dominion, allow more equitable resource allocation between the two genders and greater gender parity, along with increased uptake of higher education by women, Saudi Arabia is considered to be one of the Islamic countries achieving the highest economic development [32]. However, it is clear that women in Saudi Arabia still have few or no political and/or social rights.

The position of women in Saudi Arabia also differs from that of other Islamic communities demonstrating that the more conservative society has evolved. Taking as an example Indonesia, in comparison, Saudi women have fewer rights and freedom. In Indonesia, there is no gender segregation in relation to education and public work as is the case in Saudi Arabia [19]. Women are allowed to enjoy higher education with their male counterparts. Driving is not an issue for Indonesian women [14]. More so, travelling for higher education or for international employment does not call for the company of a male guardian. Interestingly, the Saudi government and its society see this diversity as a moral decline of the Muslims in the Indonesian community [ibid]. This points to the likelihood of changes in such practices being slow to come to Saudi Arabia, if indeed they happen at all. As a result, such methods as e-learning will provide opportunities which will appeal to both genders and satisfy the expectations of society for the foreseeable future.

3.2. The Status of Women in the Holy Book of Muslim (Qur'an)

The Holy Book of the Islamic religion, the Qur'an, has provided various teachings defining the place of women in Muslim society [10]. At some point, the Qur'an defines males as superior to women by saying that, "*Men have authority over women because God has made the one superior to the other...*" (Holy Qur'an, 4:34) It also shows men a degree above women in many ways by saying that, "*...Of course, men are a degree above them in status...*" (Holy Qur'an, 2:228). The Qur'an give each men a double share of the inheritance over what each woman gets by saying that, "*The share of the male shall be twice that of a female*" (Holy Qur'an, 4:11). It explains the roles of both males and females based on their gender, making that of males to dominate over females [10]. For instance, the Qur'an has provisions in many chapters regarding the virtues of a modest woman [11] and has appealed against female infanticide, shunning abortion as inhumane [10].

Additionally, according to the Qur'an, there must be education equity with men and women receiving education in the same way [11]. Moreover, it explains the way women should be treated by their husbands, defining extension of kindness from men to women [23] by saying that, "*...Wives have the same rights as the husbands have on them in accordance with the generally known principles*" (Holy Qur'an, 2:228). Specifically, the Holy Book describes the conduct of men explaining the character of an ideal believer in terms of best practices and deeds directed to the wives. It is the understanding of the Qur'an that has been manipulated to suit the needs of men to suppress women by exercising their dominance [ibid].

Equality has all its facets delineated in the Holy Book of Islam, which views humankind as made of equals in the eyes of Allah, without any distinction [10]. Moreover, it is plain that the equality between women and men is brought about by the mere essence of righteous deeds, which uphold the moral standing of one human being over the other and not gender disparities [ibid] by saying that, "*...the most noble of you in the sight of Allah is the most righteous of you...*" (Holy Qur'an, 49:13). Enormous respect, therefore, has been accorded to the righteous Muslim men and women described in the Qur'an, who are pious, to demarcate right from wrong in the eyes of Allah [10]. The role of women from the Islamic teachings, in the Qur'an, has historically been to serve the religious communities in diverse capacities, as leaders, health care providers and teachers as well as in the military. In interpretation, the Islamic belief explains equality, not to place men and women at the same level of dominance, but to explain their differences in terms of physical and emotional strengths to recognise their roles in their society [ibid]. Based on the above discussion, the Holy Book (Qur'an) offers capabilities that benefit women such as their right to make their own decision about which things are suitable for them in Islamic societies, but the structure of these societies gives men the power to control these capabilities and change them to serve their needs.

3.3. A Comparison between Women Place in Saudi Society and the Holy Book (Qur'an)

The concept of inferiority, which is projected onto Muslim women, is only an unconventional behavioural reduction resulting from uncouth interpretation of the Qur'an [27]. There are many indications in the Qur'an that orient women towards many spheres of life, disregarding the gender ideology, by elevating the status of Islamic women [20]. The Muslim society in Saudi Arabia, and the world at large, belittles the achievements of Islamic women by exercising norms that ensure male dominion over females in general practices, including in education [27]. The reflection of women in the Qur'an does not entail any segregation prohibiting intermingling between women and men, but in Saudi society, women are only allowed to live a private life without mixing in any way with men other than their relatives. The use of different entrances and limitations regarding the sharing of common eating places hinder women from studying subjects related to engineering and law as well as technologically oriented subjects [3].

Many practices in Saudi society, such as women not being allowed to work, travel, study and marry without first gaining authorisation from a male guardian are laws that do not have any backing from the Qur'an [27]. This indicates that the role that woman guardian play in Saudi society is fundamental and transferred from male to another. For example, when women do not have any male relatives, they do not become responsible for themselves but they become the responsibility of the judge [16]. This practice of capability should be reduced while other types must be improved like the independence of women, if it is identified as a threat to individuals in the family who feel thwarted by gender equality, or males with political power who identify gender equality as an endeavour that could render them vulnerable to power inferiority [3]. The teachings of the Holy Book and their portrayal of women regard both genders equally in many aspects of general life, however, women are not allowed to drive or travel alone in Saudi society even if it is not prohibited by the Qur'an [27].

4. CONCLUSION

Saudi society is a unique mix between religion and culture, which poses difficulties for the government over education for women. The position of women in this society is complicated and they have to face a lot of barriers to get an education as they live under male authority all the time. This situation is against their status in the Holy Book (Qur'an) which offers capabilities that benefit women, such as their right to make their own decisions about which things are suitable for them in Islamic societies, but the structure of these societies gives men the power to control these capabilities and change them to serve their needs. Therefore, the status of women in such societies needs to be enhanced by treating them with more respect and making sure their rights as human are respected as such ways would improve their chance of completing their education.

REFERENCES

1. Ahmadi, F., (2006), Islamic Feminism in Iran, 'Feminism in a New Islamic Context,' Journal of Feminist Studies in Religion, 1: pp. 34-53.

2. Al Lily, A. E. A., (2011). On line and under veil: Technology-facilitated communication and Saudi female experience within academia. Technology in Society, 33 (1-2): pp. 119-127.

3. Al-Fahad, F.N., (2010), The Learners' Satisfaction Toward Online E-Learning Implemented In The College Of Applied Studies And Community Service, King Saud University, Saudi Arabia: Can E-Learning Replace the Conventional System of Education?, Turkish Online Journal of Distance Education, 11 (2): pp. 61-73.

4. BBC, (2011), Women in Saudi Arabia to vote and run in elections [online], BBC News Middle East, 25-09-2011, available at: , [Accessed: 20/09/2014].

5. BBC, (2013), Saudi Arabia's king appoints women to Shura Council [online], BBC News Middle East, 11th January 2013, available at: http://www.bbc.co.uk/news/world-middle-east-20986428, [Accessed: 19/10/2014].

6. Brym, R. J. and Lie, J., (2010), Sociology: Your Compass for a New World, 2nd ed, Cengage Learning, USA.

7. Coleman I., (2011), Women, Islam, and the Push for Reform in the Muslim World [online], Solution Journal, 2 (2): pp. 42-51, Available at: , [Accessed: 26/11/2014].

8. Cordesman, A. H., (2003), Saudi Arabia Enters the Twenty-First Century: The Political, Foreign Policy, Economic, and Energy Dimensions. Westport, CT: Praeger.

9. Deaver, S., (1980), The contemporary Saudi women. In: Bourguignon E, ed. A world of women: anthropological studies of women in the societies of the World. New York: Praeger.

10. Doumato, E., (2000), Getting God's Ear: Women, Islam, and Healing in Saudi Arabia and the Gulf. New York: Columbia University Press.

11. Doumato, E., (2002), Women and Work in Saudi Arabia: How flexible are Islamic margins? Middle East Journal, 52 (2), Spring, 582.

12. Doumato, E., (2010), Saudi Arabia, In Sanja Kelly and Julia Breslin, eds., Women's Rights in the Middle East and North

Africa, New York, NY: Freedom House; Lanham, MD: Rowman & Littlefield, 2010', pp. 2-30.

13. Evans, M., (2011), doing gender: Gender and women's studies in the twenty first centuries, Women's Studies International Forum, 34: pp. 603-610.

14. Faiza S., (2005), Saudi women recall a day of driving, [Online], The Christian Science Monitor, [Online] available at: , [Accessed: 15/11/2014]

15. Fierke, K. M. and Jørgensen, K. E. (eds.)., (2001), Constructing International Relations: the Next Generation, Armonk: M. E. Sharpe.

16. Hamdan, A., (2005), Women and education in Saudi Arabia: Challenges and achievements. International Education Journal, 6 (1), 42-64.

17. Hurley et al., (2008), Futures studies and Feminism, FUTURES, 40: pp. 388-407.

18. Kaufman, M., (1999), Men, Feminism, and Men's Contradictory Experiences of Power, London, UK: SAGE Publications.

19. Kendall, B., (2006), Saudi Arabia's unseen reform, [online], BBC News, Middle East, 26th April 2006, Available at: . [Accessed; 17/10/2014].

20. Leslie, L. (2011) Saudi Feminism doesn't Mirror Western Ideas. Muslim Voice, [Online] Available at: <> [Accessed: 23/11/2014].

21. Lord, M., Greiter, A. and Tursunovic, Z., (2012), Feminist Theory, [online], available at www.soc.iastate.edu/sapp/Feminist.ppt, [Accessed: 10/11/2014].

22. Margot, B., (2011), From Islamic Feminism to a Muslim Holistic Feminism, IDS Bulletin, 42 (1): pp. 78-87

23. Mehran, G., (2003), The Paradox of tradition and modernity in female education in the Islamic republic of Iran, Comparative Education Review, 47 (3): pp. 269-286.

24. Metz, H. C., (1992), Saudi Arabia: A Country Study, Washington: GPO for the Library of Congress, [Online] Available at: <> [Accessed: 23/10/2014].

25. Olaniyi, S. S., (2006), E-Learning Technology: The Nigeria Experience, A paper presented at Shape the Change XXIII FIG Congress, October 8-13, Munich Germany.

26. Prokop, M., (2003), Saudi Arabia: The politics of education, International Affairs, 79(1): pp. 77-89.

27. Roy, D., (1992), Saudi Arabian education: development policy. Middle Eastern Studies, 28: pp. 477-508.

28. Saudi Gazette, (2008), Business: Kingdom's e-learning industry to reach $125 million this year. The Saudi Gazette, 26th April.

29. Sechzer, J., (2004), Islam and Woman: Where Tradition Meets Modernity: History and Interpretations of Islamic Women's Status,' Sex Roles, 51 (5/6): pp. 263-272

30. Sen, A., (2000), Social Exclusion: Concept, Application, and Scrutiny: Asian Development Bank.

31. Wajcman, J., (1991), Feminism Confronts Technology, Cambridge: Polity Press.

32. Wiseman, A.W., Sadaawi, A. & Alromi, A.H., (2008), Educational Indicators and National Development in Saudi Arabia, paper presented at the 3rd IEA International Research Conference 18-20 September, Taipei City, Taiwan.

14

CHAPTER

Impact of Foreign Investment in the Yemen's Economic Growth: The Country Political Stability as a Main Issue

Anwar Salem Musibah[1], Arfan Shahzad[1] &
Faudziah Hanim Bt Fadzil[1]

[1] Othman Yeop Abdullah Graduate School of Business, University Utara Malaysia, Malaysia

ABSTRACT

This paper investigates the moderating role of political stability in the Foreign Direct Investment (FDI) inflows into Yemen over the last two decades. Augmented Dickey Fuller (ADF) test was employed to check the stationary of the data. Following the ADF test, the standard and hierarchal regression approaches were used for the analysis. The standard regression results show that the GDP growth rate has significant negative effects on FDI inflows into Yemen while exchange rate, inflation rate, balance of payment, and gross national income have no effect on the FDI inflow in the country. However, when the moderating variable, political stability is used together with other variables such as exchange rate, inflation rate, balance of payment and gross national income, the results of hierarchical regression indicate that these variables are important determinants of FDI inflows into the country. Therefore, the results suggest that political stability is critical for the future growth of Yemen economy.

Keywords: FDI inflows, political stability, gross national income, GDP growth rate, hierarchical regression, Yemen

1 INTRODUCTION

It has been extensively known in theory and practice that foreign direct investment in a country often leads to many economic advantages such as foreign exchange improvement, technology transfer, organizational framework and managerial skills, improvement in the balance of payment, job creation and promotion of the export of the countries (Shahzad et al., 2013; UNCTAD, 2011; Crespo & Fontura, 2007; Gorg & Greenaway, 2004; Brooks et al., 2003). Few famous economists have claimed that FDI can also lead to the maximization of domestic investment via its linkages (both forward and backward) in the process of encouraging both innovation and economic growth of the country (Badr & Ayed, 2015; Musibah et al., 2014; Omri & kahouli, 2014; Temiz & Gokmen, 2014; Shahzad et al., 2013; Awan et al., 2011; Brooks et al., 2003)

The financial and economic systems integration through social and cultural aspects in a phenomenon known as globalization has transformed the world into a small village. Globalization has introduced opportunities for success, but the inherent risks associated with it have also been multiplied. In the context of the financial system, foreign direct investment (FDI) is deemed to be the core globalization component (Cho, 2004). In other words, FDI is referred to as the core globalization element in the global economy (Anyanwu, 2012). It consists of the stock purchases, earnings reinvestment, and lending of funds to a foreign subsidiary or a foreign branch (Duce, 2003). Overall, the FDI inflow is significantly to the developed and developing nations as extensively acknowledged in literature dedicated to economics. Over the last ten years of the 20th century, FDI inflows have shown an increasing trend that doubles that of the world economy, trade flows (Rajana et al., 2008; Sinani & Meyer, 2004). The FDI contribution to the host country's national economy is expected to positively influence the employment opportunities, improve the managerial productivity of capital in the industrial sector, increase foreign trade and economic growth with the corresponding increase in technology shift (UNCTAD, 2011; Ifaro et al., 2004). The FDI benefits of the economy of the host country further facilitate the superior utilization of available raw resources, improve management and marketing methods, provide access to up-to-date technologies, and improve human capital via job training and HRM strategy. Aside from the above, foreign money inflows reserves can be used to finance current account trade deficits of balance of payments. Contrary to the external debt, money inflows via FDI do not entail debt redemption and interest liabilities. In the past years, several developing nations have established sweeping reforms towards liberalization and these have led to dynamic competition among these countries on the global level.

Entry barriers and control laid down on the business activities of foreign entry in these countries are eradicated to pave way for specific incentives and business facilitating policies like tax rebates, export zones creation, among others.

A dynamic competition for the FDI inflows attraction exists among developing countries as novel challenges are encapsulating growth opportunities under the 21st century economic dynamism.

Moreover, developing countries are providing incentive packages to attract foreign investors. Countries, the world over are attempting to enhance the basis of their economic to cost on their macroeconomic policies (UNCTAD, 2010; Pajunen, 2008). Many researchers have analyzed the role of FDI in the growth of several economies to investigate the investment-growth relations. It is assumed that FDI is a significant source for obtaining capital, up-to-date technology, managerial skills, enhanced marketing know-how and output for current exports. The FDI-trade relationship is characterized by two main channels in the host country. First, countries having great degrees of openness are ostensibly attracting more FDI inflows. Technically, the openness degree is gauged via trade GDP ratio. Second, the FDI inflows can impact the trade flows via technology transfer and expansion of industrial output in the export sector (Chowdhury & Mavrotas, 2006).

As previously mentioned, FDI is extensively acknowledged as a primary basis of foreign investment in high tech industries and growth process in the context of an under developing country, and thus, it is considered to be the driver of economic growth in the global level. This holds true for both IMF and the World Bank who also advocate that FDI is a vital source of the development process, planning and programming of developing country under the aim of the 21st century globalization. Based on the World Investment Report (WIR) annually published by UNCTAD, the role and issues concerning FDI inflows in the world economy have been time and again examined. Accordingly, based on the WRI issues report, it is significant to conduct a review of the growth trend exhibited by FDI inflows and outflows in the global economy and major global economic units, like developed and developing economies. In the past twenty years, the growth of FDI on a global scale and its economic significance have been distinct and expedient compared to trade flows, particularly in the world's topmost superior industrial economies such as developed and developing economies as reported in Table 1.

Table 1. Worldwide FDI during the period of 2000-2013

Year	World	Developing Economies	Developed Economies	MENA	GCC	Yemen
2000	1,418,788	192,178	1,226,610	12,594	391	6
2001	839,780	193,559	646,221	11,656	1,957	155
2002	625,815	173,726	452,089	11,786	1,515	114
2003	598,860	183,285	415,574	20,660	6,134	-89
2004	733,597	280,770	452,827	29,500	14,145	144
2005	986,853	328,655	658,197	53,142	28,318	-302
2006	1,474,955	440,201	1,034,754	84,936	39,232	1121
2007	1,999,074	607,681	1,391,393	90,183	48,405	917
2008	1,817,004	742,906	1,074,098	107,601	61,698	1554
2009	1,216,805	535,798	681,007	87,110	51,441	129
2010	1,411,137	587,632	823,505	73,200	41,258	189
2011	1,654,283	706,035	948,248	54,497	26,275	-518
2012	1,353,930	671,825	682,105	62,553	26,368	-529
2013	1,451,676	733,135	718,541	103,278	23,888	-133

Sources: Foreign Direct Investment Inflows: UNCTAD 2013.

As noted, the majority of the studies have concentrated in certain regions and countries. For example, Mhlanga, Blalock & Christy (2010) on the Southern African Development Community, Vijayakumar, et al., (2010) on BRICS, Mohamed & Sidiropoulos (2010) on the Middle East, North African (MENA) countries, Kumar & Chadha (2009) on India, Cheung & Qian (2009) on China, Asiedu (2006) focused on Sub-Saharan Africa (SSA) and Deichmann, Karidis & Sayek (2003) on Hungary, Poland and the Baltic region. In studies providing extensive analysis, the SAARC region covering Pakistan, Sir Lanka, India, Nepal and Bangladesh has received the least attention. Only a very few studies has covered a wider range of countries and determinants. In the Middle east region covering Yemen, Saudi Arabia, Iraq, Egypt, Syria, United Arab Emirates , Jordan , Palestine, Lebanon, Oman, Kuwait, Qatar ,and Bahrain, least attention has been paid by the researchers to provide a comprehensive analysis.

Developing countries are interested in attracting FDI for many reasons. Several developing nations such as Yemen have been facing challenges in terms of closing the saving-investment gap and FDI can impact the boost the economic growth by reducing this gap, facilitating new technology relocation into the country, creating jobs for the nation and expanding national output and growth level (Kobrin, 2005; Ataullah et al., 2004). Given the advantages attributed to the employment of foreign capital in the process of developing nations, such nations are inclined to liberalize their FDI policies for the maximization of FDI inflows. On the whole, empirical analysis and theories however have resulted in mixed findings regarding the impact of FDI on economic growth in these countries. In the past twenty years, FDI exhibited a monumental expansion of inflows and outflows on a global level. The global FDI inflows are approximated to be about 4.4% for 2011 (UNCTAD, 2011).

Every nation attempts at seeking greater inflows of FDI in order to benefit from the expected advantageous effects on output production for the capital inflows, advancement of technology, management expertise, and market know-how.

In spite of the fact that Yemen is a country still undergoing a low level of FDI inflows, the Yemeni government has shown considerable interest in attracting FDIs over the past years. The Central Bank of Yemen's (CBY, 2008) report described Yemen as one of the poorest nations in the Middle East, with approximately 35% of its population living below the poverty line and with a GDP of 5.6% as at 2005 because of increased production of oil by 4% in 2004. However, such growth rate decreased to 3.2% and remained at 3.3% in 2007 due to decrease in the production of oil. During the following year, the GDP increased to 3.9% and in 2009, the move towards initiating a new liquefied natural gas project was expected to bring about a greater increase in the production of hydrocarbon. By 2010, the real GDP increased to 7.7% (CBY, 2010) but declined rapidly in 2011 to a lowest level of -12.7%. This could be due to the suffocating political crisis experienced by the Middle East countries. However, there was slight improvement in the real GDP in the following year 2012, 2013 as it increased by 2.4% and 6% respectively (UNCTAD, 2013).

With regards to its macroeconomic stability, Yemen is among the several countries that have launched reformation programs which led to the occurrence of many controversies. This includes the plan to manage the exchange rate floating. The Yemeni exchange rate experienced a dynamic fluctuated in the past twenty years. The Central Bank of Yemen (CBY) established a floating rate system in 1996 but has an evident preference for the stable Yemeni Rial (Schneider et al., 2007). With regards to the rate of inflation, Yemen is one of the nations that reported the highest price increase in the Middle Eastern region in 2008. More specifically, it reported a high and volatile rate of inflation from 2002 to 2007 (Almounsor, 2010).

The government of Yemen has made great efforts via legal framework and promotional campaigns to attract foreign investors. It made its first step in attracting FDI inflows by establishing the Yemeni General Investment Authority in 1992 and passed the Foreign Investment Law. In order to further encourage FDI, a new Foreign Investment Law was also issued in 2002. Additionally, it established a specific center to lower the time required to approve and register investments (UNCTAD, 2009). The country has also introduced other incentives to motivate FDI flows. Currently, the Yemeni government permits 100% foreign ownership, and provides income tax holidays and exemptions to import duty. Furthermore, incentives in the form of free zone, including tax profits exemptions could be allowed for 15 years with a potential extension for an additional decade.

Also, in Yemen, the private sector of foreign direct investment can play a positive role in the economic growth and development of the country. The Yemen government is playing a strategic role in attracting the flows and corresponding benefits of foreign aid. Foreign direct investment in the private sector of the country is seen to be of low order. To this extent, this study investigates the determinants of FDI inflows in the context of Yemen. With considerations of all such significant facets of the envisaged investigation of the FDI issues relating to Yemen, by and large, the present study will focus on the relationship among macroeconomic determinants, business environment on the FDI inflows and political stability.

2 MOTIVATION OF THE STUDY

Several countries have experienced a considerable FDI increase owing to its significant impacts on developed and developing nations. Nevertheless, in Yemen, low levels of FDI inflows have been experienced and the country is considered as one of the countries having the least amount of FDI inflows in the Middle East, as presented in Figure 1.

In the context of Yemen, the Inward FDI Potential Index is lower than its Inward FDI Performance Index and according to UNCTAD (2007), Yemen is among the under-performing nations. In 2008, UNCTAD stated that Yemen was among the nations that were performing lower than their potential and suggested that Yemen should engage in considerable reforms to encourage its investment environment and its share of total FDI inflows.

By 2009, UNCTAD revealed that Yemen still had low levels of FDI inflows and on top of this, its FDI inflows experienced sharp decline and had been negative for some years. This indicates repatriations of prior investments in years by foreign investors. Moreover, the General Investment Authority in Yemen reported that from 1992 to 2008, approximately 27% of the registered investment failed and foreign investments constituted the greatest portion of these failures.

UNCTAD highlighted the country's negative value of Inward FDI and attributed it to foreign investors' disinvestment. Specifically, Yemen had a negative value from 1995 to 2000, and also in 2003, 2005, 2011 and 2012. In 2013, FDI inflows in Yemen improved slightly to 560,268 YR million but remained negative.

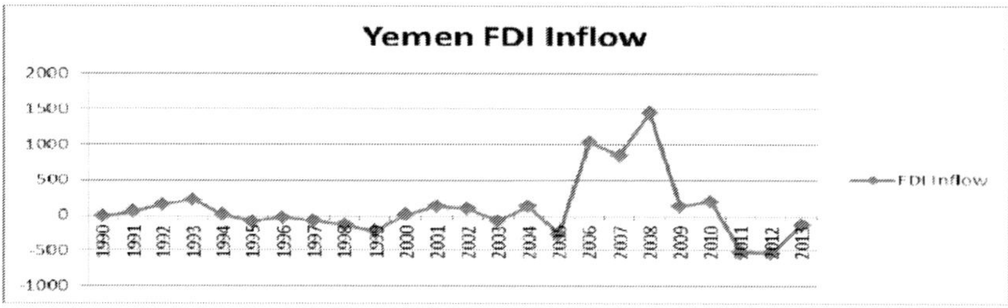

Figure 1. Yemen FDI inflow during the period 1990-2013

Source: UNCTAD, World Investment Reports, 2013

The notable low FDI and its weak contribution to the economic growth in Yemen can be explained by the international reports such as UNCTAD (2013) and World Bank (2013). Such reports confirm the undesirable effect of poor exchange rate and GDP, and corruption on the FDI inflows in Yemen. Many reasons have also been suggested for this weak contribution by the previous studies (Hela & Bouras, 2014; Musibah et al., 2014; Shahzad & Al-Swidi, 2013; AL-Shebami et al., 2013; Shahzad et al., 2012; Almsafir et al., 2011; Mahdi et al., 2011; Chami et al., 2007; Omran & Bolbol, 2003) to include the following:

1) Lack of attention placed on improving the level of openness in Yemen;

2) Oversight of the key role of the macroeconomic policy in obtaining FDI;

3) Lack of political stability to improve and reinforce FDI inflows;

4) Lack of attention placed on the business environment for the attraction of the expected degree of FDI inflows;

5) Outdated infrastructure;

6) Increasing degrees of corruption that leads to negative effects on FDI inflows in the country.

Many studies have been dedicated to the examination of the role of FDI for economic growth and the integrated determinants of FDI attraction. Generally speaking, studies have contended that FDI plays a key role in the economic growth of the country. According to Thamos et al. (2008), foreign associates of TNCs (Transnational Corporations) perform when it comes to new product development and technology adoption compared to local firms and hence, using modest competitive pressure and encouraging local firms to imitate and transform. A review of literature concerning the relationship between variables, including corruption index, business environment, political stability, and the FDI inflows reveals mixed findings. To begin with, Akcay (2001) finds no negative evidence between corruption and FDI while Habib & Zurawicki (2002) have, however, indicated that there is a negative impact of corruption on FDI. In the examination of the effect of political instability on the FDI inflows, mixed findings have also been reported. For example, Wheeler & Mody (1992) and Singh & Jun (1999) report that political instability and administrative efficiency significantly impact FDI inflow. Many other studies (Younis et al., 2008; Shahzad et al., 2012) on the other hand, have established that political instability have significant impact of FDI inflow. Because investors are sensitive to the political stability of the countries, it is assumed that the political stability can assist in attracting FDI inflows. Other researchers like; Madani, S., and Nobakht, M.(2014) Schneider and Frey (1985) and Kim (2010) state that PS that is open and welcoming to foreign investments reveals that property rights and civil rights have key role to play in the attraction of FDI into the country.

Accordingly, this study attempts to explain the issues of academic interest and to shed light on the major FDI determinants by examining some macroeconomic variables and the business environment in light of Yemen's political situation and policy making on its FDIs. This study attempts to investigate the impact of business environment's macroeconomic factors in terms of various political regimes on the country's capability of attracting FDI inflows.

3 DETERMINANTS OF FDI INFLOWS

FDI is commonly defined as a cross-border investment made by an enterprise directly in a production facility and/or in the marketing of a product. The investment is made to get a lasting interest in a foreign enterprise abroad. Dunning (1988) defines FDI to be an activity which is controlled and organized by companies in host countries. Bitzenis (2007) concludes that the "key features of the FDI are investing, acquiring and obtaining a foreign firm or asset and influencing/controlling the management operations".

In a related study, Wang (2009) examines inward FDI and growth of economies in several Asian countries for the period 1987-1997. The research obtains mixed effects which may be attributed to the used FDI as a dependent variable. However, the study suggests that FDI in manufacturing sector significantly and positively impact economic growth in the host economies. On the other hand, Wang (2009) also notes that FDI inflows in non-manufacturing areas fail to play a main role in improving the growth of the economy. In a similar study, Awan, M. Z, et al., (2011) examines the FDI impact on Pakistani economy using time series data for the period 1971-2006. The results reveal that determinant variables like degree of trade openness, gross fixed capital formation and inflation rate are statistically significant with positive signs while account balance had a negative sign.

In Yemen, AL-Shebami, et al. (2013) employs secondary data to examine the macroeconomic factors determining inflows of FDI from 1991 to 2008. These factors are categorized into five groups, including market size, cost-related factors, infrastructure, openness of trade, and human capital. Using the Autoregressive Distributed Lag (ARDL) approach, the empirical results suggests that in the long run, the most dominant factor determining FDI in Yemen is the infrastructure. This is followed by exchange rate, while other factors such as real gross domestic product per capita, trade openness, and human capital have less influence on FDI inflow. However, interest rate and the growth of real gross domestic product are found to be insignificant in influencing the FDI inflow in the long-run. On the other hand, their results also indicate that in the short run, real gross domestic product per capita, trade openness, and infrastructure have positive impacts on the FDI while the exchange rate and human capital affect FDI inflow negatively. Also in the short run, the growth of real gross domestic product and interest rate are found to be insignificant in influencing FDI.

Grass Domestic Product Growth Rate

The Grass domestic product growth rate is a significant factor considered by foreign investor while taking a decision for investment in any country. Thus, researchers have tried to study different related aspects of Grass Demostic Product growth rate and FDI inflows in their researches. A research conducted by Martinez-Zarzoso (2013) explains that higher domestic economic growth specify a high production rate along with a rise in investors' confidence to invest. Moreover, Martinez-Zarzoso & Nowak-Lehmann (2003) put forward that domestic rise in the economy usually encourage the investors from other countries to trust the host country for their business. The national economic development is termed as the GDP growth rate, which is the measure of economic performance of a country. This can be seen by the production rate, consumption, diversity and quality of goods along with various other economic facilities given in the country.

Mainly, macroeconomic factors tend to impact on the FDI inflow into a country. According to Gross & Trevino (1996), countries that have high levels of growth rate of GDP greatly tend to increase the inflow of FDI by winning the confidence of the Multinational Companies (MNCs) and encouraging them to invest specially when a steady development is recorded in the growth. However, better development in economy attracts the investors and they believe it a potential market for big profit on investments comes with higher FDI inflow (Biglaiser & DeRouen, 2011). By using panel data on 52 middle income countries for the period 1984-2012, Mina, W. (2014), found that there is the effect of GDP on FDI in addition to other factors. In india the study by Pradhan, A. K., & Kelkar, S. (2014), by using time series data over the period 1991 to 2012, indicated positive relationship between GDP and FDI. In North African countries, such as Egypt, the study by Badr, O. M., & Ayed, T. L. (2015), for the period 1961-2012, found that FDI is explained by GDP. In the context of Yemen, AL-Shebami, A., et al. (2013), found a negative correlation was revealed between Real Gross Domestic Product per Capita and FDI inflow for the period from 1991-2008. On the basis of above mentioned argument the following proposition is drawn for further examination.

H1. GDP growth rate have an impact on FDI inflow.

3.1 Exchange Rate

The exchange rate is one of the most significant issues tackled in economic research (Brixiova et al., 2014; Pan

& Song, 2014; Bilawal et al., 2014; Lily et al., 2014; Goldberg, 2009). It has been acknowledged that there is an association between FDI and exchange rate. If the currency of a country is devalued, there is a chance for foreign investors to invest in that country to buy assets at lower prices. This is especially seen in the case of foreign firms having identified specific potentiality in their targeted markets envisaged (Blonigen & Ma, 2011). Some previous studies (Nurudeen, Auta, & Wafure, 2011; Ali, Khrawish, & Siam, 2010; Adam & Tweneboah, 2009; Osinubi & Amaghionyeodiwe, 2009; Dumludag, 2009; Kaya & Yilmaz, 2003) have reported positive impact of exchange rate on FDI inflows.

The outcome of the exchange rate of FDI inflows has been documented in the literature. For example, studies

(Clare & Gang, 2010; Kiyota & Urata, 2008; Jenkins & Thomas, 2002; Erdal & Tatoglu, 2002; Love & Lage-Hidalgo, 2000; Mowatt & Zulu, 1999; Blonigen, 1997; Froot & Stein, 1991) have found that the exchange rate can lead to fluctuation of FDI by affecting the cost of acquiring foreign exchange. This is because a decrease in domestic currency value against foreign currency value or depreciation of domestic exchange rate will make it less expensive for a foreign investor to invest in the developing economy. Thus, depreciation of the exchange rate of a country will stimulate the inflows of FDI. Based on the current literature, the following hypothesis are stated for investigation.

H2. Exchange Rate has an impact on FDI inflows.

3.2 Inflation Rate

Inflation rate is considered a vital factor in a country's economic development. Rate of inflation is considered as an important element that affects the FDI inflows. The rate of inflation brings the overall financial performance of host nations to light (Hailu, 2010). Furthermore, high inflation represents the failure of the government of that country in handling its budget, and this depicts that the central bank is failed to accomplish effective monetary policy (Schneider & Frey, 1985). Generally, higher inflation rate is linked with the lower FDI inflows. Akinboade et al. (2006) draw the conclusion that the high inflation rate signifies instability in the country. Some studies such as (Bissoon, 2012; Parajuli & Kennedy, 2010; Hailu, 2010; Kok & Ersoy, 2009; Bouoiyour, 2007; Haile &Assefa, 2006; Nunes, Oscategui, & Peschiera, 2006; Asiedu, 2006; Obwona, 2001) reveal that high inflation will hinder FDI inflows. Furthermore, a positive relationship was found between inflation and FDI (Azam & Lukman, 2010; Ali, Khrawish, & Siam, 2010). In contrast, several studies (Shahzad & Al-Swidi, 2013; Anyanwu, 2012; Nurudeen, Auta, & Wafure, 2011; Parajuli & Kennedy, 2010; Vijayakumar et al., 2010; Onyeiwu, 2003; Obwona, 2001) have found that the relationship between inflation and FDI is not significant. The foregoing leads to the following hypothesis.

H3. The stable Inflation Rate has significant impact on FDI inflows.

3.3 Gross National Income

The Gross national income (GNI) is the total amount of output produced by the domestic and foreign residents of a country. This includes gross domestic product (GDP) plus net income from abroad, calculated as factor incomes earned by foreign residents minus income earned by the non-residents in the domestic economy (Todaro

& Smith, 2011). The ability of a country to sustain high growth rates in GNI determines its economic development and competitiveness. In such country, the purchasing power of the citizen increases and thus influences the FDI flows. De Mello (1999) reported that FDI has positive and significant influence on the economic growth of a country whose level of income is high. However, Antwi et al., (2013) found the association of GNI and FDI to be negative. GNI consider the following hypothesis to test with FDI.

H4. GNI has an Impact on FDI inflows.

3.4 Balance of Payment

The evidences presented in this research study show that FDI inflows have the tendency to make the position of host country better regarding the balance of payment. By taking into the consideration the data of 72 developing countries from 1970 to 2008, Majeed and Eatazaz (2009) reveal the features of the host countries that are essential in the decision making process with reference to the location of Multinational companies (MNs) in progressing countries. Various researches like (Chaudhary et al., 2009; Toda & Yamamoto, 1995) have demonstrated that FDI, one of the determinants (employed labor force, human capital index, domestic savings, and the balance of payments) ensures speedy development in economy. Furthermore, Results obtained from the research point out that the balance of payment and inflation has significant influence on FDI inflows but negative. In Pakistan, study by Shahzad, A., & Al-Swidi, A. K. (2013) by using the authentic annual data for the period 1991 to 2011 tends Balance of Payment to be a significant determinant of FDI inflows when the Political stability as moderating effect . Based on above mentioned discussion, the following hypothesis is deduced.

H5. Sufficient Balance of Payment (BOP) has an impact on FDI inflows.

4 PS and FDI Inflows

The PS has a significant impact on macroeconomic balance and in the making favorable environment for business in a country. Mainly, political risks rely on PS and good governance (Shahzad et al., 2012; Husain, 2009). Latest research carried out by Shahzad et al. (2012) accounts that political stability encourages forcing greater inflows of FDI in the developing countries. On the other hand, Yemen has been facing an unending political instability. Thus, this has badly affected the foreign and domestic investment and offer limited investment options. In this context, the country's economic development and growth process are negatively impacted by its unfavorable features on the physical and human resources. In case of political instability experienced by a country, foreign investors do not tend to start any projects except when they are confident of a favorable environment that is encouraging for investment (World Bank, 2011; UNCTAD, 2010; Brada et al., 2005).

Certainly, the decision process of foreign investments could be adversely influenced by the determinants of political risks like regime change, economic intervention by government, legislation of property rights, and the red tape (Frey & Schneider, 1985). On the other hand, the FDI decision process is extremely valuable for the foreign investors and organizations to know the status of the governance index with reference to transparency of the administration processes; reduction in corruption; and peaceful environment (World Bank, 2006). Meanwhile, Clare and Gang (2010) employed a cross-sectional time series panel comprising of 53 developed and developing nations over the period 1999-2003. They noted that political stability positively influenced FDI, but a significant influence was limited to developing countries. This indicated higher concern for political risk in the developing countries compared to their developed counterparts. Additionally, Obwona (2001) showed that foreign investors considered the political situation in Uganda because of the fact that a stable political environment is important to their investment confidence.

A more extensive study was conducted by Qian and Baek (2011) to examine whether or not political risks hinder FDI in 116 countries from 1984 to 2008. They showed that political risk significantly determined FDI in both categories of nations. A fixed effect model and a dynamic panel model were utilized by Krifa-Shneider and Matei (2010) to examine the 33 developing and transition nations from 1996-2008. They reported a negative association between political risk levels and FDI inflow. This negative association between political risk and FDI inflows was supported by Acheampong, P., & Osei, V. (2014); Burger, M., et al., (2013); Solomon &Ruiz (2012); Kim, H. (2010); and Asiedu (2006) and despite the argument that political risk could minimize FDI inflow, some authors have shown that political risks play a key role in the decision of the firm to invest abroad (Esew & Yaroson, 2014; Samimi & Rezanejad, 2013; Bitzenis, 2007; Block, 2000; Levis, 1979; Brewer, 1983). For example, Li and Resnick (2003) fail to show a significant impact of political instability on the FDI inflows. Similarly, Levis (1979) also reveals that political variables takes second place to economic ones when it comes to FDI inflows determination. A similar finding highlighted by Brewer (1983) indicated a very weak correlation between government instability and FDI. Other studies (Asiedu, 2002; Olibe & Crumbley, 1997) also fail to show a statistical association between FDI and political instability. This result is found in the context of developed countries (Jimenez et al., 2011; Bitzenis et al., 2009). According to Shahzad, A., & Kaid Al-Swidi, A. (2013), macroeconomic determinant impact by political stability. Therefore, the following hypotheses are formulated as thus:

H6: PS moderates the impact between GDP growth rate and the FDI inflows.

H7: PS moderates the impact between Exchange Rate and the FDI inflows in Yemen
H8: PS moderates the impact between Inflation Rate and the FDI inflows in Yemen
H9: PS moderates the impact between GNI and the FDI inflows in Yemen.

H10: P S moderates the impact between Balance of Payment and the FDI inflows in Yemen.

5 Research Framework

The research framework in Figure 2 is devised to trace the impact of selected macroeconomic and business environment variables on FDI in Yemen during the period 1990 to 2013.

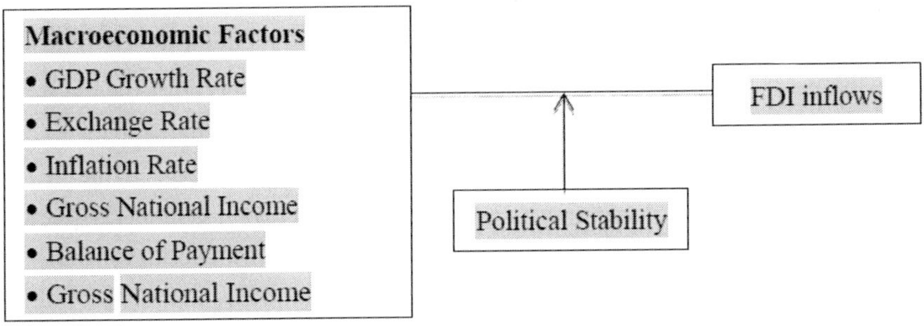

Figure 2. Research framework

The expected relationships of the macroeconomic variables with the FDI inflows and the expected level of the moderating variable, political stability are as stated earlier in the highlighted hypotheses.

6. DATA ANALYSIS AND RESULTS

Foreign direct investment inflows (FDI inflows) and gross domestic production growth rate (GDPGR) are on an annual basis and are the data is recorded from the World Bank Indicator reports. The exchange rate is considered as the rate of a nation's currency with respect to some other currency and the inflation rate corresponds to the consumer price index change in years. Gross National Income is the sum of domestic and foreign output, income owned by people of the host country, containing gross domestic product (GDP) in addition to the incomes earned by foreign residents, minus income earned in the domestic economy by non-residents. The balance of payment finds out the external balance or foreign trade position of the country. At the end, the political stability index (PSI). The data for these variables gather from the Indicator reports provided by the World Bank. In order to study the effects of these macroeconomic variables with the moderating role of PS on the FDI inflows in Yemen as mentioned during drawing the hypotheses and demonstrated in the research plan, the current study adopt the steps as follow.

6.1 Units Root Tests (ADF Test)

Spurious regression can be avoided if characteristics of time series data are analyzed at the start to know the nature of variables. These variables can either be stationary or non-stationary. Augmented Dickey Fuller (ADF) method is used in this study. Data showed in table, the dependent variable of FDI inflows and the variety of macroeconomic variables like, Gross domestic product growth rate, Exchange Rate, Inflation rate, Balance of Payment, Gross National Income, and FDI and PS are stationary.

Table 2. ADF unit root test results using the trend and intercept

	Variable	1st Diff	2nd Diff	Lagged
1	FDI	0	S	2
2	GDPGR	S	0	1
3	Exchange Rate	0	S	1
6	Inflation rate	S	0	1
7	GNI	0	S	1
8	BOP	S	0	1
9	PSI	0	S	1

Standard Regression Analysis of FDI Inflows

Having satisfied the regression assumptions, the FDI model is estimated to examine its significant predictors (GDPGR, Exchange Rate, Inflation Rate, GNI and BOP). From the results in Table 3, only GDPGR has significant negative (β= -.470, t= -2.312, $p<0.05$) impact of the FDI inflows at the 5 % level. This result, however, supports the hypothesis H1. The exchange rate, inflation rate, balance of payment, gross national income are not significant factors of the FDI inflows in the state of Yemen, These results, however, fail to support the hypothesis H2, H3, H4, and H5.

Table 3. Estimated results of the FDI inflows

Variables	Beta	T-value
GDPGR	-.470**	-2.312
Exchange Rate	-.334	-.770
INFRATE	.162	.661
GNI	.530	1.217
BOP	-.223	-.927
F value		1.906
F Sig.		.134
R^2		0.346
Adjusted R^2		0.165
Durbin Watson		2.568

Multiple Analysis of Moderating Effect

In the above mentioned model, the interaction terms lie among the macroeconomic variables, business environment variables and political stability are investigated to verify the moderating influence. The hierarchical regression outcomes are declared in steps. Foremost, the moderating influence of Political stability was examined on the already discussed relations following Frazier, Tix, & Barron (2004). Findings shown in Table 4, the exchange rate, rate of inflation and gross national income describe them as significant impact of the FDI inflows at the 0.01 level of significance whilst the balance of payment is significant at the 5 % level.

Table 4. Results of the moderating effect of PS

Variables	Predictors	T value	Moderated	T value	Interactions	T value
GDPGR	-.470**	-2.312	-.328*	-1.881	-.547**	-2.338
Exchange Rate	-.334	-.770	-.799*	-2.052	.823	1.134
INFRATE	.162	.661	.021	.100	1.162**	2.816
GNI	.530	1.217	2.024***	3.340	1.181*	2.068
BOP	-.223	-.927	-.342	-1.690	-.691**	-2.637
PSI			1.346**	3.063	1.911**	2.808
GDPGR_PSI					.171	.914
Exchange Rate _PSI					-2.853**	-2.810
INFRATE_PSI					-1.557***	-3.385
GNI_PSI					2.100***	3.204
BOP_PSI					.661**	2.446
F value		1.906		3.891		4.724
F Sig.		.143		.013		.006
R^2		.346		.579		0.812
Adjusted R^2		0.165		0.430		0.640
R^2 change		0.346		0.233		0.234
Significant F change		.143		0.007		0.056

***: p< 0.01: **:p< 0.05; *:P<0. 1

Outcomes shown in Table 4 depict the interaction terms among political stability and macroeconomic variables. Though, the interaction term lies among exchange rate (β= -2.853, t= -2.810, p<0.05), and inflation rate (β= -1.557, t= -3.385, p<0.01) is negative significant at the 0.05 level, and 0.01 respectively, and the interaction term in case gross national income is (β= 2.100, t= 3.204, p<0.01), and in case of the balance of payment is (β= .661, t= 2.446, p<0.05) is positive significant at the 0.01 level, and 0.05 respectively. These findings describe that political stability as significant moderator that influence exchange rate, inflation rate, gross national income, and balance of payment on FDI inflows. Nevertheless, these findings are in line with the hypothesis H7, H8, H9 and H10.

7 Discussions, Conclusion and Recommendations

This study's results are based on the analysis of FDI inflows in Yemen for the past two decades. In order to investigate the propositions of the study, hierarchical multiple linear regression was used. The findings obtained indicate that all the hypotheses are rejected except only one. Specifically, out of the stated hypothesis H1, H2, H3, H4 and H5, only H1 is supported with FDI inflows in Yemen. In investigating the effects of moderating variable, PS on the macroeconomic variables and FDI inflows, the results support the hypothesis H7, H8, H9 and H10. The results suggest that the political stability plays a significant role among other determinants of foreign investment in Yemen. In addition, exchange rate and gross national income nexus are influenced by the level of political system stability in the country.

A good indicator for any economy is a consistent growth of GDP because it motivates foreign investment in the host country. The GDP growth rate is an important factor determining the FDI. Therefore, Yemeni policy makers should promote the enhancement of GDP grow rate for the FDI inflow into the country. In addition, it is necessary for Yemen to provide the attractive packages which could motivate the investment of high tech companies in the county. The policy makers in Yemen should draw on the experience of the GCC countries and other neighboring countries. Favorable balance of payment of the host country also motives foreign investment in the country. This study paid attention to and stated the role of political stability as a moderating variable for macroeconomic stability. Therefore, a country with political stability, favorable balance of payments and growth in GNI will have its economic growth improved. However, political stability in Yemen has been ranked to be low compared to other developing countries like Saudi Arabia, Oman, and Djibouti. Therefore, the Yemeni policy makers should make a rule of law which would protect the foreign investment and strive to pursue a policy that will guarantee a stable political system.

To this extent, the present study investigates the parameters influencing the inflows of foreign direct investment in Yemen over the period 1990 to 2013. It could be suggested that the policy-makers of Yemen should rehash the FDI policy which would stimulate more investment into the country in order to address the declining trend in the FDI inflow. Selective FDI policies could be made to channel FDI inflows into the country by including a set of positive and negative lists of action. Positive list in this sense implies some sectors where FDI should be encouraged and promoted while the negative list refers to some sectors where FDI inflows should be discouraged or disallowed, for example, defines good and the service sector. The adequate decision should be made on the approval procedure and screening mechanism to achieve the objective of FDI policy. Indeed, it is necessary for a developing country like Yemen to design a well-planned FDI policy that could greatly enhance the country's economic growth with stable macroeconomic goals. Such policy should be flexible for the practical determination f FDI inflows in the future.

With respect to future researches, one of the key suggestions are to examine in-depth the moderating effect of the economic stability between various determinants and the other variable related to business with FDI inflows.

REFERENCES

1. Acheampong, P., & Osei, V. (2014). Foreign Direct Investment (FDI) Inflows into Ghana: Should the Focus Be on Infrastructure or Natural Resources? Short-Run and Long -Run Analyses. *International Journal of Financial Research, 5*(1). http://dx.doi.org/10.5430/ijfr.v5n1p42

2. Adam, A. M., & Tweneboah, G. (2009). Foreign Direct Investment and Stock market Development: Ghana's Evidence. *International Research Journal of Finance and Economics, 26*, 178-185.

3. Akcay, S. (2001). Is Corruption an Obstacle for Foreign Investors in Developing Countries? Cross Country Evidence. *Yapi Kredi Economic Review, 12*(2), 27-34.

4. Akinboade, O. A., Siebrits, F. K., & Roussot, E. N. (2006). *Foreign Direct Investment in South Africa.*

5. Alfaro, L., Chanda, A., Kalemli-Ozcan, S., & Sayek, S. (2004). FDI and Economic Growth: The Role of Local

6. Financial Markets. *Journal of International Economics, 64*(1), 89-112. http://dx.doi.org/10.1016/S0022-1996(03)00081-3

7. Ali, Khrawish, H., & Siam, W. Z. (2010). Determinants of Direct Foreign Investment: Evidence from Jordan.

8. *Business and Economic Horizons, 1,* 67-75. http://dx.doi.org/10.15208/beh.2010.10

9. Almounsor, A. (2010). Inflation Dynamics in Yemen: An Empirical Analysis. *IMF Working Papers, 10*(144), 1.

10. http://dx.doi.org/10.5089/9781455201273.001

11. AL-Shebami, A., Almsafr, M., & Shaari, M. (2013). A Bounds Testing Approach to Co-integration: Determinants of Foreign Direct Investments Inflows to Yemen. *Journal of Advanced Social Research, 3*(7).

12. Antwi, S., Mills, E. F. E. A., Mills, G. A., & Xicang, Z. H. A. O. (2013). Impact of Foreign Direct Investment on Economic Growth: Empirical Evidence from Ghana. *International Journal of Academic Research in Accounting, Finance & Management Sciences, 3*(1), 18-25.

13. Anyanwu, J. C. (2012). Why does Foreign Direct Investment Go where it Goes? New Evidence From African Countries. *Annals of Economics and Finance, 13*(2), 433-470.

14. Asiedu, E. (2006). Foreign Direct Investment in Africa: The Role of Natural Resources, Market Size, Government Policy, Institutions and Political Instability. *World Economy, 29*(1), 63-77. http://dx.doi.org/10. 1111/j.1467-9701.2006.00758.x

15. Ataullah, A., Cockerill, T., & Le, H. (2004). Financial Liberalization and Bank Efficiency: A comparative Analysis of India and Pakistan. *Applied Economics, 36*(17), 1915-1924. http://dx.doi.org/10.1080/000368404200068638

16. Awan, M. Z., Khan, B., & uz Zaman, K. (2011). Economic Determinants of Foreign Direct Investment (FDI) in commodity producing sector: A case Study of Pakistan. *African Journal of Business Management, 5*(2), 537-545.

17. Awan, M. Z., uz Zaman, K., & Khan, B. (2010). Determinants of Foreign Direct Investment in Services Sector of Pakistan: An Econometric Approach. *Global Financial Crisis: Causes, Emerging Trends and Strategy, 5*(2), 167.

18. Azam, M., & Lukman, L. (2010). Determinants of Foreign Direct Investment in India, Indonesia and Pakistan: A quantitative Approach. *Journal of Managerial Sciences, 4*(1), 31-44.

19. Badr, O. M., & Ayed, T. L. (2015). The Mediator Role of FDI in North Africa: Case of Egypt. *Journal of Advanced Management Science,* 1-7. http://dx.doi.org/10.12720/joams.3.1.1-7

20. Biglaiser, G., & DeRouen, K. (2011). How Soon is Now? The Effects of the IMF on Economic Reforms in Latin America. *The Review of International Organizations, 6*(2), 189-213. http://dx.doi.org/10.1007/s11558- 011-9123-8

21. Bilawal, M., Ibrahim, M., Abbas, A., Shuaib, M., Ahmed, M., Hussain, I., & Fatima, T. (2014). Impact of Exchange Rate on Foreign Direct Investment in Pakistan. *Advances in Economics and Business 2*(6), 223-231.

22. Bissoon, O. (2012). Can Better Institutions Attract More Foreign Direct Investment? Evidence from Developing Countries. *International Research Journal of Finance and Economics, 82*, 142-158.

23. Bitzenis, A. (2006). Decisive FDI Barriers that Affect Multinationals' Business in A transition Country. *Global Business and Economics Review, 8*(1), 87-118.

24. Bitzenis, A., Tsitourasb, A., & Vlachosa, V. A. (2009). Decisive FDI Obstacles as an Explanatory Reason for limited FDI Inflows in an EMU Member State: The Case of Greece. *The Journal of Socio-Economics, 38,* 691-704. http://dx.doi.org/10.1016/j.socec.2009.03.001

25. Block, S. (2000). Integrating Traditional Capital Budgeting Concepts into an International Decision-Making Environment. *The Engineering Economist, 45*(4), 309-325. http://dx.doi.org/10.1080/00137910008967555

26. Blonigen, B. A. (1997). Firm-Specific Assets and the Link between Exchange Rates and Foreign Direct Investment. *The American Economic Review*, 447-465.

27. Blonigen, B., & Ma, A. C. (2011). *China's Growing Role in World Trade: Please Pass the Catch-Up: The Relative Performance of Chinese and Foreign Firms in Chinese Exports.*

28. Bouoiyour, J. (2007). The Determining Factors of Foreign Direct Investment in Morocco. *Saving and Development, 31*(1), 91-106.

29. Brada, J. C., Kutan, A. M., & Yigit, T. M. (2005). *The Effects of Transition and Political Instability on Foreign Direct Investment in ECE Emerging Market.* Paper Presented at the United Nations Economic Commission for Europe (UNECE) Spring Seminar.

30. Brewer, T. L. (1983). The Instability of Governments and the Instability of Controls on Funds Transfers by Multinational Enterprises: Implications for Political Risk Analysis. *Journal of International Business Studies, 14*(3), 147-157. http://dx.doi.org/10.1057/palgrave.jibs.8490534

31. Brixiova, Z., Egert, B., & Essid, T. H. A. (2014). The Real Exchange Rate and External Competitiveness in Egypt, Morocco and Tunisia. *Review of Middle East Economics and*

Finance, 10(1), 25-51. http://dx.doi. org/10.1515/rmeef-2013-0014

32. Brooks, D. H., Fan, E. X., Sumulong, L. R., & Bank, A. D. (2003). *Foreign Direct Investment in Developing Asia: Trends, Effects, and Likely Issues for the Forthcoming WTO Negotiations.* Asian Development Bank.

33. Burger, M., Ianchovichina, E., & Rijkers, B. (2013). *Risky Business: Political Instability and Greenfield Foreign Direct Investment in the Arab World.* Policy Research Working Papers. http://dx.doi.org/10.1596/1813-9450-6716

34. Central Bank of Yemen (CBY). (2008). *Annual Report 2008.* Yemen. Retrieved from http://www.centralbank.gov.ye/App_Upload/annl_rep2008_en.pdf

35. Central Bank of Yemen (CBY). (2010). *Annual Report 2010.* Yemen. Retrieved from http://www.centralbank.gov.ye /App_Upload/annl_rep2010_en.pdf

36. Chaudhary, A. R., Iqbal, A., & Gillani, S. Y. M. (2009). The Nexus between Higher Education and Economic Growth: An Empirical Investigation for Pakistan. *Pakistan Journal of Commerce and Social Sciences, 3*, 1-9.

37. Cheung, Y. W., & Qian, X. (2009). Hoarding of International Reserves: Mrs Machlup's Wardrobe and the Joneses.

38. *Review of International Economics, 17*(4), 824-843. http://dx.doi.org/10.1111/j.1467-9396.2009.00850.x Cho, J. W. (2004). Foreign Direct Investment: Determinants, Trends inflows and Promotion Policies. *Investment Promotion and Enterprise Development Bulletin for Asia and the Pacific, 1*, 99-112.

39. Chowdhury, A., & Mavrotas, G. (2006). FDI and Growth: What Causes What? *World Economy, 29*(1), 9-19. http://dx.doi.org/10.1111/j.1467-9701.2006.00755.x

40. Clare, G., & Gang, I. N. (2010). Exchange Rate and Political Risks, Again. *Emerging Markets Finance and Trade, 46*(3), 46-58. http://dx.doi.org/10.2753/REE1540-496X460303

41. Crespo, N., & Fontoura, M. P. (2007). Determinant Factors of FDI Spillovers-What Do We Really Know? *World Development, 35*(3), 410-425. http://dx.doi.org/10.1016 /j.worlddev.2006.04.001

42. De Mello, L. (1999). Foreign Direct Investment-led Growth: Evidence from Time Series and Panel Data. *Oxford Economic Papers, 51*(1), 133-151. http://dx.doi.org/10.1093 /oep/51.1.133

43. Deichmann, J., Karidis, S., & Sayek, S. (2003). Foreign Direct Investment in Turkey: Regional Determinants.

44. *Applied Economics, 35*(16), 1767-1778. http://dx.doi.org/ 10.1080/0003684032000126780

45. Duce, M. (2003). *Definitions of Foreign Direct Investment (FDI): A Methodological Note.* Paper for the Committee on the Global Financial System Working Group, Banco Deespana, Madrid.

46. Dumludag, D. (2009). An Analysis of the Determinants of Foreign Direct Investment in Turkey: The Role of the Institutional Context. *Journal of Business Economics and Management, 10*(1), 15-30. http://dx.doi.org/10. 3846/1611-1699.2009.10.15-30

47. Dunning, J. H. (1988). The Eclectic Paradigm of International Production: A Restatement and Some Possible Extensions. *Journal of International Business Studies, 19*(1), 1-31. http://dx.doi.org/10.1057/palgrave. jibs.8490372

48. Erdal, F., & Tatoglu, E. (2002). Locational Determinants of Foreign Direct Investment in an Emerging Market Economy: Evidence From Tukey. *Multinational Business Review, 10*, 21-27.

49. Esew, N. G., & Yaroson, E. (2014). Institutional Quality and Foreign Direct Investment (FDI) In Nigeria: A Prognosis. *IOSR Journal of Humanities and Social Science, 19*(6), 37-45. http://dx.doi.org/10.9790/0837- 19653745

50. Froot, K. A., & Stein, J. C. (1991). Exchange Rates and Foreign Direct Investment: An Imperfect Capital Markets Approach. *The Quarterly Journal of Economics, 106*(4), 1191-1217. http://dx.doi.org/10.2307/2937961

51. Goldberg, L. S. (2009). Exchange Rates and Foreign Direct Investment. *The Princeton Encyclopedia of the World Economy, 1*, 393-396.

52. Gorg, H. (2004). Much Ado about Nothing? Do Domestic Firms Really Benefit from Foreign Direct Investment?

53. *The World Bank Research Observer, 19*(2), 171-197. http://dx.doi.org/10.1093/wbro/lkh019

54. Grosse, R., & Trevino, L. J. (1996). Foreign Direct Investment in the United States: An Analysis by Country of Origin. *Journal of International Business Studies, 27*(1), 139-155. http://dx.doi.org/10.1057/palgrave.jibs.8490129

55. Habib, M., & Zurawicki, L. (2002). Corruption and Foreign Direct Investment. *Journal of International Business*

56. *Studies, 33*(2), 291-307. http://dx.doi.org/10.1057 /palgrave.jibs.8491017

57. Haile, G. A., & Assefa, H. (2006). *Determinants of Foreign Direct Investment in Ethiopia: A time-series analysis.*

58. Hailu, Z. A. (2010). Demand Side Factors Affecting the Inflow of Foreign Direct Investment to African Countries: Does Capital Market Matter? *International Journal of Business and Management, 5*(5), 104-116. http://dx.doi.org /10.5539/ijbm.v5n5p104

59. Hela, B. (2014). Knowledge Economy, Governance and FDI: Case of Tunisia. *Journal of Business Management and Economics, 5*(2), 52-62.

60. Husain, I. (2009). The Role of Politics in Pakistan's Economy. *Journal of International Affairs, 63*(1), 1-18. Javed, K., Falak, S., Awan, R., & Ashfaq, M. (2012). Foreign Direct Investment, Trade and Economic Growth: A

61. Comparison of Selected South Asian Countries. *International Journal of Humanities and Social Science, 2*(5).

62. Jenkins, C., & Thomas, L. (2002). *Foreign Direct Investment in Southern Africa: Determinants, Characteristics and Implications for Economic Growth and Poverty Alleviation.* CSAE, Univ. of Oxford.

63. Jimenez, A., de la Fuente, J. M., & Duran, J. J. (2011). Is there an East-West Structure in the Location of FDI in Europe? the Role of Institutions and Political Risk. *Research in Economics and Business: Central and Eastern Europe, 3*, 5-23.

64. Kaya, & Yılmaz (2003). Turkiye'de Dogrudan Yatırımların Belirleyicileri: 1970-2000. *AtatUrk Universitesi BF Dergisi, 17*(3-4), 39-56.

65. Kim, H. (2010). Political Stability and Foreign Direct Investment. *IJEF, 2*(3), 59. http://dx.doi.org/10.5539/ijef.v2n3p59

66. Kiyota, K., & Urata, S. (2008). The Role of Multinational Firms in International Trade: The Case of Japan. *Japan and the World Economy, 20*(3), 338-352. http://dx.doi.org/10.1016/j.japwor.2007.03.003

67. Kobrin, S. J. (2005). The Determinants of Liberalization of FDI Policy in Developing Countries: A cross-Sectional Analysis, 1992-2001. *Transnational Corporations, 14*(1), 67-104.

68. Kok, R., & Ersoy, A. B. (2009). Analyses of FDI Determinants in Developing Countries. *International Journal of Social Economics, 36*(1/2), 105-123. http://dx.doi.org/10.1108/03068290910921226

69. Krifa-Schneider, H., & Matei, I. (2010). Business Climate, Political Risk and FDI in Developing Countries: Evidence from Panel Data. *International Journal of Economics and Finance, 2*(5), 54-65. http://dx.doi.org/10.5539/ijef.v2n5p54

70. Kumar, N., & Chadha, A. (2009). India's Outward Foreign Direct Investments in Steel Industry in a Chinese Comparative Perspective. *Industrial and Corporate Change, 18*(2), 249-267. http://dx.doi.org/10.1093/icc/ dtp004

71. Levis, M. (1979). Does Political Instability in Developing Countries Affect Foreign Investment Flow: An Empirical Examination. *Management International Review (MIR), 19*(3), 59-69.

72. Li, Q., & Resnick, A. (2003). Reversal of Fortunes: Democratic Institutions and Foreign Direct Investment Inflows to Developing Countries. *Int. Org., 57*(1), 175-211. http://dx.doi.org/10.1017/S0020818303571077

73. Lily, J., Kogid, M., Mulok, D., Thien Sang, L., & Asid, R. (2014). Exchange Rate Movement and Foreign Direct Investment in Asean Economies. *Economics Research International,* 1-10. http://dx.doi.org/10.1155/2014/ 320949

74. Love, J. H., & Lage-Hidalgo, F. (2000). Analysing the Determinants of US Direct Investment in Mexico. *Applied Economics, 32*(10), 1259-1267. http://dx.doi.org/10.1080/000368400404416

75. Madani, S., & Nobakht, M. (2014). Political Regimes and FDI Inflows: Empirical Evidence from Upper Middle Income Countries. *Journal of Finance and Economics, 2*(3), 75-82. http://dx.doi.org/10.12691/jfe-2-3-4

76. Mahdi, O. R., Almsafir, M. K., & Yao, L. (2011). The Role of Knowledge and Knowledge Management in Sustaining Competitive Advantage within Organizations: A review. *African Journal of Business Management, 5*(23), 9912-9931.

77. Majeed, M. T., & Ahmad, E. (2009). An Analysis of Host Country Characteristics that Determine FDI in Developing Countries: Recent Panel Data Evidence. *The Lahore Journal of Economics, 14*(2), 71-96.

78. MartÃnez-Zarzoso, I., & Nowak-Lehmann, F. (2003). Augmented Gravity Model: An Empirical Application to Mercosur-European Union Trade Flows. *Journal of Applied Economics, 6*(2), 291-316.

79. Martínez-Zarzoso, I. (2013). The Log of Gravity Revisited. *Applied Economics, 45*(3), 311-327. http://dx.doi.org /10.1080/00036846.2011.599786

80. Mhlanga, N., Blalock, G., & Christy, R. (2010). Understanding Foreign Direct Investment in the Southern African Development Community: An Analysis based on Project-level Data. *Agricultural Economics, 41*(3-4), 337-347. http://dx.doi.org/10.1111/j.1574-0862.2010.00440.x

81. Mina, W. (2014). But Most of All We Love Each Other: Does Social Cohesion Pay off? *Evidence from FDI Flows to Middle Income Countries International Center for Public Policy, Working Paper Series, 8.*

82. Mowatt, R., & Zulu, T. (1999). *Intra-Regional Private Capital Flows in Eastern and Southern Africa: A study of South African investment in the Region.* ACREFSA/FDI workshop on Intra-Regional Private Capital Flows in Eastern and Southern Africa, Harare.

83. Musibah, A. S., Arfan, S., & Faudziah, H. B. F. (2014). *The Role of Foreign Investment Inflow in the Yemen's Economy Growth.* In Comparison with the MENA Countries,

International Congress on Economy, Finance and Business (ICEFB, 2014). Nagoya, JAPAN.

84. Nunes, L. C., Oscategui, J., & Peschiera, J. (2006). *Determinants of FDI in Latin America: Document De Trabajo, 252*, 1-12.

85. Nurudeen, A., Auta, E. M., & Wafure, O. G. (2011). Determinants of Foreign Direct Investment in Nigeria: An Empirical Analysis. *Global Journal of Human Social Science, 10*(1), 26-34.

86. Obwona, M. B. (2001). Determinants of FDI and their Impact on Economic Growth in Uganda. *African Development Review, 13*(1), 46-81. http://dx.doi.org/10.1111/1467-8268.00030

87. Olibe, K. O., & Crumbley, C. L. (1997). Determinants of US Private Foreign Direct Investments in OPEC Nations: From Public and Non-Public Policy Perspectives. *Journal of Public Budgeting Accounting and Financial Management, 9*, 331-355.

88. Omran, M., & Bolbol, A. (2003). Foreign Direct Investment, Financial Development, and Economic Growth: Evidence from the Arab Countries. *Review of Middle East Economics and Finance, 1*(3), 231-249. http://dx.doi.org/10.1080/1475368032000158232

89. Omri, A., & kahouli, B. (2014). The nexus among foreign investment, domestic capital and economic growth: Empirical evidence from the MENA region. *Research in Economics, 68*(3), 257-263. http://dx.doi.org/10.1016/j.rie.2013.11.001

90. Onyeiwu, S. (2003). *Analysis of FDI Flows to Developing Countries: Is the MEN a region Different?* Paper Presented at the ERF 10th Annual Conference, December, Marrakech, Morocco.

91. Osinubi, T. S., & Amaghionyeodiwe, L. A. (2009). Foreign Direct Investment and Exchange Rate Volatility in Nigeria. *International Journal of Applied Econometrics and Quantitative Studies, 9*(2), 83-116.

92. Pajunen, K. (2008). Institutions and Inflows of Foreign Direct Investment: A fuzzy-set Analysis. *Journal of International Business Studies, 39*(4), 652-669. http://dx.doi.org/10.1057/palgrave.jibs.8400371

93. Pan, W., & Song, Y. (2014). Empirical analysis for the impact of RMB real effective exchange rate on foreign direct investment in China. *Journal of Chemical & Pharmaceutical Research, 6*(5).

94. Parajuli, S., & Kennedy, P. L. (2010). *The Exchange Rate and Inward Foreign Direct Investment in Mexico.*

95. Paper Presented at the Southern Agricultural Association, Florida, USA.

96. Pradhan, A. K., & Kelkar, S. (2014). Macroeconomic Determinants of Foreign Direct Investment in India: An Empirical Investigation (1991-2012). *Jour. Comm. and Manag. Thou., 5*(4), 530-544. http://dx.doi.org/10.5958/0976-478X.2014.00002.0

97. Rajana, R. S., Rongalab, S., & Ghoshc, R. (2008). *Attracting Foreign Direct Investment (FDI) to India.* World Scientific Press.

98. Salman, A., & Feng, H. X. (2010). FDI in Pakistan: Impact on GNP and Capital Financial Account. *2010 International Conference on Financial Theory and Engineering.* http://dx.doi.org/10.1109/ICFTE.2010. 5499389

99. Samimi, A. J., & Rezanejad, A. G. Z. (2013). Financial Development, FDI and Governance in Mena Regio.

100. *Middle-East Journal of Scientific Research, 17*(9), 1285-1289.

101. Schneider, F., & Frey, B. S. (1985). Economic and Political Determinants of Foreign Direct Investment. *World Development, 13*(2), 161-175. http://dx.doi.org/10.1016/0305-750X(85)90002-6

102. Schneider, T., Ben Ltaifa, N., Ahmed, F., & Chami, S. (2007). Yemen: Exchange Rate Policy in the Face of Dwindling Oil Exports. *IMF Working Papers, 7*(5), 1. http://dx.doi.org/10.5089/9781451865691.001

103. Shahzad, A., & Al-Swidi, A. K. (2013). Effect of Macroeconomic Variables on the FDI inflows: The Moderating Role of Political Stability: An Evidence from Pakistan. *Asian Social Science, 9*(9). http://dx.doi.org/10.5539/ass.v9n9p270

104. Shahzad, A., Al-Swidi, A. K., Mithani, D. A., Bt Fadzil, F. H., & Bin Golamuddin, A. G. (2012). An Empirical Investigation on The Effect of Business Environment Factors on The FDI Inflows in Pakistan: The Moderating Role of Political Stability. *Business and Economic Research, 2*(2). http://dx.doi.org/10.5296/ber. v2i2.2597

105. Sinani, E., & Meyer, K. E. (2004). Spill overs of Technology Transfer from FDI: The Case of Estonia. *Journal of Comparative Economics, 32*(3), 445-466. http://dx.doi.org/10.1016/j.jce.2004.03.002

106. Singh, H., & Jun, K. W. (1999). *Some New Evidence on Determinants of Foreign Direct Investment in Developing Countries.* Policy Research Working Papers. http://dx.doi.org/10.1596/1813-9450-1531

107. Solomon, B., & Ruiz, I. (2012). Political Risk, Macroeconomic Uncertainty, and the Patterns of Foreign Direct Investment. *The International Trade Journal, 26*(2), 181-198. http://dx.doi.org/10.1080/08853908.2012. 657592

108. Temiz, D., & Gökmen, A. (2014). FDI inflow as an international business operation by MNCs and economic growth: An empirical study on Turkey. *International Business Review, 23*(1), 145-154. http://dx.doi.org/10.1016/j.ibusrev.2013.03.003

109. Toda, H. Y., & Yamamoto, T. (1995). Statistical Inference in Vector Auto regressions with Possibly Integrated Processes. *Journal of Econometrics, 66*(1-2), 225-250. http://dx.doi.org/10.1016/0304-4076(94)01616-8

110. Todaro, & Smith. (2011). *Economic development todaro smith* (11th ed.), 44.

111. UNCTAD. (2007). *World Investment Report 2007: Transnational corporations, extractive industries and development.* New York and Geneva: United Nations.

112. UNCTAD. (2009). *World Investment Report 2009: Transnational Corporations, Agricultural Production and Development.* New York and Geneva: United Nations.

113. UNCTAD. (2010). *World Investment Report.* United Nations, New York. UNCTAD. (2011). *World Investment Report.* United Nations, New York.

114. UNCTAD. (2013). *World Investment Report 2013: Transnational Corporations, Extractive Industries and Development.* New York and Geneva: United Nations.

115. Vijayakumar, N., Sridharan, P., & Rao, K. C. S. (2010). Determinants of FDI in BRICS Countries: A panel analysis. *International Journal of Business Science and Applied Management, 5*(3), 1-13.

116. Wang, M. (2009). Manufacturing FDI and economic growth: Evidence from Asian economies. *Applied Economics, 41*(8), 991-1002. http://dx.doi.org/10.1080/00036840601019059

117. Wheeler, D., & Mody, A. (1992). International investment location decisions. *Journal of International Economics, 33*(1-2), 57-76. http://dx.doi.org/10.1016/0022-1996(92)90050-T

118. *World Bank Report.* (2006). United State, New York.

119. *World Bank Report.* (2011). United State, New York.

120. World Bank. (2013). *Country Data: Link to Foreign Direct Investment definition.* Retrieved from http://devdata.worldbank.org/external/CPProfile.asp?SelectedCountry=YEM&CCODE=YEM&CNAME=Y emen%2C+Rep.&PTYPE=CP

121. Younis, M., Lin, X. X., Sharahili, Y., & Selvarathi, S. (2008). Political Stability and Economic Growth in Asia.

122. *American J. of Applied Sciences, 5*(3), 203-208. http://dx.doi.org/10.3844/ajassp.2008.203.208

Copyrights

15

CHAPTER

Gender and Islam in Development Policy and Practice in Yemen

EWA Strzelecka

RÉSUMÉS

The present paper discusses the intersection and inter-connection of Islam, gender, and development policy and practice in Yemen since the 1990s. Special attention is paid to the complexity of how gender work reflects tension and continuity between aspiration and reality in the context of shifting meanings and perspectives in current human development theory. Not only are women from developing countries placed at the centre of development processes, but so their cultures are also discussed, as they are finally visible. In a number of developmental projects in Yemen, Islam now appears as an interesting means for gender and development advancement. However, there is still a gap between theory and practice when implementing these new perspectives in international development. The article spotlights how Yemeni women's agency shaped and was shaped by a complex combination of shifting meanings, uses and effects of Islam, gender and development. It leads to the conclusion that religious and cultural considerations need to be taken into account, but with close attention paid to power relations and ensuing gender implications in terms of bargaining power. Research findings reaffirm the crucial role of the women's movement in the process of social change towards gender transformations in Yemen.

Entrées d'index

Motsclés: genre, développement, islam, culture, féminisme, droits des femmes, droits humains,

mouvement féminin, autonomisation des femmes, action féminine

Keywords: gender, development, Islam, culture, feminism, human rights, women's movement,

TEXTE INTÉGRAL

This research This research explores the intersection and inter-connection of Islam, gender, and development policy and practice in Yemen in a context where a new paradigm for development studies is being shaped. The previously prevailing approach of emphasizing political economy shifted in the 1990s to include other areas of study such as feminist and cultural studies. According to this new paradigm, not only are women from developing countries now at the centre of development and global processes, but their cultures are also discussed. This results in the political statement that human development is only possible if gender equality and local cultures are embraced. The central question is this: how has this new paradigm of development studies been put into practice in the context of developing countries and in particular, within the various Muslim communities found in Yemen? To what extent are these development actions consistent with the latest gender and development theories and political statements? In addition, there is also the question of how this new paradigm has been interpreted, redefined and renegotiated from a local perspective by women's human rights activists and gender practitioners.

I examine these questions in the context of contemporary Yemen - from its unification in 1990 until the present —focusing especially on gender and development policies and practices reflecting perspectives of human development, gender equality and cultural sensitivity relating to Muslim identity. In particular, I am interested in specific projects that consider Islam a powerful tool and means for gender and development advancement. Most such initiatives have been implemented in Yemen since the second half of the 1990s by local NGOs and women's organizations, and have been funded by international donors. I analyse these projects to find out the different ways in which recent international development theory on gender and development has influenced, impacted and been implemented in local policies and practices, in dealing with women's empowerment and human rights. I place special emphasis on examining the opinions of women's human rights activists and gender practitioners, and their direct experiences, to better understand the complexity and diversity of gender issues in Yemen. I also draw attention to the political and social implications of using 'Islam' in developmental work, specifically to the Islamic views on women's rights laid down by opinion-makers and religious scholars, both of whom may resist or, on the contrary, promote culture transformations aimed at women's empowerment and social change. These Islamic discourses are embedded in the specific socio-economic, historical and political context of Yemen, and are seen as resulting from power struggles between different groups with various social positions and interests. Power relations play an important role in shaping the capacities of communities and the associated social change processes, as cultural systems frequently confer power and privileges on some by denying rights and access to resources to others. These power relations are reproduced and legitimised by cultural mechanisms, including socialization according to prevalent Islamic standards and representations concerning gender models and women's rights. In this framework, projects aimed at promoting women's rights and gender equality through woman-friendly interpretations of Islam challenge the patterns in opposing ideologies justifying gender inequalities. Nevertheless, the meaningful impact of these projects will depend on their willingness to achieve feminist goals of women's empowerment and the transformation of gendered power structures.

INCORPORATING ISLAMIC FEMINIST VIEWS INTO GENDER AND DEVELOPMENT POLICY AND PRACTICES IN YEMEN

The starting point of my research focuses on the above-mentioned shift in international development theory - from understanding development merely in terms of economic growth to the new paradigm based on human development and considering culture and gender. Several authors, such as Amartya Sen, Mahbub ul Haq and Martha Nussbaum, have helped theorize this innovative perspective, which resulted in a normative approach to development policy promoted by the UN and Western donor agencies. However, this shift in developmental discourse and policy has not necessarily been accompanied by meaningful changes in development actions or their impact assessment. In particular, there is still a persistent gap between actual gender and development discourse and its implementation pattern on the ground. A large body of literature on the topic shows how feminist concepts that were captured or co-opted by international agencies have lost their radical or critical edge. In that sense, the language of gender and development has been criticized for turning into "buzzwords". An example of this is the developmental use of the term "women's empowerment"**1**. As this concept underwent a process of institutionalization by development agencies in the 1990s it was emptied of its original meaning connected to feminist politics and the transformation of gender power relations. Despite the depolitization of such concept, spaces for contestation and resignification of meaning have never been completely closed.**2** In this context, I was particularly interested in exploring how ideas relating to Islamic feminism have shaped and been shaped by gender and development policy and practice in Yemen.

Since the second half of the nineties, international trends in culture, gender and development approaches started being reflected in Yemen's local projects relating to women's rights and Islam. In line with UN and Western donors discourse and policy, more focus has been placed on funding project proposals that promote women's rights and gender equality from a culturally sensitive perspective, taking more into account Islamic concepts and collaborating with faith-based organizations and religious leaders. With the shift from the WID to the GAD approach[3], donor interest focused on funding projects aimed at "women's empowerment in Muslim contexts" in line with the GAD strategy, rather than merely "incorporating Muslim women into development", as required by the WID approach. The cultural dimensions of development were also brought to the donors´ attention. Culture was no longer seen as a homogeneous and static unit hindering development, but rather as a dynamic and diverse entity in a constant state of flux, driven by both internal and external forces. As such, culture was recognized as a potentially powerful tool that had to be taken into consideration in development processes aimed at social change and at advancing gender equality. Consequently, increasing attention was paid to positive aspects of religious and traditional practices that could be utilized as powerful vehicles for the promotion of women's rights and empowerment. In line with this discursive framework for development, an international dialogue within the Islamic feminist movements could now be set up.

The term "Islamic feminist" itself has been the subject of controversy and disagreement, due to diverging political positions as to whether it is possible to reconcile feminism with Islam or not. Scholars who use this concept also draw attention to its development and plurality of meaning, ranging from evolutions and fragmentation in the theory to the diversity of local Islamic feminist movements. In Margot Badran's view, despite the range of Islamic feminisms, we can still consider their driving core principles and core ideas to have remained the same, and that they are connected to a message of full human equality, including gender equality and social justice.[4] Contemporary Islamic feminist scholars, such as Amina Wadud, Asma Barlas, Azizah al-Hibri, Riffat Hassan, Leila Ahmed and Fatima Mernissi, have produced refined research on the topic and initiated important efforts to propound egalitarian models of Islam. They have been advocating an emphasis on reinterpreting religious texts in the light of feminist human rights perspectives, rather than patriarchal ones, in order to guarantee equal rights to Muslim women within the Islamic framework. The idea that Islam and feminism are compatible and complementary in nature has been seen as a new opportunity to advocate for women's rights within Muslim societies. As such, it has nourished and innovated gender and development strategies applied particularly in countries where Sharia-based laws are enforced. Data from Yemen has not contradicted this trend.

One of the first initiatives in Yemen inspired by this new approach on Islam, gender and development was a project entitled "Muslim Women and Development Action Research" (MWDAR). The project was implemented in 1999-2000 by the Yemeni Women's Union and the Dhamar Women's Health Centre, funded by the Dutch government through the Royal Tropical Institute(KIT). The project aimed to develop insights into the ways in which Muslim women use religious and cultural resources in supporting their rights to reproductive health and education. A further aim was to use these insights to develop approaches to gender and development that empower women and see them as agents of change rather than victims of patriarchal culture.**5** Riffat Hassan, a Pakistani-born scholar and one of the most prominent Islamic feminists, was the principal consultant on this project, providing an Islamic framework to women's human rights advocacy. She believes that the most effective way of empowering Muslim girls and women is through human rights education based on a feminist reading of the Quran. She argues that if women acquire the competency to use religious texts in support of their fundamental rights, they will be equipped to take a stand against negative cultural practices and gender-based violence. The research data of the MWDAR project was interpreted in line with this argument. The study findings focused on a few humble women from the rural areas of Aden and Dhamar that were able to use some positive religious and cultural resources to advocate their rights and freedoms. They applied it to situations where they had to defend their traditional way of living in the face of recent ultra-conservative Islamic speeches that had spread to local villages through extremist mosque preachers and people having received a conservative religious education in school.**6** The analysis of these cases shows that mere access to education is not enough for women's empowerment; above all, it requires an access to quality knowledge and religious information so that women can use these to assert their rights and overcome their reluctance to defending what they consider to be a rightful way of life. Consequently, the study recommended a new strategy for development enhancing women's empowerment through access to religious knowledge in support of women's rights.**7**

A few years later, Brenda Bartelink and Marjo Buitelaar (2006) took up the debate on the MWDAR project to draw attention to its shortcomings and to problematize the question of Islam as a tool for women's empowerment. They believed that the MWDAR project did not meet expectations or project goals, because it failed to go beyond an essentialist view of Muslim women.**8** This had led to an ill-informed conceptualization of the role of Islam in development. A renewed analysis of the life stories of the rural women depicted in the MWDAR project, suggests that the role of religion was mainly relative to the configuration of their everyday lives and positions, and that it was not necessarily more important than other cultural, political and socio-economic factors or knowledge. Although references to Islam are often used when talking, it would be erroneous to think this usage is helpful when dealing with women's empowerment. It can be interpreted, for instance, as a way of reaffirming their Muslim identities or to highlight their faith as a source of inspiration, motivation, and hope. Trust in God and Islamic messages may even help a number of them to endure precarious and difficult situations, but this is mainly a coping mechanism. The idea of 'moving into positions of power', central to the concept of empowerment, was lacking**9**. Empowerment, in feminist theory, is the process by which women, individually and collectively, become aware of the gendered power relations and gain the ability to develop effective strategies to challenge these inequalities and shift power imbalances. Unlike coping mechanisms, empowerment strategies deal not only with patriarchal restrictions, but also have the potential to challenge an oppressive system of male domination and power. From this perspective, a woman-friendly interpretation of Islam can only be a helpful tool in gender development if it is used in the pursuit of feminist political ends. In that sense, the importance of Islamic feminism is not only in religious advocacy of women's rights, but also in its political implications such as tackling those patriarchal ideologies seeking to legitimize gender inequalities in the name of religion. Women's involvement in such gender politics and transformative actions is crucial. Therefore, a key question, discussed in this article, concerns the dynamics of power relations and the recognition of women's agency.

STORIES FROM THE FIELD: BEYOND ESSENTIALIST VIEWS OF MUSLIM WOMEN AND ISLAM

Cassandra Balchin contends,

> *"in current international development policy, religion is simultaneously seen as the biggest developmental obstacle, the only developmental issue, and the only developmental solution. The co-existence of these three —seemingly contrary— approaches, which can often be found within a single bilateral or international development agency or NGO, is possible because they all stem from the same Orientalist presumption about the 'underdeveloped Other' (Said, 1978)."* **10**

This reflexion is particularly useful in relation to the debate on women and Islam in development work, since it has often been trapped between two opposing and contradictory discourses. The first depicts Islam as a barrier to development and as a source of oppression for Muslim women, while the second discourse portrays it as a vehicle for social change and women's empowerment. The problem of both positions lies in their essentialist views of Muslim women as well as in the depiction of Islam as a static and monolithic entity. What is identified as 'Islamic' in both discourses is wrongly represented as something affecting all Muslim women in the same way. Women are depicted as a homogenous group, deprived of power and individual voices, treated as the objects, not the subjects of development. This corresponds with Chandra Tolpade Mohanty's notion of the "third world woman", represented particularly in Western views as a victim without agency, who is always in need of external help.**11**

Despite the influence of religious factors, it cannot be assumed that the situation of women in Yemen is determined solely by Islamic ideologies, norms or beliefs. And, as such, that these situations can be changed simply by replacing conservative interpretations of Islam with more moderate ones that are supportive of women's rights. Although a woman-friendly interpretation of Islam can be a helpful tool in gender and development, it is necessary to bear in mind that there is nothing in 'Islam' intrinsically capable of changing gendered power relations.**12** Moreover, focusing squarely on Islam and the religious identity of Yemeni women in development projects can result in hindering a deeper analysis of their situations in the broader context of economic, political, cultural, social, and gender relations. In my interviews with Yemeni women's rights activists and leaders from various women's non-Islamist networks and NGOs based in Sana´a, Taiz and Aden, I realized that their primary concerns were not religious, but rather related to the lack of opportunities and basic services, poverty, difficulties in accessing and controlling resources, gender-based violence, early marriage, under-representation in the political sphere and in decision-making positions, among others. When asked about religious problems, they expressed worry about the political and social power that Islamic extremist groups and conservative Islamist parties have gained in relatively recent times in Yemen. In particular, they talked about the negative changes that had been observed in women's lives and rights due to the influence of ultra-conservative ideologies that are Wahhabism and Salafism. They also pointed to the influence of conservative party al-Iṣlāḥ in political circles, which had affected many of the progressive social and legislative reforms concerning women's issues in Yemen after unification in the 1990s. The impact of these conservative trends hindered, for instance, the promulgation of a new law that would have made 17 the minimum legal age for marriage. It also affected Yemen's Family Code of 1992, based on Islamic Sharia law, and modified in 1998, 1999 and 2002 with more conservative amendments.

11The life stories of women's rights activists also remind us of the historical difference between women in the South and in the North of Yemen as well as of the diverse sets of values along which both societies were organized. Susanne Dahlgren in her study of Adeni society of the late 1980s has suggests three co-existing frameworks that should have been taken into consideration when analysing the social life of the former capital of South Yemen. These frameworks are: *'adāt wa taqālid* (customs and traditions), *dīn* (religion), and *thawra* (revolution). Regarding religion, Dahlgren specifies, *"'*dīn*' alone does not stand for Islam, since custom and revolution are influenced by it, too, contributing to the local variations of Islam. Rather, '*dīn*' is a specific understanding of Islam that presents this particular religious discourse as the only rightful way of life."***13**

The above-mentioned three major ideologies continue to exist side by side in Aden until present. However, I would suggest that religious discourse has become particularly strong after Yemen's unification in 1990, and has affected the whole Yemeni society. This is how women's rights activists, and in particular those originally from Taiz and Aden, remembered the abrupt shift in gender relationships that took place in Yemeni society after the 1990s:

*"Everything started to change when Yemeni workers returned to Yemen from Saudi Arabia during the Gulf Crisis in the 1990s... Many of them came back with a Wahhabi mentality. At that time, we were in Taiz like that: women without veils ... we didn't wear any black things or cover our faces... Everything changed in just two years, after the Gulf Crisis, in the mountains and in the city."***14**

*"When Wahhabis and Salafis entered Yemen, everything changed. They changed our culture... When I was young everything was different... When I was in the market [in Taiz], I remember it as an open and colourful place, but with the passage of time, the market started getting more closed in upon itself, women started wearing black clothes, everything started to be cloaked in darkness, women and men stopped working together, people started saying: '*ḥaram, ḥaram*' [forbidden, forbidden]... They changed our culture, it went from joyful and colourful to a black Wahhabi and Salafi culture...This Wahhabi culture is killing our spirit, our freedoms."***15**

"In the South [in Aden], we were Muslims... But, because of the communist regime there, after the unification [of South and North Yemen], we were accused of not being Muslim. Before, I was like you, without a veil. I wear the veil only because my colleagues here said that I was not a Muslim... Everything the

previous state had done to improve women's rights, collapsed after unification." **16**

As mentioned above, Yemeni women are particularly concerned about the specific conservative discourses of "*dīn*" that have gained in influence and induced specific sociocultural changes in Yemen since the 1990s. As a consequence, a number of women's rights activists decided to engage in religious debates to run counter the ultra-conservative Islamic influence. In addition, the events of September 11, 2001 represented a turning point in the history of developmental initiatives aiming to tackle Islamist extremism and promote moderate Islam, since Western donor interest in funding such projects in Yemen had grown. This has also had an influence on the project proposals that seek solutions to gender inequality by promoting and enhancing women's human rights through modern interpretations of Islam, and by working side by side with moderate religious leaders and faith-based organizations.

A QUESTION OF JUSTIFICATION: CONNECTING DEVELOPMENT PROJECTS WITH THE GOALS OF ISLAMIC FEMINISM

14A development programme entitled "Women's Rights in Islam" started in 2002, shortly after September 11, and finished in 2008. It was implemented by the Taiz-based NGO "Women's Forum for Research and Training" (WFRT), and funded by the German Agency for Development (GTZ). Its main goal was to raise awareness of women's human rights through the lens of Islam. The strategy consisted of training female and male leaders in woman-friendly interpretations of the Quran and Sunna in order to gain their support and mobilize them to advocate human rights and gender equality in Yemen. Particular attention was paid to imams, preachers and other religious authorities to strengthen their commitment to a human rights perspective on argumentative topics such as polygamy, political participation, the state, inheritance, wergild, equal citizenship, social justice, and equal rights and duties. Project activities consisted mainly of seminars, training sessions, workshops, research studies and publications.

15An in-depth analysis of the "Women's Rights in Islam Programme" shows how gender and development actions can be connected to, but also disconnected from feminist meanings and strategies for women's empowerment. The project was drafted and implemented by the WFRT, which is considered a Yemeni women's NGO. According to the project leader, this initiative aimed to end the male monopoly on the interpretation of Islam and to challenge patriarchal religious power:

> *"It is very important to take the risk of analyzing women's rights from an Islamic perspective. We cannot leave it to imams and to all these religious people. We have to bring all these issues to the table and ask what Islam is. We have to know if Islam is against women or not, and why. Imams and some others keep saying that Islam is not against women. However, we have to know, we have to verify that... Because in real life —it seems to be against women, because they made it so. So we have to know if the problem is with Islam or if it is because of their interpretation of Islam... It is very important to talk about women's rights and Islam, especially when the debate comes from women's organizations... They [male religious scholars] are used to women just keeping silent when they say that this or that is* ḥaram *[forbidden]. Women have always done what they told them to do since it came from Islam, because they told them that was Islam. But when you bring all these issues to the table and discuss them... It is a good thing, because women now can stand up and say: 'No, you are not right, Islam doesn't say such things'."***17***

16The project was driven by the level of women's interest in politics and aimed to reclaim and reinterpret religion from an Islamic feminist perspective in order to advocate for women's rights and gender equality. Due to the highly politicized context of Yemen regarding women's issues, having development practitioners adapt Islamic language and arguments was also seen as a matter of legitimacy needed to justify their work and struggle for women's emancipation.

> *"Yemeni society is strongly influenced by religion", says Suad al-Qadasi, chairwoman of the WFRT. "Any talk of gender equality or the emancipation of women is almost*

> *automatically branded here as western colonialism or un-Islamic. But it is not right to pretend that the emancipation of women is a privilege reserved for the West. Women have rights in Islam too - you just have to read the texts correctly."***18**

The issue of women's rights, as Deniz Kandiyoti put it for the Muslim world, is invariably

> "part of an ideological terrain where broader notions of cultural authenticity and integrity are debated and where women's appropriate place and conduct may be made to serve as boundary markers."**19**

That is why many Yemeni activists, both secular and religious, applied an Islamic framework to human rights and gender equality in answer to those who wished to perpetuate the notion of an East/West split and use the label "western" to discredit progressive moves to implement human rights and women's freedoms. Furthermore, the promotion of women's rights through Islam has been seen as a culturally sensitive approach that helps to connect with wider segments of Yemeni society.

A QUESTION OF POWER IN ISLAMIC HERMENEUTICS

19One of the contributions of the Islam-inspired gender projects in Yemen was to prove and promote compatibility between Islam and women's human rights, as defined by the Convention on the Elimination of All Forms of Discrimination against Women (CEDAW), through the use of feminist interpretations of Islamic texts. The above-mentioned WFRT project published two training manuals in Arabic supporting women's human rights authored by female experts in the field of Islamic jurisprudence and philosophy. The first guide was prepared by Zeinab Radwan (2004), an Egyptian academic scholar and successful politician, member of parliament. The second one was edited by Farida Bennani (2005), a Moroccan feminist researcher and university professor of Islamic law. Similar publications relating to women's human rights and Islam were also developed by other Yemeni women's organizations, including the Women's National Committee and the Yemeni Women's

Union. Consequently, women's rights as stipulated in international human rights treaties and ratified by Yemen, were reaffirmed as valid and legitimate from an Islamic perspective. In particular, among women's rights confirmed as being fundamental to Islam are the following: the right to life, dignity, education, justice, freedom, work, income and property, to live in safety and security, and to participate in all affairs pertaining to women's personal well-being and that of their families, communities and societies.

20The women's reinterpretations of Islamic texts and teachings in accordance with international standards of human rights challenge conventional patriarchal views on gender relations in Islam, and are a threat to male dominance and power. Therefore, such practices often meet with religiously grounded opposition and are the target of attacks from conservative religious factions. The WFRT project was no exception to such a dynamic. As one project leader recalls,

> "The first minister who contacted me when he read about the project was the Minister of Awqāf [Religious Endowments] from Saudi Arabia. He sent twenty copies of books about Islam to my office... These people, when they get to know about projects like that, they become afraid. They want to keep you within their interpretation of Islam. For us, it was a sign that our project was on the right track. I even put those books in the library, I don't hide them... It is a measure of our project. We didn't know that the project could be a problem for them. But it was... It caused them a lot of problems... Even Zindānī ['Abd Abd al-Majīd al-Zindānī, conservative Yemeni cleric from the Iṣlāḥ Party]wrote a fatwa against one of our researchers [Muḥammad Sayf al-'Udaynī], who wrote a book about ten obstacles standing in the way of women's rights in Islam... Things calmed down, because he [Muḥammad al-'Udaynī] is from Iṣlāḥ too... But, what do you think would have happened if al-'Udaynī had not been with Iṣlāḥ? If he had been just a researcher at the university or from any other modern organization? They let him off the hook, because he was from their organization."**20**

21There is no doubt that feminist interpretations of the Quran, along with other training and social re-education activities dealing with such points of view of Islam, points of view amenable to human rights and gender equality perspectives, play a part in gender politics and dynamics of power. The renegotiation of gender power relations involves conflict and resistance. However, I would argue that without a real commitment to the feminist goals of women's empowerment and the radical readjustment of patriarchal power structures, these strategies can easily lose their initial meanings and intentions in terms of transformative actions in development work. The crucial questions of *how*, *why* and *who* is implementing these strategies make all the difference in determining their success in terms of final project outcomes and progress toward the goal of gender equality and social justice.

ENGAGING WITH ISLAM TO PROMOTE WOMEN'S RIGHTS: OPPORTUNITIES AND SHORTCOMINGS IN DEVELOPMENT PROJECTS

22The "Women's Rights in Islam Programme", according to WFRT and GTZ reports, succeeded in engaging Yemeni women with leadership potential and from different professional backgrounds (such as lawyers, teachers, journalists, preachers and NGO representatives) in project activities. The training provided them with sound arguments about their rights in Islam, and with the skills to participate in public debates with the media, judiciary, university scholars and religious leaders. The project aim was to generate a ripple effect by mobilizing them to train other women and discuss specific issues relating to gender and Islam from a woman-friendly interpretation of the Quran and hadiths. There are no available references in the project documents to measure the real impact and changes incurred as a result of these activities. As I was told, the women, mainly preachers and teachers, refused to be observed and evaluated when they had meetings with other women, mostly in private houses and schools. Still, post-project interviews with the outstanding Yemeni women involved in the WFRT project as coordinators or as participants, suggest certain positive impacts on their personal sense of empowerment thanks to the knowledge acquired on women's human rights in Islam and other related topics. The woman-friendly interpretations of Islam were seen as an important tool to give legitimacy to their public work and to enhance their motivation to pursue their personal goals. However, it was not the religious knowledge in itself that had prepared them and propelled them to their leadership positions.

23The experience of empowerment was seen as a process. It was not due to just one project but instead to many factors that shaped their personal, relational and professional life. Training on women's rights from a reform-oriented Islamic perspective was relevant in gaining an insight into the distinction between normative Islam, and its cultural interpretations tied to a local political and economic context. It helped by enhancing women's freedom to make choices. For example, Tawakkul Karmān, laureate of the Nobel Peace Prize 2011 and founder of the organization "Women Journalists without Chains", decided in 2004 to take off her *niqāb*, the cloth covering her face, to make a point that fully covering your face is not dictated by Islam, but is Yemeni tradition. Other well-known women who were involved in the WFRT project, like Raḥma Ḥujayra, founder of the Media Women's Forum, or Misk al-Junayd, who now works for international organizations, made similar remarks, and removed their face veils in the process of empowering themselves. It is difficult to attribute this kind of personal choice to the WFRT project. However, according to one of the WFRT leaders, such a choice should be recognized as a result of the awareness raised in Yemen by such initiatives. Personally, she considers that her particular knowledge of Islam along with the critical thinking skills was useful in defending her rights and freedoms in the face of religious conservatism:

> "I know a lot about Islam. I can discuss it with imams. If they say one thing, I can answer back and give them other arguments from the Quran or hadiths... However, if you want to challenge them, you have to know what you're talking about. These people are very tough. They will fight for what they have. If you don't have something to make them question themselves, then you have failed."**21**

Other activists from non-Islamist women's networks in Sana'a present two different, but complementary points of view. In their statements, they claim that a faith-based approach is politically necessary in Yemen, even if the way the strategy is currently implemented is a topic of controversy in the women's rights movement. A number of women focus on the potential of Islam as a positive resource for gender equality. They claim women have a right to interpret their religion in accordance with modern times and with the principles of equality, justice and freedom in mind. Their declarations clearly go against patriarchal interpretations, made by mostly male religious scholars. As one of the Yemeni female university scholars says,

> "Women should have the right to interpret Islamic texts to lay down our rights very clearly. They should sit with men and say, 'these are our rights according to this book [in the Quran], why are you hiding them?' I, as a Muslim woman, I know Islam by myself, I practice what I know, and I never accept any advice or speech from any imam or religious men. I don't accept them at all, because they are not clear and not honest in their visions... I am not a specialist in this area... But, there are women who are specialists of Islam, and who have the power to teach about these issues... Internationally, we should set up a system where women are visible and they interpret their religion. Women should interpret religion for other women. We should have access to their books to read them... Unfortunately, there are also women who are specialists of Islam, but they are extremists, and they ask other women to be invisible, more than they are now. They are dangerous... We need women who can teach women-friendly interpretations of Quran... I am a Quranist, I believe in the Quran and in a few hadiths only. I don't believe in all the hadiths, because they were created by people, and some seem to be against women."**22**

There are also Yemeni women's rights activists who think the current talk about Islam only shifts the focus away from other debates relating to modern, cultural, intellectual and social dynamics in the country. This resulted in their voices not being heard in current gender and development policy and practice. These secular Muslim activists prefer promoting human rights and gender equality from a non-religious perspective. Most of them are highly critical of the ways in which Islam-inspired gender projects are implemented in Yemen. According to them, that sort of strategy does more harm than good. It overlooks the problem of power relations and seeks a solution to discrimination against women through religious preaching and education. Although these opinions are still limited in number, they are based on women's professional experience in gender and development work in Yemen. One of these women identified the following shortcomings in the projects on which she worked:

> "We have very weak education in Yemen. The only knowledge that the society has access to comes from religious perspectives. There is no effort to give people a different kind of education... And, development organizations have never made any effort to change that... From my point of view, the main problem is not religion, but the lack of services and opportunities... Here... they use religious awareness for family planning... When they want to stop a woman from having too many children, they give her religious speeches. Do you think this can give her access to contraceptives? That is not the way to go. We have to give her contraceptive services. We have to have more powerful women, women with income and a good education, and also stop the conflicts."**23**

Another women's rights practitioner, while talking about her experiences in dealing with the religious approach in the UNFPA Gender-based Violence Programme, came to the similar conclusion that religion and Islamic scholars are not the key issues in enhancing women's empowerment and in implementing women's rights in Yemen. She was concerned with the strategy itself as well as with the ways in which the project was implemented:

> "There are no real follow-up mechanisms... When we finished the project, we ended with some recommendations to be implemented. But, nobody has used these recommendations to start from where we finished... Everybody is always starting from square one... The second point is that we have to work on services... We need to support women with services free of charges... We were talking about how women should use these services, and we worked on women's awareness about the system. It was like

> the first stage… but the problem is that we didn't develop these services… We were discussing whether women should go directly to court, to the police station or to the hospital. But, these places are not gender-sensitive at all, and you have to have money to pay for them. What if you don't have money?… The majority of women don't have their own money… They need help with services."**24**

The above-mentioned declarations of Yemeni women's rights practitioners draw attention to the complexity of Islam-inspired gender projects in a context of development machinery. On the one hand, a number of women activists recognize the positive value of promoting women's rights within the legitimate framework of Islam. They see it as a positive strategy to raise awareness about women's rights and to connect with broader segments of Yemeni society. On the other hand, there are limitations. Gender equality advancement and women's empowerment do not necessarily take place in the targeted or expected directions. From the feminist perspective, it is questionable if any meaningful impact on the advancement of women's empowerment and gender equality can be attributed to such development projects. In reality, all these are specific and isolated activities, the impact of which does not necessarily go beyond the information gained during the training sessions, workshops, seminars, mosque-based activities or awareness raising campaigns through mass media. The main shortcoming of these programmes is in their inability to implement a holistic strategy that would empower women and provide them with the necessary resources and services to put into practice the knowledge acquired during awareness-raising activities. For Yemeni women's rights activist, the holistic strategy requires, as a minimum, access to good quality education, control over resources, providing services, and the power of decision making.

RUNNING THE RISK OF LOSING SIGHT OF FEMINIST GOALS IN PROJECTS RELATED TO GENDER AND ISLAM

These missed opportunities for women's empowerment within Islam-inspired development projects are due to the way in which "gender" has been deployed within them, resulting in the de-politicization of feminist commitments. While in feminist theory, "gender" refers to male-female power relations, and its goal is to transform these hierarchical relations in order to generate more equality and justice for women, the usage of this concept in development practice has often been misleading. Authors like Sally Baden and Anne Marie Goetz (1997) show how "gender" has become a synonym for "women" in development work. My concerns lie elsewhere, and point to practice where "gender" gets men and women jointly involved in development projects, but fails to integrate consciously and consistently gender analysis**25**, which creates a disconnect between this advance and feminist goal of eliminating gender discrimination and inequalities. Involving men into gender and development policy and practice is of unquestionable importance. However, this integration should not be mainly interpreted as a mean of increasing number of men in existing gender projects, inadvertently at the expense of women's participation and advancement. It is more about assuming equal responsibilities in transforming gender power relations to make the world a better place for both men and women.

Yemen-based projects relating to women and Islam can give an insight into challenges that lay ahead of this "gender" trend. Projects goals are the promotion of women's rights and empowerment, but do not necessarily focus on strengthening women's movements, instead they target influential men. Getting male leaders involved in women's rights advocacy stems from an assumption that they have an advantage over women as influential community members who are perceived as trustworthy and who people will listen to. The change in strategy of the WFRT project on "Women's rights in Islam" was partly motivated by this belief.**26** In 2005, the project shifted from a woman-oriented approach to a gender-oriented one. Consequently, influential groups of men were targeted, including imams, religious scholars, mosque preachers, university professors, journalists, lawyers and human rights activists. The aim was to turn them into supporters of women's issues in Yemen. As explained in the project documentation,

> "the gender issue was placed in a general human rights and democracy context. The original concept was modified such that special training courses [focusing on citizenship, democracy and women's rights in Islam] were offered to men

alone, so that they too could support the process of rethinking."**27**

30Engaging men in the process was acclaimed by development agencies as good practice to achieve successful results in gender work. However, little efforts have been made to critically analyse the outcome of this strategy in Yemen, to measure its real contribution to feminist goals of women's empowerment and gender equality.

The data from the WFRT project documents raise questions. The WFRT report on the last phase of the programme (September 2007–December 2008), for instance, shows that men, and not women, were the major beneficiaries of the project. The first activity of that phase consisted of a research meeting in Taiz, in September 2007, held to prepare a study design on equal citizenship in Yemen. Eight researchers took part in that meeting, all men. Three of them ended up writing research studies sponsored by the WFRT project. As a result, three books were published, namely: *Citizenship and the Paradox of State in Islamic Thinking* by Abdulkarim Kassem, *Equal Citizenship in Islam* by Mohammed al-Lotaify, and *Equal Citizenship in Light of Sharia Objectives* by Abdulaziz al-Usaly. Following the new gender strategy, the language deployed in the project also changed. There were no workshops on "women's rights" anymore, but on "equal citizenship", so that the title of the topic was more attractive for both sexes. In fact, it was appealing to men, who represented the majority of training participants. Concretely, the targeted number of beneficiaries in the first workshop on equal citizenship, held in Sana'a in December 2007, was 46: 66.6% males and 33.3% females. In the second workshop, carried out in Sana'a in March 2008, there were 21 participants: 63.15% males and 36.85% females. The majority of lecturers in both workshops were also men. In the first one, there was only one woman out of eight lecturers. In the second one, the main trainer was a male expert on human rights in the Arab world, who carried out eleven sessions. A woman, the chair of the WFRT, held two sessions only. The rest of the projects' activities consisted of lectures presented mostly by male scholars. As a result, in the last phase of the programme, most of the 276 direct beneficiaries were men, although it is hard to find out the exact number due to a lack of sex-disaggregated data. The total number of indirect beneficiaries, those to whom direct beneficiaries of the program imparted their knowledge, was 16143: 5120 women and 11023 men.**28** The fact that the majority of beneficiaries in the last phase of the project were men means that they also benefited the most from that stage of the project. The training courses provided them with qualifications, skills and contacts that were helpful in enhancing their public profile and in getting job opportunities. A number of male religious scholars and leaders were employed as trainers in other projects, including other WFRT initiatives. Some got a chance to travel abroad to receive more training or to spread success stories of their experiences in gender programmes.

32The lack of an equity policy regarding the problem of gender distribution and power relations raises questions of missed opportunities for women in such gender projects. Instead of promoting women, they involuntarily promote men. Incorporating religious leaders and scholars as development partners in gender projects in Yemen is another illustration of this issue. The justification for mobilizing religious men and faith-based organizations in women's rights advocacy is based on the assumption that they could play a leading role in influencing public opinion and stimulating social change. In Yemen, the United Nations Population Fund (UNFPA) has one of the longest-running experiences in dealing with gender initiatives implemented in partnership with faith-based organizations and religious communities. Since 1998, the UNFPA has been working with Yemen's Ministry of Awqāf and Religious Guidance and other religious institutions to raise public awareness and social change in the fields of reproductive health, family planning, HIV/AIDS, early marriage, female genital mutilation and gender-based violence. Initiatives involved male imams, scholars and preachers who were supposed to promote women's empowerment through the use of women-friendly Islamic resources. Nevertheless, these projects never intended to challenge the fact that women are excluded from the most important religious leadership positions in Yemen, and that certain Islamic teachings continue to be widely used to justify this exclusion. There are no female imams or women having attained decision-making positions in prominent religious institutions in Yemen. As of now, female preachers mostly operate at grassroots levels. This goes against the fact that there are female precursors in religious leadership positions in other Muslim countries and in Muslim communities in Europe and in the United States. The case of Amina Wadud, an American scholar and Islamic feminist, who asserted the right to be an imam for a mixed-gender congregation, is emblematic, for instance, of the debate on women as imams in Islam.

"Recent increases in the ability of Muslim women to publicly speak as preachers, teachers, scholars or interpreters of religious texts represent a significant shift in Islamic leadership and authority".**29** These women, and especially Islamic feminists, are challenging male dominance, drawing on their knowledge, beliefs and practices in creative and innovative ways. The WFRT programme on "Women's rights in Islam" dealt with a similar experience when it first started. Leading female Islamic scholars, such as Zeinab Radwan from Egypt and Farida Bennani from Morocco, were involved in the early phases of the project. Despite their controversial appearance as unveiled Muslim women**30**, they are acknowledged as prominent Islamic scholars, and male religious preachers and leaders take part in their training courses and workshops. WFRT's first initiative relating to gender and Islam was to organize a training workshop on Islam in Lebanon for a mixed group of potential leaders from Yemen. The trainers were mostly women and their reform-oriented teachings were progressively accepted by Yemeni male imams. As one of the WFRT leaders remembers,

> "Mūna come from Egypt and another trainer from Tunisia, both women came to train male imams. It was a shock for them, 'female trainers on modern Islam!' And then, they had that long workshop, maybe 10 days, and they always came on time, they sat and listened to these women...This is what we first did —we took 25 imams, among others, to Lebanon. Why? If we had started here [in Yemen], we would not have succeeded. But, because we took them to Beirut, it made a difference."**31**

Getting back to the debate on the role of male religious leaders and scholars in development programmes, there is no in-depth research on the impact of their involvement in gender projects on empowering women and on gender equality. A number of developmental practitioners in Yemen believe that cooperating with religious leaders as advocates and partners in promoting women's rights is a successful strategy. However, to what extent are their opinions influenced by current development discourses rather than based on facts? If we question the details of how the approach was implemented, limitations show up. My concern goes further, as even the most moderate imams that I interviewed in Yemen - acting as project stakeholders - were sometimes reluctant to break with certain conventional Islamic teachings on gender models, regarding differences between women's and men's rights and freedoms. This is in opposition to international commitments to gender equality and women's human rights as declared in CEDAW.

In 2011, I paid a visit to the National Organization for Developing Society (NODS) in Taiz, founded by Shawqī al-Qāḍī, moderate imam and Iṣlāḥ Member of Parliament. Previously, I had had the opportunity to evaluate a project carried out by the same organization in partnership with the Yemeni Women's Union. The project was entitled "Leadership for Strengthening Women's Political Participation through Dialogue in Yemen", and was implemented in 2008–2009. Its goal was to improve the political and social integration of women through consensus and network building in support of women's political rights across a broad spectrum of political and civil society actors. It is one of many projects, in which NODS has collaborated in support of women's rights in Yemen. Nevertheless, NODS' area of expertise is in projects targeting imams and other religious people in an effort to embrace democracy and human rights as well as combat religious extremism and faith-based violence. The NODS is well known for the effectiveness of its strategies in that field and its achievements in re-educating ultra-conservative men in accordance with moderate teachings of Islam. The contribution of such initiatives to social change and for a better society is indubitable. However, the extent to which these male religious leaders and scholars play an important role in women's empowerment and in transforming gender power relations is unclear. Do they offer any alternative to traditional and conservative gender models in Yemen? The case of Muḥammad**32**, a 35-year-old imam who currently works for international organizations and trains youth on human rights in Islam, is an illustrative example of a Salafi turned moderate Islamist. Because he received training on women's human rights from the WFRT and other development organizations, questions have been raised about the impact that these gender courses have had on his life and his way of thinking. In a conversation, he listed his public contributions to the promotion of women's rights in Yemen, and in particular to the national campaigns against early marriage and gender-based violence. On a personal level, he mentioned how his perceptions of Yemeni women working for international organizations had changed positively. Previously, he used to have a negative opinion of them, based on stereotypes of 'modern' women's behaviour, particularly women's rights activists. In Yemen, female activists are often the victims of discrediting tactics, one of which is to falsely accuse them of being agents of the West and of subverting Islamic values. In short, Muḥammad's discourse on women's rights and freedoms tended to be progressive. However, a closer look at his private life revealed certain contradictions between his moderate discourse and his actual practice. He considers that there are still certain men's rights and privileges that cannot be revoked since they are given by Islam. His recently contracted multi-wife marriage, which was undoubtedly made in good faith, is an example of men's exclusive rights which he asserts cannot be changed and are considered sacred.

36In my interviews with Yemeni women's rights activists a part of the urban elite of well-educated professionals who mostly work for International Organizations (IO) and NGOs, having male imams and Islamic scholars promote new models of masculinity and the full realization of gender equality is greeted with scepticism. Yemeni religious leaders, with the exception of one or two, are not seen as the best role models for other boys and men to promote gender equality and new conceptions of masculinity. A number of women's rights activists believe that they should not been seen as key people to work with on women's empowerment. Their criticism concerns the fact that too much importance has often been given to male religious leaders and scholars, at the expense of other stakeholders, including Yemeni women. They recognize, however, that it is politically important for women's organizations and development workers to set up strategic alliances with religious leaders and faith-based organizations to advocate reforms of Sharia-based laws and other related issues. Yemeni women's rights activists point out the advantages of using religious strategies in Muslim contexts, but also show the limitations and possible dangers of approaches to women's advocacy relying solely on religious discourses and actors. While speaking about the sensitive gender issues in Islam, like equal rights and spousal duties, inheritance, and so on, one of the Yemeni activists said:

> "Yes, maybe they [male religious leaders and scholars] don't believe in all rights for women, but some of them... Very few of them, who are open-minded, they believe in women's rights... But me, I don't believe that they will accept ever all of women's rights. You know, Yemen ratified CEDAW, but some issues are untouchable, nobody will touch them, because they will say that these rights are for men and are given by Allah. Even some women believe that... I don't want to generalize, but men always fight for women's rights if it doesn't get in the way of their own interests. Their own interests have to be prioritized, and then if women can get other rights —it is fine [laughs]. That is why the Quran is interpreted in keeping with the interests of men. Who interprets the Quran? All of them are men. The preachers are men, so they give the community what they want, and they pass on the idea of the Quran and its verses based on their interests."**33**

37My research findings suggest that the religious scholars, preachers and imams who were selected for and successfully passed the gender and human rights training workshops, organized by NGOs and IOs across Yemen, are able to accept women's rights and freedoms, and even become partners in promoting them, unless this implies a subversion of their own position within the hierarchy of patriarchal power. It means that certain women's rights are more easily accepted than others. In fact, Islamic jurisprudence recognizes many women's rights, but still promotes significant gender differences in freedoms and responsibilities in people's daily lives, for marriage and its dissolution. This, along with granting men privileges such as polygamy, unilateral divorce (*ṭalāq*) and a larger part of inheritance, constitutes a sensitive issue when dealing with Islamic leaders from CEDAW gender equality perspective. When talking about these issues, cultural and religious differences are frequently claimed to justify patriarchal models of gendered power relations. It seems like these cultural and religious claims merely serve as justification for women's oppression. Within this system women can obtain certain privileges and rights by coping, strategizing or bargaining with patriarchy. However, their strategies do not necessary mean the subversion of the whole structure of men's power. If social change only occurs at men's convenience, and in clear opposition to the real recognition and implementation of gender equality in rights, responsibilities, freedoms and opportunities, the patriarchal system will not collapse, but will be revived in a new form. Its survival depends on its capacity to extend within the limits of women's rights and freedoms. It can be useful at certain levels to promote gender equality by dealing with male Islamic religious leaders, scholars and preachers; however it is likely to have limited results in terms of real transformation of gender power relations and women's empowerment.

CONCLUSIONS

38Through an analysis of selected gender development projects and in-depth interviews with women's rights activists, I have tried to verify to what extent gender and development practice in Yemen is consistent with the current theory and policy on 'culture, gender equality and human development'. I was particularly interested in analyzing the ways in which new developmental thought and policy reconsider Islam as a potential tool and means to promote women's rights and empowerment, and how it has been adapted and implemented in Yemen. I also paid attention to the ways in which women's rights activists were involved and dealt with issues of renegotiation of gender power relations and resignification of gender concepts in the light of Islamic feminism. The main research findings confirm a persistent gap between gender, culture and development theory and practice. Academic efforts and political statements hardly translate into effective action. Discourses in international development have changed, but initiatives on the ground are still very often guided by outdated developmental thought. Stereotypical representations of others and of their cultures as well as North-South power relationships determine the main orientations in development work. Cultural considerations in Muslim countries have frequently been reduced to religious aspects only. Furthermore, my research findings suggest that there is still an inadequate understanding of how "Islam" may affect the empowerment or disempowerment of Yemeni women. Although gender and development projects created within an Islamic framework have been inspired by Islamic feminisms, they are not necessarily consistent with the political implications of promoting "women's empowerment" and "gender equality". Once deployed in development, these concepts are used as buzzwords to get funding and justify development intervention. As a result, they easily lose their original feminist meaning during project implementation. Despite good intentions, many Yemen-based projects relating to gender and Islam did not succeed in achieving their goals of gender transformation and women's empowerment. In my argumentation, the problem is that they ignored the question of power and undermined women's agency. These projects mainly consisted of training and social re-education in woman-friendly interpretations of the Quran and Sunna.They undoubtedly contributed to raising gender awareness and also provided useful arguments with which to defend women's human rights from an Islamic perspective. Nevertheless, access to information and knowledge does not necessarily guarantee that women's rights will be fully exercised and gender equality implemented. Raising awareness through training and workshops can be considered a first step in that direction, but certainly not the last. Unfortunately, a number of projects in Yemen end before moving past the beginning stages, hoping that social change will come about automatically, regardless of the shortage of effective strategies to transform patriarchal power structures. Despite the use of gender and development discourses, most of the projects mentioned in the article failed when they were being implemented, more specifically, they failed in applying the feminist strategic vision of gender and power transformations. They used an Islamic framework and got religious leaders involved as a strategy to promote women's rights and freedoms. However, little effort was made to critically analyse the possible dangers and assumptions that are behind that approach. My concern lies in privileging faith-based approaches over more secular strategies to advocate women's rights in Yemen. In particular, there is a problem with the instrumentalization of religion to advance certain political agendas. The use of 'Islam', either by Islamic feminists or by opposing fundamentalist clerics, results in competing religious visions over gender relationships and women's rights. In fact, when dealing with 'Islam' and women's issues, it is necessary to take into consideration the power relations that shape and are re-shaped by highly contextualized and dynamic aspects of Yemeni culture and politics, which determine the gender interests of the different social groups. Power relations are continuously overlooked in the process of mobilizing male religious leaders and scholars in development projects to advocate women's rights and enhance women's empowerment. Partnering with them without challenging patriarchal power structures means women's exclusion from religious leadership and other decision-making positions, traditionally male-dominated, remain unchanged and reproducing the *status quo* in Yemen.

Religious and cultural considerations need to be taken into account, but with close attention paid to power relations and their gender implications for bargaining power. Having male religious scholars, imams and other opinion-makers as allies in efforts to enhance women's rights and gender equality is seen as politically necessary by Yemeni activists and development practitioners. However, due to the fact that funding allocations in collaboration with religious entities are often made at the expense of directly supporting women and women's movements, Yemeni women's rights activists find this strategy particularly controversial. As one of my interviewees said, *"by supporting and engaging religious leaders in gender and developmental projects, we also empower them."* **34** To be consistent with feminist meanings of gender and development, the priority of investment should go to empowering women rather than male religious leaders. Dealing with the latter yields unreliable results. Especially now, with the emerging women's movement as part of Yemen's Revolution of 2011-2012 there is a new opportunity to re-engage with feminist goals. Although women's agency was internationally and locally recognized in the 'Arab Spring' and symbolically acknowledged by awarding the 2011 Nobel Peace Prize to Tawakkul Karmān, there is still a gap between this recognition and the feminist-oriented empowerment of the women's movement. This very agency has framed women's ability to resist oppression in Yemen and lead cultural and social transformations. As soon as it engages within a strong feminist movement, it will also provide meaningful answers about the political strategies and creative power needed to successfully challenge gender inequalities in Yemen and shed light on how to overcome deep-rooted patriarchal structures.

Notes

1 BATLIWALA, 2010, p. 111-120.

2 CORNWALL, 2010, p. 14.

3 The WID (or Women in Development) approach emerged in the 1970s and called for greater attention to women in development policy and practice. It brought into the spotlight the need to integrate women into development projects not only as "needy" beneficiaries, but above all as active agents. As a result, the women's productive contribution to development was made visible, and their reproductive role was downplayed. From a WID perspective, women's subordination was seen in terms of their exclusion from the marketplace, and their limited access to and control over resources. It was, therefore, assumed that if women were more fully brought into the productive sphere, not only would they make a positive contribution to development, but they would also be able to improve their status vis-à-vis men. By focusing on women alone, the WID approach failed to bring in men, and the question of male power over women. The GAD (or Gender and Development) approach emerged as a preferable alternative to WID, as it suggested the importance of power, conflict and gender relations in understanding women's subordination. An international commitment to GAD at the 1995 Beijing World Conference on Women has recognized it as a necessary consideration in current development policy and practice. It proposes two complementary strategies to be simultaneously addressed in order to tackle the root causes of gender inequalities: "women's empowerment" and "gender mainstreaming". Both strategies are aimed at challenging persisting gender gaps and to subvert patriarchal structures of power. In general, programmes informed by a WID approach addressed women's practical needs by, for example, creating employment and income-generating opportunities, improving access to credit and to education. In contrast, a GAD approach is aimed to meet both women's practical gender needs and more strategic gender needs by challenging existing gender role divisions and power relations.

4 BADRAN, 2010, p. 2. See also on the variety of Islamic feminism, LATTE ABDALLAH, 2010.

5 KIT, 2000, p. 3.

6 Personal Interview with a women's rights practitioner, a MWDAR project researcher (W-7), Sana´a, 2011/04/05.

7 MUKHOPADYA, 2001, p. 17.

8 BARTELINK and BUITELAAR, 2006, p. 351-361.

9 BARTELINK and BUITELAAR, 2006, p. 356.

10 BALCHIN, 2010, p. 83.

11 MOHANTY, 1991.

12 BARTELINK and BUITELAAR, 2006, p. 358.

13 DAHLGREN, 2007, p. 330.

14 Personal interview with a woman's rights practitioner (W-10), Taiz, 10 May 2011.

15 Personal interview with a woman's rights practitioner (W-1), Sana'a, 11 March 2012.

16 Personal interview with a woman's rights practitioner (W-3), Sana'a, 13 June 2011.

17 Personal interview with Yemeni women's rights practitioner (W-10), Taiz, 10 May 2011.

18 SABRA, 2008, p. 39.

19 Abu Lughod, 1998, p. 3.

20 Personal interview with a woman's rights practitioner (W-10), Taiz, 10 May 2011.

21 Personal interview with a woman's rights practitioner (W-10), Taiz, 10 May 2011.

22 Personal interview with a woman's rights practitioner (W-7), Sana'a, 5 April 2011.

23 Personal interview with a woman's rights practitioner (W-14), Sana'a, 14 June 2011.

24 Personal interview with a woman's rights practitioner (W-4), Sana'a, 7 June 2011.

25 Gender analysis refers to "the systematic gathering and examination of information on gender differences and social relations in order to identify, understand and redress inequities based on gender" (Reeves and Baden, 2000, p. 6).

26 Personal interview with a woman's rights practitioner (W-10), Taiz, 2011/05/10.

27 Sabra, 2008, p. 40.

28 WFRT, 2009, p. 36.

29 Dr Hilary Kalmbach, co-author of *Women, Leadership and Mosques: Changes in Contemporary Islamic Authority*, http://www.ox.ac.uk/media/news_stories/2012/120309.html, accessed 25/02/2013.

30 Zeinab Radwan and Farida Bennani do not usually use a *ḥijāb*, a headscarf, which is a practice that would hardly be accepted by religious conservatives since, according to conventional Islamic teachings, a Muslim woman should wear a veil and modest clothing.

31 Personal interview with a woman's rights practitioner (W-10), Taiz, 2011/05/10.

32 The name has been changed to protect the informant's identity.

33 Personal interview with a woman's rights practitioner (W-8), Sana'a, 18 September 2011.

34 Personal interview with a woman's rights practitioner (W-15), Sana'a, 2011/07/11.

BIBLIOGRAPHIE

1. ABU LUGHOD L. (ed.), *Remaking Women. Feminism and Modernity in the Middle East,* Princeton University Press, Princeton, 1998.

2. AHMED L., "Feminism and Feminist Movements in the Middle East, a Preliminary Exploration. Turkey, Egypt, Algeria, People's Democratic Republic of Yemen", *Women's Studies International Forum,* No. 5(2), 1982, p. 153-168.

3. AHMED L., *Women and Gender in Islam. Historical Roots of a Modern Debate,* New Haven and London, Yale University Press, 1992.

4. BADEN S. and GOETZ A. M., "Who Needs 'Sex' When You Can Have 'Gender'? Conflicting Discourses on Gender at Beijing", *Feminist Review,* No. 56, 1997, p. 3-25.

5. BADRAN M., "Unifying Women. Feminist Pasts and Present in Yemen", *Gender & History,* No. 10(3), 1998, p. 498-518.

6. BADRAN M., *Feminism in Islam. Secular and Religious Convergences,* Oxford, Oneworld, 2008.

7. BADRAN M., "An Historical Overview of Conferences on Islamic Feminism. Circulations and New Challenges", in St. Latte Abdallah (dir.), *Féminismes islamiques, Revue des mondes musulmans et de la Méditerranée,* No. 128, 2010 http://remmm.revues.org/6824.

8. BALCHIN C., "The F-word and the S-word —too much of one and not enough of the other", in A. Cornwall and D. Eade (eds.), *Deconstructing Development Discourse. Buzzwords and Fuzzwords,* Oxford, Oxfam, 2010, p. 81-88.

9. BALCHIN C., "Religion and Development. A Practitioner's Perspective on Instrumentalisation", Gender, Rights and Religion at the Crossroads, *IDS Bulletin*, No. 42(1), 2011, p. 15-20.

10. BARTELINK Br. and BUITELAAR M., "The challenges of incorporating Muslim women's views into development policy. Analysis of a Dutch action research project in Yemen", *Gender and Development,* No. 14(3), 2006, p. 351-362.

11. BATLIWALA Sr., "Taking the power out of empowerment —an experiential account", in A. Cornwall and D. Eade (eds.), *Deconstructing Development Discourse. Buzzwords and Fuzzwords,* Oxford, Oxfam, 2010, p. 111-120.

12. BENNANI F., *Ḥuqūq al-Nisā' fi al-Islam (Women´s right in Islam). Training manual 2,* Taiz, Women's Forum for Research and Training (WFRT) and GTZ Yemen, 2005.

13. BHAVNANI K.-K., FORAN J. and KURIAN P., *Feminist Futures. Re-imagining Women, Culture and Development*, London, Zed Books, 2000.

14. CARAPICO Sh., *Civil Society in Yemen. The Political Economy of Activism in Modern Arabia,* London, Cambridge University Press, 1998.

15. COLBURN M., *Gender and Development in Yemen,* Bonn, Friedrich Ebert Stiftung, 2002.

16. CORNWALL A. and EADE D. (eds.), *Deconstructing Development Discourse. Buzzwords and Fuzzwords,* Oxford, Oxfam, 2010.

17. DAHLGREN S., "Islam, Custom and Revolution in Aden. Reconsidering the Background to the Changes of the Early 1990s", in K. A. Mahdi, A. Würth & H. Lackner (eds.), *Yemen into the Twenty-first Century. Continuity and Change,* Reading, Ithaca Press, 2007, p. 327-345.

18. DESTREMAU Bl. and GRABUNDZIJA M., *Women and Civil Society. Capacity Building in Yemen. A Research Perspective on Development,* Sana'a, CEFAS, 2011.

19. DE REGT M., *Pioneers or Pawns? Women Health Workers and the Politics of Development in Yemen,* New York, Syracuse University Press, 2007.

20. JOLLY S., *Gender and Cultural Change. Supporting Resources Collection,* Brighton, BRIDGE, Institute of Development Studies, University of Sussex, 2002.

21. KABEER N., *Reversed Realities. Gender Hierarchies in Development Thought,* London, Zed Press, 1994.

22. KANDIYOTI D., "Bargaining with patriarchy", *Gender and Society,* Vol. 2, No. 3, 1988, p. 274-290.

23. KIRMANI N., "Re-thinking the Promotion of Women's Rights through Islam in India", Gender, Rights and Religion at the Crossroads, *IDS Bulletin,* No. 42(1), 2011, p. 56-66.

24. KIT, *Muslim Women and Development Action Research Project. Fieldwork phase I,* Royal Tropical Institute (KIT), Women, Gender and Development Programme, Amsterdam, 2000.

25. LEACH F., "Gender, education and training. An International Perspective", *Gender and Development,* Vol. 6, No. 2, 1998, p. 9-18.

26. LATTE ABDALLAH St. (dir.), Féminismes islamiques, *Revue d'Études sur le Monde Musulman et la Méditerranée,* n°128-2, 2010.

27. MARCHAND M. and PARPART J. (eds.), *Feminism, postmodernism, development,* London, Routledge, 1995.

28. MERNISSI F., *Beyond the Veil. Male-Female Dynamics in Modern Muslim Society,* Revised edition, Boomington, Indiana University Press, 1987.

29. MERNISSI F., *The Veil and the Male Elite. A feminist interpretation of women's rights in Islam*, New York, Addison-Wesley, 1991.

30. MOHANTY Ch. T., "Under Western Eyes. Feminist Scholarship and Colonial Discourses", in C. T. Mohanty, A. Russo and L. Torres (eds.), *Third World Women and the Politics of Feminism,* Bloomingdale, Indiana University Press, 1991, p. 51-80.

31. MOJAB Sh., "Theorizing the Politics of Islamic Feminism", *Feminist Review,* Winter 2001, No. 69 (1), 2001, p. 124-146.

32. MOLYNEUX M., "Women's rights and political contingency. The case of Yemen 1990-1994", *The Middle East Journal,* No. 49, 1995, p. 418-443.

33. NUSSBAUM M. C. and GLOVER J., *Women, Culture, and Development. A Study of Human Capabilities,* Oxford, Clarendon Larendon, 1995.

34. MOGHADAM V. (ed.), *Gender and National Identity. Women and Politics in Muslim Societies*, London, Zed Books, 1994.

35. MUKHOPADYA M. (dir.), *Synthesis Report of the Muslim Women and Development Action Research Project. Annex 8 - Yemen,* Amsterdam, Royal Tropical Institute (KIT), 2001.

36. MOSER C., *Gender Planning and Development. Theory, Practice and Training*, London, Routledge, 1993.

37. PALUCH M., *Yemeni Voices. Women Tell Their Stories,* Sana'a, The British Council, 2001.

38. RADWAN Z. and AL-QADASI S., *Huquq al Nisa fi al Islam (Women´s right in Islam). Training manual 1*, Taiz, Women's Forum for Research and Training (WFRT) and GTZ, 2004.

39. REEVES H. and BADEN S., *Gender and Development. Concepts and Definitions,* Brighton, Bridge, Institute of Development Studies, University of Sussex, 2000.

40. SABRA M., *On the way to improved legal reality*, Eschborn, GTZ, 2008.

41. SAID E., *Orientalism. Western Conceptions of the Orient*, New York, Pantheon, 1978.

42. SAUNDERS Kr. (ed.), *Feminist Post-development Thought. Rethinking Modernity, Post-colonialism and Representation*, New York, Zed Books, 2007.

43. SEN A., *Development as Freedom*, Oxford, Oxford University Press, 1999.

44. STRZELECKA E., "Género, desarrollo y diversidad cultural", in Molina, Estefanía & Nava San Miguel (eds.), *Nuevas líneas de investigación en género y desarrollo*, Madrid, Autonomous University of Madrid, 2009.

45. TADROS M., "Introduction. Gender, Rights and Religion at the Crossroads", *IDS Bulletin: Gender, Rights and Religion at the Crossroads*, Vol. 42(1), 2011, p. 1-9.

46. UNDP, *Human Development Report. Cultural Liberty in Today's Diverse World*, New York, United Nations Development Programme, 2004.

47. UNFPA, *Culture Matters. Working with Communities and Faith-based Organizations. Case Studies from Country Programmes*, New York, UNFPA, 2005.

48. WADUD A., *Qur'an and Woman. Rereading the Sacred Text from a Woman's Perspective,* Oxford, Oxford University Press, 1999.

49. WADUD A., *Inside the Gender Jihad. Women's Reform in Islam,* Oxford, Oneworld Publications, 2006.

50. WFRT, *Final Report of Women's Rights in Islam Programme. The Third Phase,* Taiz, Women's Forum for Research and Training (WFRT) and GTZ, 2009.

Index